About Island Press

Island Press is the only nonprofit organization in the United States whose principal purpose is the publication of books on environmental issues and natural resource management. We provide solutions-oriented information to professionals, public officials, business and community leaders, and concerned citizens who are shaping responses to environmental problems.

In 2003, Island Press celebrates its nineteenth anniversary as the leading provider of timely and practical books that take a multidisciplinary approach to critical environmental concerns. Our growing list of titles reflects our commitment to bringing the best of an expanding body of literature to the environmental community throughout North America and the world.

Support for Island Press is provided by The Nathan Cummings Foundation, Geraldine R. Dodge Foundation, Doris Duke Charitable Foundation, Educational Foundation of America, The Charles Engelhard Foundation, The Ford Foundation, The George Gund Foundation, The Vira I. Heinz Endowment, The William and Flora Hewlett Foundation, Henry Luce Foundation, The John D. and Catherine T. MacArthur Foundation, The Andrew W. Mellon Foundation, The Moriah Fund, The Curtis and Edith Munson Foundation, National Fish and Wildlife Foundation, The New-Land Foundation, Oak Foundation, The Overbrook Foundation, The David and Lucile Packard Foundation, The Pew Charitable Trusts, The Rockefeller Foundation, The Winslow Foundation, and other generous donors.

The opinions expressed in this book are those of the author(s) and do not necessarily reflect the views of these foundations.

About The Conservation Fund

The Conservation Fund, a national nonprofit organization, acts to protect the nation's legacy of land and water resources in partnership with other organizations, public agencies, foundations, corporations, and individuals. Since its founding in 1985, The Conservation Fund has helped its partners safeguard wildlife habitat, working landscapes, community "greenspace," and historic sites totaling more than 3.5 million acres throughout the nation. Headquarters are in Arlington, Virginia: telephone 703-525-6300; www.conservationfund.org.

LAND CONSERVATION
FINANCING

MIKE McQUEEN
EDWARD McMAHON

THE CONSERVATION FUND

ISLAND PRESS

WASHINGTON • COVELO • LONDON

Library of Congress Cataloging-in-Publication data.
McQueen, Mike, 1950–
Land conservation financing / Mike McQueen, Ed McMahon.
     p. cm.
Includes bibliographical references.
     ISBN 1-55963-481-2 (pbk. : alk. paper)
1. Land use—United States—States—Planning. 2. Land use—Government policy—United States—States. 3. Land trusts—United States—States. 4. Open spaces—United States—States—Finance. 5. Conservation of natural resources—United States—States—Finance. I. McMahon, Edward, 1947– II. Title.
     HD205.M37 2003
     333.73′16′0973—dc21

                                                           2003011302

British Cataloguing-in-Publication data available.
Book design: Teresa Bonner
Printed on recycled, acid-free paper ✷

Manufactured in the United States of America
10 9 8 7 6 5 4 3 2 1

CONTENTS

CHAPTER 7 158
Protecting Land Conservation Funding in Tough Economic Times

FOREWORD BY LARRY SELZER, PRESIDENT OF THE CONSERVATION FUND

Southern New England where I grew up was a green place. The landscape was defined by small towns, broad expanses of woodlands and farmlands, and in the south, long stretches of beach, interlaced with wetlands. A mosaic of natural communities covered the New England landscape. In the spring and summer I criss-crossed the state enjoying the great outdoors, especially bird watching in my beloved East Rock Park squarely within the city of New Haven. Today, rampant, haphazard growth is consuming the landscape I treasured as a child, leaving isolated parcels of open space of limited recreational or biological value. Wetlands, farmlands, and forests are disappearing. Residential and commercial development is sprawling across the landscape. To a greater or lesser degree this scenario is playing out all across America.

Sure we have lots of greenscape left, but today land is being developed faster than ever before. According to the Natural Resources Conservation Service's *1997 National Resources Inventory,* over the fifteen-year period from 1982 to 1997 the total acreage of developed land in the United States increased by 34 percent (25 million acres). From 1982 to 1992, land was converted at 1.4 million acres per year, but from 1992 to 1997, land was converted at 2.2 million acres a year—more than one and one-half times the pace of the previous ten years. What's more, open space is being consumed at a rate almost three times faster than our population growth. According to a July 2001 report from the Brookings Institution's Center on Urban and Metropolitan Policy, between 1982 and 1997 the amount of urbanized land in the United States increased by 47 percent. However, during the same period, the nation's population grew by only 17 percent.

In major metropolitan acres, greenspace is rapidly disappearing. The Atlanta metropolitan area, for example, has lost 25 percent of its tree cover since 1973—nearly 350,000 acres. This loss equals nearly 35 acres of trees every day.

To address the accelerating consumption and fragmentation of open land, local and state governments have proposed a wide variety of programs and policies. Smart growth, sustainable development, transit-oriented development, traditional neighborhood development, brownfield redevelopment, mixed-use development, and coordination of land use and transportation have become twenty-first-century buzzwords. All these approaches have been tried in one location or another, but the most politically popular response to sprawl and the accelerating consumption of open land has been an explosion of programs and funding designed to protect open space.

As this book goes to press, America is engaged in a global struggle against terrorism and tyranny. Our economy is lagging and budgets are tight, yet few programs have attracted more popular support than open space funding. In the general election on November 5, 2002, voters approved conservation-related bonds and tax increases worth about $6.9, including almost $3 billion in local and state funding for land acquisition and restoration. What's remarkable is that these measures enjoyed a higher rate of voter approval than almost anything else Americans had voted on in the preceding five years. It is also worth noting that these conservation measures enjoyed widespread support among African Americans, Hispanics, and other minorities, which is significant given America's changing demographics.

Land Conservation Financing describes the many innovative programs and funding sources being used to protect parks, open spaces, wildlands, forests, and farmland across America. Some are the result of ballot measures, but many important land conservation programs have been legislated at the state and local level. Even more remarkable is that these funding programs are not limited to government. National conservation organizations, the land trust community, and private foundations have invested hundreds of millions of dollars of private capital to finance land protection projects. In addition, a few states and localities are taking a more strategic approach to land conservation based on the concept of "green infrastructure, an interconnected network of greenspace that conserves natural ecosystem values and functions while providing associated benefits to people." The Conservation Fund has helped to foster this shift in emphasis through its Center for Conservation and Development and our partnerships with state and local governments and the U.S. Forest Service.

In the mid-nineteenth century, French statesman Alexis de Tocqueville described the spirit of citizen involvement he found in his trip across America. Today this spirit is still alive and well in America, not only in the countless conservation organizations and the booming land trust movement but in the efforts of countless state and local governments. Together, these endeavors ultimately enrich people, wildlife, and the economy.

Arlington, Virginia
May 2003

ACKNOWLEDGMENTS

Many people have left their mark on this book. First and foremost, The Conservation Fund gratefully acknowledges the funding assistance of the George Gund Foundation; the Jackson Hole Preserve, Incorporated; the Surdna Foundation; the Peter J. Sharp Foundation; and the Tucker Foundation. Without their generous support this publication would not have been possible. Special thanks also go to Patrick F. Noonan, chairman of The Conservation Fund, and to Henry L. Diamond, for recognizing the need for this book and for their solid support in helping us to get it into the hands of those who need it.

This book could not have happened without the hard work, diligent research, and thoughtful writing of Mike McQueen, who took the lead in interviewing, recording, and translating the ideas of dozens of people from state and local governments, land trusts, foundation and conservation organizations around the country for the book. The Conservation Fund also wishes to thank Chuck Savitt and Heather Boyer at Island Press for their skills in bringing this book to publication; Sue Dodge for her outstanding design skills; Mark Benedict for his helping in writing Chapter 6 on Green Infrastructure; and Leigh Anne McDonald, whose efficiency, resourcefulness, and cheerfulness contributed to this project in untold ways. Finally, I wish to thank Larry Selzer for his inspiration and leadership in guiding The Conservation Fund into the twenty-first century.

Ed McMahon, The Conservation Fund
July 2003

ACKNOWLEDGMENTS

There have been moments while writing this book when the amount of cooperation it has taken to complete it comes home to me, when I think of the people, most of whom I don't know and will never meet, who nevertheless have helped to make this a better book. I've spoken with hundreds of individuals from state and local governments, land trusts, foundations, and conservation organizations around the county, along with photographers and graphic artists. Dozens of people have taken the time to review sections of the text. A thank-you to all who have helped bring this book into being. This network of conservationists has done great work to preserve land across the nation.

Thanks also go to Patrick Noonan and Lawrence Selzer at The Conservation Fund, for their support; to James Nuzum, Heather Boyer, Cecilia González, and Meg Weaver at Island Press, for their skills in bringing this book to publication. Mary Anne Stewart's copyediting measurably improved the manuscript. Sue Dodge has done great work illustrating many of the book's figures. Margaret Barton West's painting of the treasured open space we have here in Albemarle County, Virginia, appears on the cover. My parents, Arthur and Alice McQueen, are a continuing inspiration. And a special thanks to my wife, Jane, and son, Lucas, who have heard more about this book than anyone else on Earth, except my dog, Abby, whose upbeat attitude during our daily walks through the woods inspired me to finish writing this book on time (almost).

Mike McQueen
Earlysville, Virginia
July 2003

CHAPTER I

PROTECTING
OPEN SPACE

A generation ago, talk of spending over $1 billion to protect important open space in the United States was the stuff of dreams. Congress passed the 1964 Land and Water Conservation Fund Act (LWCF) with the idea that $100 million or $200 million of federal funding annually would suffice to revolutionize the availability of parks and open space across America.

Flash forward to the dawn of the twenty-first century. From 1998 through 2002, voters in states and local communities across the United States approved 670 ballot measures to spend more than $25 billion on parks and open space (see Table 1.1). And in March 2002, California voters approved a huge $2.6 billion park and environmental bond issue, the largest such bond in the nation's history. Remarkably, support for the bond was widespread across ethnic, racial, economic, and educational levels, with overwhelming majorities of whites, blacks, Latinos, and Asians backing the measure. Heeding the call of the grassroots groundswell of support for land conservation, Congress has boosted LWCF funding since fiscal year 2000, particularly for state grants, after two decades of neglect.

Clearly, public financing to acquire and protect parks and open space has experienced a sea change. Land protection is now big business. The

TABLE I.I.

State and local land conservation ballot measures, 1998–2002

Year	Number of Measures	Number Approved	Percentage Approved	Funding Approved
1998	150	126	84%	$8.3 billion
1999	102	92	90%	$1.8 billion
2000	209	174	83%	$7.5 billion
2001	196	137	70%	$1.7 billion
2002	189	141	75%	$5.7 billion
Total 1998–2002	846	670	79%	$25.0 billion

Sources: Adapted from Land Trust Alliance, 1998, 1999, and 2000 *Referenda Results;* and Trust for Public Land and Land Trust Alliance, *LandVote 2001* and *LandVote 2002.*

dollar figures involved are huge, and land development pressures have never been greater. At the same time, the variety of land conservation financing tools available from Main Street to the U.S. Capitol continues to expand.

Land Conservation Financing profiles some of the nation's best land conservation programs located in eight states—California, Colorado, Florida, Illinois, Maryland, Massachusetts, Minnesota, and New Jersey. As these forward-looking states have created impressive state land conservation financing programs, citizens and legislators in counties, cities, and towns across the United States have responded in kind. They have approved local ballot measures to leverage the state funding by dedicating sales taxes, property taxes, and other local revenue sources to boost the state land conservation efforts at the local level.

The Land and Water Conservation Fund

Although state and local governments have set aside land for parks and recreation for a very long time, the modern movement to protect open space can be traced to a little-known report, *Outdoor Recreation for America,* released in January 1962 by the Outdoor Recreation Resources Review Commission. The fifteen-member commission, created in 1958 by Congress and President Dwight D. Eisenhower and chaired by Laurance Rockefeller, requested that a federal funding program should be established to provide grants to states that would stimulate and assist them to meet new demands for outdoor recreation and to pay for additions to the federal recreation estate.

The commission owed its birth to forces in American society unleashed after World War II.[1] From the end of the war into the 1950s, the United States witnessed a swift expansion in the demand for outdoor recreation. The baby boom and rapid urbanization coupled with increases in disposable income, leisure time, and mobility coalesced into a national awareness that the nation needed more access to parks, open space, and other areas for outdoor recreation.

Spurred by the commission's recommendations, President John F. Kennedy on February 14, 1963, proposed the creation of a Land and Water Conservation Fund. In a letter to Congress accompanying the legislation, Kennedy wrote:

> The Nation needs a land acquisition program to preserve both prime Federal and State areas for outdoor recreation purposes. The growth of our cities, the development of our industry, the expansion of our transportation systems—all manifestations of our vigorous and expanding society—preempt irreplaceable lands of natural beauty and unique recreation value. In addition to the enhancement of spiritual, cultural, and physical values resulting from the preservation of these resources, the expenditures for their preservation are a sound financial investment. Public acquisition costs can become multiplied and even prohibitive with the passage of time.[2]

After Kennedy's assassination in November 1963, President Lyndon B. Johnson urged speedy approval of the bill, which received broad bipartisan support. Congress approved the legislation in the late summer of 1964 and sent the bill to the president, who signed it into law on September 3, 1964, as Public Law 88–578.

The law establishing the Land and Water Conservation Fund stipulated that up to 60 percent of all appropriations for the fund could be devoted to the new state grant program, but at least 40 percent should be set aside for federal land acquisition. Congress tapped four sources of revenue to fund the program: (1) the sale of surplus federal property, (2) an existing motor boat fuel tax, (3) a new system of entrance and recreation user fees at national parks and on other federal lands, and (4) annual appropriations of $60 million a year for eight years, which were to be paid back. Because the user fees never raised more than $16 million in the early years, Congress bolstered the original funding sources in 1968 by including a portion of federal revenue from offshore oil and gas drilling, which has become the key funding source for the Land and Water Conservation Fund. Congress saw its use of offshore drilling revenue as a means to recycle money generated from a depleting natural resource to rejuvenate other natural resources. Lawmakers increased the program's authorized funding level to $200 million a year in FY 1969, $300 million in FY 1971, and $900 million in FY 1978, where it stands as of 2003.

Four decades after its creation, the impact of this program can be seen in every county and major city in America.[3] Millions of acres of recreation land in the United States—from parks and playgrounds in every state and territory to the magnificent national parks spanning the country from Cape Cod to Point Reyes—owe their existence to the Land and Water Conservation Fund Act. From FY 1965 through FY 2002, Congress appropriated $11.8 billion from the Land and Water Conservation Fund to provide monies for federal acquisition of park and recreation lands and matching grants to state and local governments for recreation planning, land acquisition, and park development.

All or a major part of dozens of our national parks and forests, wildlife refuges, and river and trail systems were acquired through the $8.2 billion that Congress has devoted to federal acquisitions under the Land and Water Conservation Fund program. In addition to creating new protected areas, the fund has helped expand existing areas through acquisitions of key recreation and conservation sites in almost every national forest and wildlife refuge east of the Rocky Mountains (see Box 1.1). Through FY 2001, over 4.5 million acres of federal land have been protected through the program.

Besides the federal acquisitions, from FY 1965 through FY 2002, Congress also appropriated $3.6 billion in grants to state and local governments to plan, acquire, and develop park and recreation land. These grants leveraged an additional $3.6 billion in state and local matching funds that acquired more than 2.3 million acres of recreation land, funded 37,000 state and local projects, and developed 27,000 recreational facilities spread throughout every county, state, and territory in the nation.

Although Congress authorized a spending level of $900 million a year for the Land and Water Conservation Fund, actual annual appropriations have never approached the authorized amount (see Figure 1.1).

BOX 1.1.

*Sampling of public land acquired with Land and Water
Conservation Fund appropriations from
FY 1965 through FY 2000*

In addition to grants to state and local governments, the Land and Water Conservation Fund has provided more than $8.2 billion to acquire new federal recreation lands. Following are some of the areas added to national park, forest, wildlife refuge, river, and trail systems from FY 1965 through FY 2000 for which all or a major part of land purchases were funded by the federal side of the Land and Water Conservation Fund. In addition to new areas, the fund has helped expand existing areas through acquisition of key recreation and conservation sites in almost every national forest and wildlife refuge east of the Rocky Mountains.

Apostle Islands National Lakeshore, Wisconsin
Appalachian National Scenic Trail, Maine to Georgia
Assateague Island National Seashore, Maryland
Atchafalaya National Wildlife Refuge, Louisiana
Big Cypress National Preserve, Florida
Big South Fork National River, Kentucky, Tennessee
Big Thicket National Preserve, Texas
Biscayne National Park, Florida
Bluestone National Scenic River, West Virginia
Buffalo National River, Arkansas
Canaveral National Seashore, Florida
Cape Cod National Seashore, Massachusetts
Cape Lookout National Seashore, North Carolina
Chattahoochee River National Recreation Area, Georgia
Chesapeake & Ohio Canal National Historical Park, District of
    Columbia, Maryland and West Virginia
Chickasaw National Recreation Area, Oklahoma
Congaree Swamp National Monument, South Carolina
Cumberland Island National Seashore, Georgia
Cuyahoga Valley National Recreation Area, Ohio
Delaware National Scenic River, Pennsylvania, New Jersey
Flaming Gorge National Recreation Area, Utah, Wyoming

Gulf Islands National Seashore, Texas
Indiana Dunes National Lakeshore, Indiana
Jean Lafitte National Historic Park and Reserve, Louisiana
Lowell National Historic Park, Massachusetts
Lower Rio Grande Valley National Wildlife Refuge, Texas
Lower Suwanee National Wildlife Refuge, Florida
Martin Luther King, Jr., National Historic Site, Georgia
Minnesota Valley National Wildlife Refuge, Minnesota
Mississippi National River and Recreation Area, Minnesota
Missouri National Recreational River, Nebraska, South Dakota
Natchez Trace National Scenic Trail, Tennessee
New River Gorge National River, West Virginia
North Cascades National Park, Washington
Obed Wild and Scenic River, Tennessee
Oregon Dunes National Recreation Area, Oregon
Ozark National Scenic Riverway, Missouri
Padre Islands National Seashore, Texas
Pictured Rocks National Lakeshore, Michigan
Pinelands National Reserve, New Jersey
Point Reyes National Seashore, California
Redwoods National Park, California
Rio Grande Wild and Scenic River, Texas
Santa Monica Mountains National Recreation Area, California
Sawtooth National Recreation Area, Idaho
Sleeping Bear Dunes National Lakeshore, Michigan
St. Croix and Lower St. Croix National Scenic Rivers, Minnesota, Wisconsin
Steamtown National Historic Park, Pennsylvania
Voyageurs National Park, Minnesota

Source: National Park Service. www.nps.gov/lwcf/Fed_state.html

The total amount that could have been appropriated to the Land and Water Conservation Fund between FY 1965 and FY 2002 was $25.4 billion, but only $11.8 billion was appropriated for land acquisition. (Between FY 1998 and FY 2002, Congress appropriated another $658

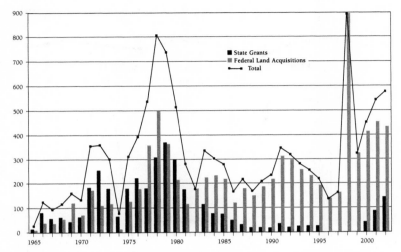

FIGURE I.I. Land and Water Conservation Fund appropriations, FY 1965–FY 2002 (in millions of dollars). *Source:* Department of the Interior, National Park Service. Figure by Sue Dodge. *Note:* FY 1976 appropriation includes extra funding for July–September 1976 because of the adoption of a new fiscal year calendar. Fiscal year 1998 appropriation includes $627 million in special land acquisition funding under Title V of Interior appropriations bill. FY 2000 appropriation includes $177.5 million in special land acquisition funding under Title VI of Interior appropriations bill. FY 2001 appropriation includes $228.5 million in special land acquisition funding under Title VIII of the Interior appropriations bill.

million of LWCF funds for purposes other than land acquisition.) As a result of this lack of appropriations, the Treasury Department estimated in 2002 that it held a paper "balance" for the Land and Water Conservation Fund of about $12.9 billion (see Figure 1.2).

Except during the Carter administration (1977–1980), when appropriations exceeded $500 million each year and reached a high of $805 million in FY 1978, LWCF spending has approached the authorized level of $900 million only once, in FY 1998.[4] (Appropriations exceeded $900 million in FY 2001, but almost half the amount—$456 million—was for purposes other than land acquisition.) Between FY 1981 and FY 1999, annual appropriations generally ranged between $150 million and $350 million.

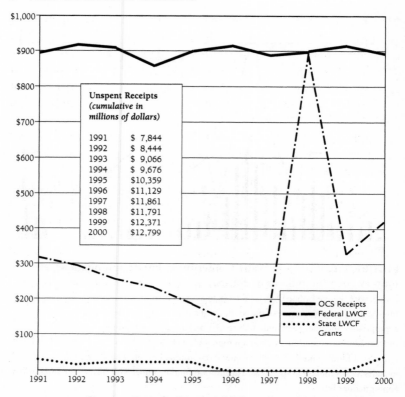

FIGURE 1.2. Receipts into the Land and Water Conservation Fund versus federal and state Land and Water Conservation Fund appropriations, FY 1991–FY 2000 (in millions of dollars). *Source:* Department of the Interior, National Park Service. Figure by Sue Dodge. *Notes:* The Land and Water Conservation Fund receives $900 million a year in receipts from surplus property sales, motorboat fuel taxes, and revenue from oil and gas production on the outer continental shelf. OCS: Outer Continental Shelf receipts from federal royalties, rents, and bonuses on oil and gas production. LWCF: Land and Water Conservation Fund.

State Grant Funding

With a few exceptions, state grant appropriations from the Land and Water Conservation Fund were on the upswing from 1965 until the early 1980s, particularly during the Carter presidency, when state grants peaked in FY 1979 at $370 million. But program spending dropped when President Ronald Reagan chose James Watt to head the Interior Department.[5] Armed with a mandate to cut taxes and reduce the size of the federal government, President Reagan successfully cut off all state LWCF grants for FY 1982. The federal side fared better that year, but its funding was cut significantly, to $167 million from a high of $490 million in FY 1978.

Although Congress continued to provide between $140 million and $329 million for federal acquisitions from the Land and Water Conservation Fund annually through the rest of the 1980s and 1990s, the state grant program went into a tailspin, ending with no funding from FY 1996 through FY 1999 (see Figure 1.2). However, Congress revived the program in FY 2000 with a $41 million appropriation, followed by $90 million in FY 2001 and $144 million in FY 2002.

The cuts in the LWCF program, dating to the Reagan years, exposed an underlying weakness: although billions of dollars had been spent on the program in cities and states around the country, governors, mayors, and mainline environmental groups had voiced little opposition when the cuts came. "One of the great failures was the failure to develop a constituency," said Washington, D.C., attorney Henry Diamond, a longtime proponent of the program who had edited the final 1962 report of the Outdoor Recreation Resources Review Commission. "When it was gutted, there wasn't much of a hue and cry."[6]

Development Pressures

The downturn in Land and Water Conservation Fund funding coincided with mounting land development pressures around the country. From 1982 to 1997, 25 million acres of open space were developed in the United States—a 34 percent increase in just fifteen years, representing more than one-quarter of the 98.3 million acres developed since colonial times. And the pace of development continued to accelerate: 6.3 million acres were developed between 1982 and 1987, 7.5 million acres between 1987 and 1992, and a staggering 11.2 million acres between 1992 and 1997, according to the Natural Resources Conservation Service (NRCS), an agency of the United States Department of Agriculture, which has documented the upswell in developed land in surveys it has conducted every five years since 1977.[7]

TABLE 1.2.

1997 National Resources Conservation Service inventory of developed and undeveloped nonfederal land in the United States, 1982–1997

		1992–1997			1982–1992		1982	1997
Rank	State	Acreage Developed	Annual Rate of Development (acres)	Rank	Acreage Developed	Annual Rate of Development (acres)	Percentage of State Land Developed (%)	Percentage of State Land Developed (%)
1	Texas	893,500	178,700	1	1,387,000	138,700	3.8	5.2
2	Georgia	851,900	170,380	5	738,400	73,840	6.8	11.4
3	Florida	825,200	165,050	2	1,088,200	108,820	10.6	16.9
4	California	553,400	110,680	4	764,700	76,470	7.7	10.3
5	Pennsylvania	545,100	109,020	6	619,300	61,930	10.1	14.3
6	North Carolina	506,600	101,320	3	933,100	93,310	8.4	13.6
7	Tennessee	401,900	80,380	7	464,000	46,400	6.0	9.5
8	Ohio	364,800	72,960	8	463,700	46,370	10.8	14.1
9	Michigan	364,100	72,800	9	456,100	45,610	8.2	10.8
10	South Carolina	362,000	72,400	11	386,400	38,640	7.4	11.6
11	Virginia	343,500	68,700	10	441,000	44,100	8.2	11.7
12	New York	317,600	63,520	24	230,200	23,020	8.8	10.7
13	Alabama	315,300	63,060	13	320,400	32,040	5.2	7.2
14	Illinois	246,500	49,300	19	245,800	24,580	7.7	9.1
15	Washington	240,800	48,160	17	287,000	28,700	5.0	6.8
16	Kentucky	237,100	47,420	12	355,100	35,510	4.7	7.2
17	Minnesota	231,800	46,360	21	233,800	23,380	3.6	4.6
18	Missouri	224,200	44,840	25	209,300	20,930	5.0	6.0
19	New Mexico	217,200	43,440	28	154,500	15,450	1.5	2.3
20	New Jersey	213,600	42,720	15	299,100	29,910	27.7	39.1
21	Massachusetts	211,800	42,360	22	233,400	23,340	21.2	30.4
22	Mississippi	206,400	41,280	29	147,400	14,740	4.0	5.3
23	Indiana	195,300	39,060	23	230,300	23,030	8.2	10.1
24	Wisconsin	188,200	37,640	20	240,500	24,050	6.1	7.4

25	Maryland	177,600	35,520	31	145,100	14,510	15.1	20.4
26	West Virginia	176,800	35,360	33	112,900	11,290	4.1	6.2
27	Oklahoma	176,700	35,340	27	156,100	15,610	3.7	4.5
28	Arkansas	168,900	33,780	36	96,800	9,680	3.8	4.7
29	Louisiana	133,600	26,720	18	256,300	25,630	4.7	6.2
30	Arizona	113,800	22,760	16	289,000	28,900	2.6	3.5
31	Colorado	112,500	22,500	14	302,700	30,270	2.9	3.9
32	Maine	111,100	22,220	37	91,400	9,140	2.6	3.7
33	Oregon	103,900	20,780	26	162,800	16,280	3.2	4.1
34	Kansas	96,500	19,300	32	124,900	12,490	3.3	3.8
35	Idaho	91,900	18,380	34	112,800	11,280	2.8	3.9
36	Utah	81,300	16,260	35	110,200	11,020	2.6	3.6
37	Montana	76,300	15,260	40	77,400	7,740	1.3	1.6
38	Iowa	69,100	13,820	44	50,800	5,080	4.5	4.8
39	New Hampshire	62,600	12,520	30	147,000	14,700	7.6	11.9
40	South Dakota	57,800	11,560	41	64,500	6,450	1.8	2.1
41	Nebraska	55,100	11,020	45	39,300	3,930	2.3	2.5
42	Connecticut	39,400	7,880	38	83,900	8,390	24.5	28.6
43	Wyoming	34,400	6,880	43	59,400	5,940	1.6	1.9
44	North Dakota	32,800	6,560	48	24,800	2,480	2.2	2.3
45	Nevada	26,700	5,340	39	82,500	8,250	2.6	3.6
46	Delaware	23,100	4,620	46	35,400	3,540	13.8	18.6
47	Vermont	11,500	2,300	42	63,300	6,330	4.4	5.8
48	Hawaii	6,800	1,360	49	23,700	2,370	3.9	4.8
49	Rhode Island	6,600	1,320	47	26,500	2,650	25.6	30.5
Total		11,217,000	2,243,400		13,788,900	1,378,890	4.9	6.6

Source: Adapted from USDA Natural Resources Conservation Service, 1997 National Resources Inventory; www.nrcs.usda.gov/technical/NRI.
Note: Alaska data not available.

Texas outpaced all other states by developing 2,280,500 acres of open space between 1982 and 1997, or 152,033 acres each year. Florida (1,913,400 acres), Georgia (1,590,300 acres), North Carolina (1,439,700 acres), California (1,318,100 acres), and Pennsylvania (1,164,400 acres) also topped the million-acre mark over the fifteen-year period (see Table 1.2).

Grassroots Response

The most important polling in a democracy is that done in the voting booth. And where voters are asked to protect open space, the record shows that the voters approve.
—RUSSELL SHAY,
Director of public policy, Land Trust Alliance

As development accelerated over the last two decades, federal aid to states to acquire parks and open space evaporated. But the dramatic rise in grassroots support for open space stunned even seasoned conservationists. From 1998 through 2002, voters in states and localities across the U.S. approved 670 referenda, devoting more than $25 billion to parks and open space (see Table 1.1).

In 1998 alone, voters approved 126 state and local open space ballots, including 8 of 10 state initiatives, which funneled $8.3 billion to open space protection.[8] In fast-growing Florida, 75 percent of the state's voters endorsed the state's authority to sell bonds for land conservation, opening the door to a second $3 billion installment of land preservation called Florida Forever, the successor to Preservation 2000. Likewise, in New Jersey, voters dedicated $98 million annually in state sales tax for thirty years for open space acquisition after then-governor Christine Whitman called for preserving 1 million acres in the nation's most densely populated state. By the end of 2002, residents of 20 of the state's 21 counties and 187 of its 566 municipalities had approved funding for local open space and recreation plans to raise up to $158 million annually to match the new state funding.[9]

In 1998 in the Denver metro region, Jefferson County residents authorized $160 million in bond authority to acquire open space. On Cape Cod, Massachusetts, voters in all fifteen towns approved a 3 percent surcharge on property taxes that could raise $250 million over twenty years to fund a "land bank" to acquire and protect land. And in

Austin, Texas, voters approved two propositions authorizing $45 million in bonds to acquire open space and protect their water supply.[10]

Although 1999 was an off-year for elections, interest in land conservation continued to build.[11] Of 102 state and local ballot measures on open space, 92 were approved, a higher percentage than in 1998. Voters committed more than $1.8 billion for land conservation, including a major effort by residents of Phoenix, Arizona, who raised their sales tax by one-tenth cent to provide $256 million for preserving important land. In Boulder County, Colorado, voters extended their one-fourth cent sale tax for ten years to raise $123.5 million for land acquisition. In Mecklenburg County, North Carolina, residents approved bonds totaling $272 million for parks, open space, and greenways. In Suffolk County, New York, voters extended a one-fourth-cent sales tax to raise $140 million to protect drinking water supplies; and voters in Franklin County, Ohio, agreed to a property tax hike to pay for prairie, forest, and wetland acquisition.

The year 2000 was another "on-year" for elections, in which voters approved 174 ballot measures committing $7.5 billion to open space.[12] Californians alone agreed to a $2.1 billion bond referendum for a variety of parks, open space, clean water, clean air, and coastal protection projects, as well as a $1.97 billion bond measure devoted to safe drinking water, water quality, watershed, and flood protection projects.

San Francisco residents approved $150 million in new property taxes to acquire and maintain greenspace, gardens, and recreation areas. In response to Florida's renewed commitment of $3 billion for land preservation, residents of nine Atlantic Coast cities and counties in the state approved $802 million in spending for a variety of park, open space, and water protection projects, including Broward County, Florida, residents, who voted by nearly a three-to-one margin in favor of a $400 million bond to acquire and improve their parks.

Elsewhere in the South, residents of Gwinnett County outside Atlanta agreed to extend their one-cent sales and use tax for two years and dedicated $320.6 million of the proceeds for recreation, open space, and park land acquisition. In the Midwest, voters in the St. Louis, Missouri, area agreed to spend more than $400 million of a new retailers' occupation tax to create a park district and fund water quality improvements, open space preservation, and recreation. And, in a statewide vote, Ohioans authorized the issuance of $400 million in bonds for a range of conservation and environmental restoration projects.

In 2001, another supposedly slow "off-year," voters approved 137 of 196 open space measures that were scattered across twenty-four states.[13] In Massachusetts, where legislators approved a statewide Community Preservation Act in 2000, residents of thirty-six cities and towns voted to increase their property taxes to raise $112.8 million for land conservation, historic preservation, and affordable housing, making them eligible for $26 million annually in matching funds from the state. In predominantly African American DeKalb County, Georgia, voters by a three-to-two margin approved a $125 million bond to acquire and improve parks and to protect natural areas and greenspace.

In the Rocky Mountain West, Colorado voters approved $115 million in bonds from lottery proceeds to continue funding the state's Great Outdoors Colorado program, which funds open space, park, wildlife, and recreation projects around the state. Residents of Douglas County, Colorado, the fastest-growing county in the nation, agreed to $43 million in bonds for parks and trails, open space, wildlife habitat, agricultural land, scenic vistas, and recreation. And in California, residents of Santa Clara County approved a $20-per-house assessment to raise $160 million for acquiring, preserving, and developing open space, parks, trails, and waterways.

To top off a remarkable four-year run, California voters in March 2002 approved a $2.6 billion park and environmental bond issue, the largest such bond in the nation's history, followed by a $3.44 billion water bond in November, including hundreds of millions of dollars to preserve land along water.

The California vote on the parks bond was particularly instructive. The *Los Angeles Times* found broad support for the huge bond measure, all the more remarkable because it occurred during the state's economic downturn and just two years after residents had approved a similar $2.1 billion measure. Exit polling by the *Times* found that 77 percent of blacks, 74 percent of Latinos, 60 percent of Asians, and 56 percent of white voters endorsed the park and environmental bond.[14] Three in four voters whose family income was less than $20,000 supported the measure—the highest percentage of any income group— and 61 percent of those with a high school education or less voted for the park bond, the highest percentage among education levels. The widespread minority group support for the bond "demolishes the myth that parks are a luxury and that lower income communities don't care about the environment," said Robert Garcia, an attorney in Los Angeles at the Center for Law in the Public Interest.[15]

Land Trusts on the Rise

Another indication of the nation's growing support for open space preservation is the explosive growth in the number of land trusts during the 1990s. In its 2001 *National Land Trust Census,* the Land Trust Alliance reported that Americans created 376 land trusts in the 1990s (see Figure 1.3).[16] A record 1,263 local and regional land trusts were operating in the United States in 2000, protecting 6.4 million acres of open space in all fifty states. The acreage, which doesn't include the millions of acres protected by national conservation organizations such as The Nature Conservancy, The Conservation Fund, and the Trust for Public Land, represented a 226 percent increase over the 1990 census total of 1.9 million protected acres. California, New York, and Montana led the nation in acreage protected by local and regional land trusts with 1.25 million, 552,220, and 505,659 acres, respectively.

The land trust movement truly turned national in scope in the 1990s. For the first time since the birth of the movement in 1891 when the first nonprofit land trust was founded in the United States, land trusts protected open space in all fifty states, the District of Columbia, and Puerto Rico. Although the Northeast and the West continued to lead the nation in the number of land trusts—Massachusetts had 143, California 132, and Connecticut 112—the South experienced the most rapid growth in land trusts in the 1990s, with Texas alone home to 22. In terms of acreage protected, land trusts outside of the Northeast and California also shone. By 2000, in the southwestern states of Arizona, Colorado, New Mexico, and Utah, land trusts protected 923,603 acres, up from just 40,403 acres a decade earlier. In the southcentral states of Arkansas, Louisiana, Oklahoma, and Texas, land trusts protected 105,967 acres, up from a mere 7,341 acres in 1990.

Private Foundation Support

As voters increased state and local spending on land protection and land trusts helped protect millions of acres of land, private foundations also made a dramatic entrance into land conservation. The 1990s saw

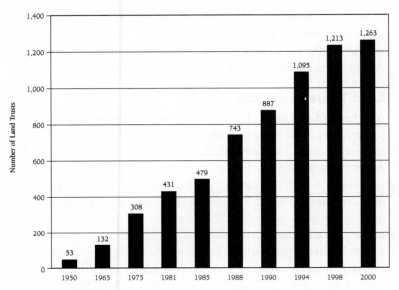

FIGURE 1.3. Growth of land trusts in the United States, 1950–2000
Source: Land Trust Alliance. Figure by Sue Dodge.

a strong increase in grants for the environment, with hundreds of millions of dollars specifically devoted to the protection of open space. The Richard King Mellon Foundation and the David and Lucile Packard Foundation alone donated more than $500 million to protect more than 1.5 million acres of land. And newer foundations, including the Doris Duke Charitable Foundation, the Arthur M. Blank Family Foundation, and the Gordon and Betty Moore Foundation, also have chosen to support land conservation initiatives in their grants.

Demand for Open Space Funding

As these new state, local, and private sector players have brought their money and energy into the protection of land in America, the demand for state grants under the original Land and Water Conservation Fund has not abated. In an effort to measure the current need for outdoor recreation facilities and open space acquisition at the state and local level, in November 2002 the National Park Service asked each state to estimate its total request for Land and Water Conservation funds for FY 2000 through FY 2002 (see Table 1.3). Of the forty-five states responding, 70 percent reported an unmet funding need exceeding 50 percent. Overall, the National Park Service received grant requests of $3.3 billion for the $268.8 million available for state LWCF grants in this period, leaving 92 percent of the need unmet.

The Rise of Green Infrastructure

As state and local governments took center stage with their efforts to fund parks and open space, other conservationists and land use planners were arguing that land conservation needed to be more strategic by better linking open space preservation with efforts to manage urban growth and preserve biodiversity. Their goal was to have individual tracts of preserved lands fit into larger landscapes, watersheds, and ecosystems. For example, Ed McMahon and Mark Benedict of The Conservation Fund argue that many conservation efforts have been reactive, site-specific, narrowly focused, and not well integrated with other land planning efforts.[17-20] By looking at how watersheds operate as systems and exploring how plants and animals depend on their habitats, conservationists can work with land use planners to see how human development can thrive in concert with existing natural systems. Technological advances in geographic information systems have enabled ecologists and planners to envision growth scenarios and estimate their effects not just on society's so-called gray infrastructure—the road, utility and water systems that are essential to modern life—but the green infrastructure, an interconnected network of greenspace that conserves natural ecosystem values and functions while providing associated benefits to people.

Planning for green infrastructure represents a new approach that allows land planners and conservation biologists to forge a stronger link between the use of land and its preservation. A handful of states— notably Florida, Maryland, and Massachusetts—have taken the lead in overhauling such haphazard planning and in elevating greens infrastructure closer to equal footing with their gray infrastructure. And, in one of the largest green infrastructure applications in the nation, state and federal officials are developing a green infrastructure plan for the entire 64,000 square miles of the Chesapeake Bay watershed.

TABLE 1.3.
Charting the need for the Land and Water Conservation Fund,
FY 2000–FY 2002

State	Grant Requests[a] ($)	LWCF Assistance[b] ($)	Unmet Need (%)
Alabama	$30,000,000	$4,447,334	85%
Alaska	6,891,814	2,377,743	65%
Arizona	25,415,924	4,971,170	80%
California	68,976,784	23,004,391	67%
Delaware	83,394,069	2,545,722	97%
Florida	22,815,256	11,498,562	50%
Georgia	13,442,311	6,256,490	53%
Hawaii	2,767,000	2,767,639	0%
Idaho	7,772,107	2,637,218	66%
Illinois	102,062,407	9,271,320	91%
Indiana	19,108,636	5,352,450	72%
Iowa	8,148,351	3,396,578	58%
Kansas	16,050,000	3,398,256	79%
Kentucky	13,379,532	3,934,901	71%
Maine	11,964,414	4,630,236	61%
Maryland	24,282,192	5,322,044	78%
Massachusetts	61,116,000	6,034,098	90%
Michigan	361,471,914	7,846,015	98%
Minnesota	39,034,735	4,682,297	88%
Mississippi	6,085,116	3,262,043	46%
Missouri	25,000,000	5,020,239	80%
Montana	21,232,037	2,454,472	88%
Nebraska	6,287,024	2,900,619	54%
Nevada	5,855,036	3,174,270	46%
New Hampshire	5,605,275	2,711,350	52%
New Jersey	1,165,525,699	7,399,988	99%
New York	164,091,943	13,484,994	92%
North Carolina	16,069,604	6,155,760	62%
North Dakota	4,700,000	2,390,333	49%
Ohio	32,000,000	8,628,469	73%
Oklahoma	7,304,971	3,808,733	48%
Oregon	7,036,536	3,912,315	44%
Pennsylvania	80,700,000	9,270,059	89%
Rhode Island	36,449,994	2,736,799	92%
South Carolina	22,083,445	4,190,560	81%
South Dakota	1,806,203	2,410,663	0%
Tennessee	195,350,548	5,028,432	97%
Texas	139,173,961	13,900,244	90%
Utah	14,375,500	3,303,612	77%
Vermont	92,224,957	2,339,203	97%
Virginia	15,993,551	6,006,627	62%

TABLE I.3. (*Continued*)

Charting the need for the Land and Water Conservation Fund,
FY 2000–FY 2002

State	Grant Requests[a] ($)	LWCF Assistance[b] ($)	Unmet Need (%)
Washington	127,329,816	5,459,728	96%
West Virginia	5,433,104	2,900,549	47%
Wisconsin	73,903,730	4,901,260	93%
Wyoming	4,650,000	2,298,880	51%
Other States/ Territories	69,655,243[c]	24,379,335	65%
Total	$3,264,016,739	$268,804,000	92%

Source: National Park Service, "Land and Water Conservation Fund: State Assistance Program Summary, 2000–2002; see www.nps.gov/lwcf.

Note: Since Land and Water Conservation funds are available to states for three years following appropriation, some states have not fully implemented their apportioned funding.

[a]Estimated total state request for Land and Water Conservation funds for fiscal years 2000 through 2002. If a state typically combines Land and Water Conservation funds with similar state grant programs, estimate includes the total demand for all programs.

[b]Total LWCF state apportionment for fiscal years 2000 through 2002.

[c]Estimate based on the average need of 65 percent for reporting states. (Arkansas, Colorado, Connecticut, Louisiana, and New Mexico did not report.)

CHAPTER TWO

FINANCING STATE LAND CONSERVATION PROGRAMS

The evolution in thinking about the conservation of land in America has been driven by two inescapable issues. One, the consumption of environmentally valuable land is an accelerating problem. The pace of development is outstripping efforts by state and local governments to preserve open space, greenways, and trails, wildlife habitat, and agricultural land, while protecting water supplies and providing recreational opportunities for a burgeoning population. Two, state and local officials have joined conservationists who have realized that a haphazard, piecemeal approach to land conservation isn't effective. A more systematic approach is needed that elevates the protection of open space to an equal footing with other long-term land use goals of states and localities. That approach requires a stable funding source.

This chapter profiles eight states that have emerged as national leaders in the preservation of land. These states have committed billions of dollars to protect the lands they know will be lost unless they commit the resources to protect them. As more states decide to fund land conservation from bonds and general fund appropriations, they also have embraced other approaches, including the use of lottery proceeds in Colorado and Minnesota, tobacco taxes in California and Minnesota, and real estate transfer taxes in Florida and Maryland (see Table 2.1). And in states like New Jersey, Florida, and Colorado, the availability of dedicated funding for land conservation at the state level has helped spur local governments to create their own land conservation programs as a means of matching the state grant funding. Their efforts provide models for other states as they face the reality of a disappearing and irreplaceable resource (see Appendix A).

Massachusetts

Visitors to many of Massachusetts's towns and cities are struck by their village greens, visually attractive downtowns, and compact, pedestrian-friendly layouts. Although the village-center pattern of development is centuries old in the Bay State, sprawl has muscled its way in. From 1950 to 1990, the state's population grew 28 percent while developed land mushroomed by 188 percent. Alarm over this trend has grown in the past two decades, prompting legislators in 2000 to develop an innovative tool for communities to recapture their past as a means to invigorate their future.

The early success of Massachusetts's Community Preservation Act (CPA), which was enacted in September 2000, is shaping up as a textbook example of how state financial incentives can engage local communities to create a vision of their future.[1] As of November 2002, just two short years after Massachusetts legislators dangled $26 million in annual matching grants in front of the state's 351 towns and cities, 58 of them had agreed to raise property taxes up to 3 percent in order to raise just over $26 million each year for three purposes: acquiring open space, providing affordable housing, and preserving historic sites and buildings (see Map 2.1). If the remaining 293 communities follow suit, the state's towns and cities could raise between $184 million and $230 million for community preservation activities.

The Community Preservation Act complements the state's Community Preservation Initiative, which the Executive Office of Environmental Affairs began in 1999. Among other actions, the initiative has developed "build-out maps," which portray currently developed and protected land in each of the state's communities, along with projections of what they would look like if the remaining undeveloped land was built out according to what current zoning allows. In addition,

TABLE 2.1.
Selected funding sources for state land conservation programs,
1960–2003

Bonds

States (25 total)	Years
Alabama	1998
California	1974, 1976, 1980, 1982, 1984, 1988, 1990, 1996, 2000, 2002
Colorado	2001
Connecticut	1986–1992, 1998–2002
Delaware	1990
Florida	1964, 1968, 1972, 1986, 1987, 1990, 1999
Georgia	1992–1999
Illinois	1985, 1995
Louisiana	1990
Maine	1987, 1999
Maryland	1998–2003
Massachusetts	1982, 1983, 1987, 1992, 1994, 1996, 2000, 2002
Michigan	1998
Minnesota	1987, 1990, 1991, 1992, 1994
Nevada	1990, 2002
New Hampshire	1987, 2000
New Jersey	1961, 1971, 1974, 1978, 1983, 1987, 1989, 1995, 1996, 1998
New Mexico	1988
New York	1960, 1962, 1972, 1986, 1996
Ohio	1993, 2000
Pennsylvania	1993
Rhode Island	1986, 1987, 1989, 1996, 1998, 2000
Vermont	1990, 1992
Virginia	1992, 2002
Wisconsin	1989

General Fund Appropriations

States (23 total)	Years
Arizona	1994, 2001–2011
California	1989, 1991, 1996
Connecticut	2000, 2002
Delaware	1994, 1995, 1998–2000
Florida	1990–2000
Georgia	1994, 1999–2002
Hawaii	1987–1991
Illinois	1986
Indiana	1984, 2000, 2001
Iowa	1989–1999
Kentucky	1990, 1992, 1993
Nebraska	1990–1992

TABLE 2.1. (*Continued*)
Selected funding sources for state land conservation programs,
1960–2003

General Fund Appropriations (*Continued*)

New Hampshire	1987–1989
New Mexico	1994
New York	1993
North Carolina	1987, 1988, 1996
North Dakota	1995–1997
Pennsylvania	1988, 1990, 1999
South Carolina	1976
Utah	1998
Vermont	1987, 1988
Virginia	1988, 1999, 2000
Washington	1987, 1989, 1990–2003

Environmental License Plate Sales

States (29 total)	**Years**
Arizona	1990
California	1971
Connecticut	1993
Delaware	1995
Florida	1990
Georgia	1997
Indiana	1993
Illinois	1994
Iowa	1994
Kentucky	1994
Maine	1995
Maryland	1990
Massachusetts	1994
Michigan	2001
Minnesota	1995
Mississippi	1997
New Hampshire	2000
New York	1996
North Carolina	1989
Oklahoma	1995
Ohio	1995
Pennsylvania	1995
South Carolina	1993
Tennessee	1993
Texas	1999
Utah	1993
Virginia	1992
West Virginia	1996
Wisconsin	1995

TABLE 2.1. (*Continued*)
Selected funding sources for state land conservation programs,
1960–2003

Real Estate Transfer Tax

States (14 total)	Years
Arkansas	1986
Delaware	1990, 2001
Florida	1982
Hawaii	1993
Illinois	1989, 1996
Maryland	1990
New York	1993
North Carolina	1991
Pennsylvania	1993
Rhode Island	1986
South Carolina	1986
Tennessee	1986
Vermont	1988
Washington	1987–1989

Lottery

States (7 total)	Years
Arizona	1990
Colorado	1982, 1992
Iowa	1986, 1989–1999
Maine	1996
Minnesota	1988, 1998
Nebraska	1992
Oregon	1995, 1998

Cigarette Tax

States (5 total)	Years
California	1988
Minnesota	1963, 1969
Nebraska	1965, 1980
Pennsylvania	1991
Texas	1987–1993

Environmental Penalty Money

States (4 total)	Years
Alaska	1992–2003
Kentucky	1994
Montana	1987
Utah	1994

TABLE 2.1. (*Continued*)
Selected funding sources for state land conservation programs,
1960–2003

Gas Tax

States (2 total)	**Years**
California	1989, 1999
Idaho	1996

Sales Tax (Conservation Tax, Sporting Goods Tax)

States (4 total)	**Years**
Arkansas	1996
Missouri	1984, 1996
New Jersey	1998
Texas	1994

Oil/Gas/Mineral

States (8 total)	**Years**
Alabama	1992–2012
California	1997
Florida	1979, 1987
Kentucky	1994
Louisiana	1988
Michigan	1976
Montana	1975
New Mexico	1988, 1992

Adapted and updated from *Preserving California's Natural Heritage* (California Resources Agency, 1998); http://ceres.ca.gov/planning/conservation_guidebook/OtherStates.pdf.

then-governor Jane Swift signed Executive Order 418, which provided up to $30,000 in planning services to each community to draft a community development plan. The plans will include image-based maps that municipalities can generate to portray their future growth through the identification of open space, housing, commercial, industrial, and transportation needs.

To help translate planning into action, the Community Preservation Act allows communities, through local referenda, to create Community Preservation Trust Funds financed by up to 3 percent surcharges on property taxes. At least 10 percent of the money must be set aside each year for each of the three spending categories: acquiring open space,

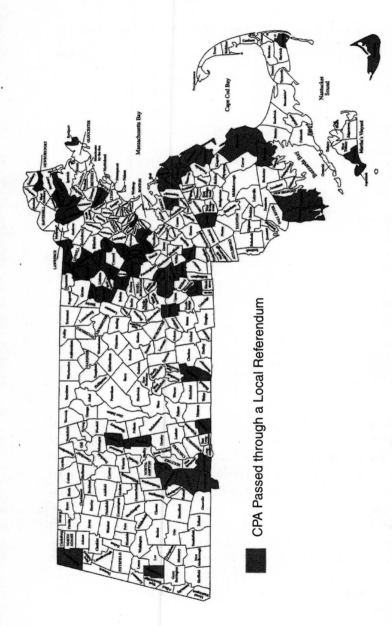

■ CPA Passed through a Local Referendum

MAP 2.1. As of November 2002, fifty-eight communities (shaded) in Massachusetts have approved 3 percent property tax surcharges that raise $26 million annually for community preservation activities under the state's Community Preservation Act program. *Map courtesy of the Community Preservation Coalition; www.communitypreservation.org.*

providing affordable housing, and preserving historic sites and buildings. Local communities can decide how to split the remaining 70 percent among the three emphasis areas.

The state's carrot for local government approval of the surcharge is access to $26 million each year in state matching grants. The state money comes from surcharge fees of $20 on each recording fee and $10 on the recording of a municipal lien certificate, collected by the registrar of deeds and assistant recorders. The annual state match will range from 10 percent to 100 percent of the local surcharge, based on the amount of money collected at the local level by participating communities, with communities that adopt the maximum 3 percent surcharge eligible for higher matches.

Under the open space component, CPA funds may be used to purchase land, easements, or restrictions to protect existing and future water supply areas, agricultural and forest land, coastal lands, frontage to inland water bodies, wildlife habitat, nature preserves, and scenic vistas. Towns and cities also can buy land for recreational use, including land for parks, trails, playgrounds, community gardens, and noncommercial youth and adult sports. Flexibility built into the legislation allows communities to spend the CPA money outside their boundaries to protect water supplies and heritage corridors, or to partner in other regional open space efforts. The new open space funding already has allowed municipalities such as Bedford, Boxford, Harvard, Rowley, and Weston to protect farmland and water supplies that probably would have been out of reach financially without the new funding sources.

To help administer the program, the law requires communities to create Community Preservation Committees that assess community preservation needs and make recommendations to local officials regarding how to spend the CPA money. The Community Preservation Act money ties in with two other state programs. If a community passes the CPA, it will receive 10 bonus points in its application evaluation in two other state open space and recreation acquisition programs—called the Self-Help and Urban Self-Help funding programs.

SELF-HELP PROGRAM

The state established the Self-Help Program in 1961 to help municipal conservation commissions acquire land for natural resource and passive outdoor recreation purposes. The program, which is funded by environmental bond bills approved by the state legislature, received $21.25 million in grant money in 2002, to be spent over three to five years. Municipalities must have a five-year open space and recreation plan to be eligible for Self-Help grants. Eligible lands include trails; wildlife habitat; unique natural, historic, or cultural resources; water resources; and forest and farm land. Under the Self-Help Program, the state pays for the acquisition of land or conservation easements and associated acquisition costs. During the FY 1998–FY 2002 period, the program awarded $26.3 million in grants to fund 132 projects that protected 7,640 acres.

URBAN SELF-HELP PROGRAM

The Urban Self-Help Program was established in 1977 to give grants to communities for the acquisition of land, and the construction, restoration, or rehabilitation of land for park and outdoor recreation purposes, such as playgrounds, game courts, swimming pools, and athletic playfields. The Urban Self-Help Program, which also is funded by environmental bond bills, received $22.2 million in August 2002 for grants to be spread over three to five years.

New Jersey

New Jersey faces a daunting challenge as it struggles to protect its remaining conservation lands. The fifth smallest state in the Union and the ninth most populous, New Jersey easily outpaces all other states in terms of population density, with more than a thousand people for every square mile in the state. Fully 40 percent of the 4.8-million-acre state already is developed, by far the highest percentage among all states. But Garden State residents have long supported land conservation initiatives, beginning in 1961 with the creation of the Green Acres Program, the first of its kind in the nation. Between 1961 and 1995 state residents approved nine bond referenda totaling $1.6 billion for open space and recreation (see Table 2.2).

Despite the state's impressive record for passing bonds to preserve open space, state officials had long sought a dedicated source of funding. In 1997, the Governor's Council on New Jersey Outdoors recommended a dedicated funding source to preserve an additional 1 million

TABLE 2.2.

Funding for New Jersey Green Acres, Farmland Preservation, and Historic Preservation Programs, 1961–1999 (in millions of dollars)

Year	Program/Purpose	Amount (millions of dollars)
1961	Green Acres Land Acquisition Act	$60
1971	Green Acres Land Acquisition Act	$80
1974	Green Acres Land Acquisition and Recreation Opportunities Act	$200
1978	Green Acres Bond Act	$200
1981	Farmland Preservation Bond Act	$50
1983	Green Acres Bond Act	$135
1987	Green Acres, Cultural Centers and Historic Preservation Bond Act	$35 (GA), $25 (HP)
1989	Open Space Preservation Bond Act	$230 (GA), $50 (FP)
1992	Green Acres, Clean Water, Farmland and Historic Preservation Bond Act	$200 (GA), $50 (FP), $25 (HP)
1995	Green Acres, Farmland and Historic Preservation, and Blue Acres Bond Act	$250 (GA), $50 (FP), $30 (BA), $10 (HP)
1998	Supplemental appropriation in budget	$25 (GA), $25 (FP)
1998	Constitutional amendment providing stable source of funding for Land and Historic Preservation approved by voters	$98/year for 10 years for GA, FP, and HP
1999	Garden State Preservation Trust Act becomes law, providing program guidance for SSF	$6 (HP), $92 (60%/40% GA/FP)

Source: New Jersey Department of Environmental Protection, Green Acres Program.
BA = Blue Acres Program; FP = Farmland Preservation Program; GA = Green Acres Program; HP = Historic Preservation Program; SSF = stable source of funding.

acres in the state on top of the 900,000 acres already preserved. Then-governor Christine Whitman championed the idea of devoting $98 million a year in state's sales tax revenue for open space acquisition and protection. An overwhelming two-thirds of voters agreed in November 1998, and the state is now committed to spending up to $3 billion in state sales taxes over thirty years to achieve the ambitious goal. If reached, it would mean that nearly 40 percent of the state's total land area would be protected from development.

The idea has caught fire locally as well. By 2003, residents of 20 of the state's 21 counties and 187 of its 566 municipalities had approved funding for local open space and recreation plans to match the new state funding. Based on the open space tax rates, counties and municipalities anticipated collecting more than $158 million in 2003 to preserve open space.

GARDEN STATE PRESERVATION TRUST

To implement the $3 billion open space plan approved by voters, legislators passed the Garden State Preservation Trust Act, which then-governor Whitman signed into law in June 1999.[2] The law created the Garden State Preservation Trust, whose mission includes overseeing the preservation of an additional 1 million acres in the state. The trust reviews and recommends preservation projects to the governor and the state legislature that have been proposed by the state's three key preservation agencies—the Office of Green Acres, the State Agricultural Development Committee, and the New Jersey Historic Trust. It also ensures that adequate funding and financing are available for the preservation projects. As approved by voters, state legislators can appropriate up to $200 million annually through 2009 for open space, farmland, and historic preservation projects. The appropriations come from the $98 million in annually dedicated state sales taxes, and up to $1 billion in bonds that may be issued for the same purposes, to be paid off by the dedicated sales tax funding available through 2029.

As part of its mission, the trust reviews all conservation projects recommended by the state's three preservation programs to monitor how well they meet the state's preservation goals. These goals include the protection of the state's water supplies, preservation of its agricultural land base, protection of contiguous and diverse wildlife habitats and greenways, and provision of recreational opportunities throughout the state.

GREEN ACRES PROGRAM

The state Green Acres Program, which has protected more than 507,000 acres since 1961, receives $120 million each year from the Garden State Preservation Trust to administer four land preservation programs.[3] Half the total ($60 million) is earmarked each year for state-initiated acquisitions or additions to state parks, forests, natural areas, and wildlife management areas.

About 40 percent ($48 million each year) goes for grants and loans to counties and municipalities to fund their land preservation and recreational development projects. For counties and municipalities that have adopted a local open space and recreation plan and an open space tax to implement it, the agency's Planning Incentive Program provides 50 percent matching funds along with a streamlined application process and flexibility in the use of the funds for land acquisition projects. Towns and counties that don't have local open space and recreation plans and haven't approved a local open space tax receive only 25 percent matching funds for specific open space projects, along with a 2 percent loan for part of the remaining costs of the project.

To promote open space and recreation development in larger cities, the agency offers a separate 75 percent match to so-called Urban Aid municipalities, with 2 percent loans available to fund remaining costs. The remaining $11.5 million (10 percent) of the Garden State Preservation Trust money is reserved for a 50 percent matching grant program (with a $500,000 cap per project) for environmental nonprofit groups that are acquiring land or conservation easements or developing recreational facilities.

FARMLAND PRESERVATION PROGRAM

As part of New Jersey's ambitious goal to preserve an additional 1 million acres, the state quadrupled funding for farmland preservation in FY 1999, with a long-term goal to protect 500,000 acres of the state's agricultural land. The State Agriculture Development Committee receives about $80 million a year from the Garden State Preservation Trust to administer the state's five farmland land preservation programs.[4] As of January 2003, the state had preserved 808 farms, comprising 101,126 acres of farmland, including approximately 26,346 acres (284 farms) since it started expending Garden State Preservation Trust funding in 2000. The total preserved acreage represents approximately 12 percent of the estimated 830,000 acres of available farmland in New Jersey—ranking it first among all states in the preservation of available land base.

The eleven-member public–private committee, chaired by the state secretary of agriculture, sometimes buys farms outright and resells them with agricultural deed restrictions. Second, the committee may purchase development rights directly from the landowner. Third, the committee provides grants to counties to cover between 60 percent and 80 percent of their costs in purchasing development rights from landowners. And, as in the Green Acres Program, the committee provides Planning Incentive Grants to counties or municipalities to fund easement purchases to protect blocks of land included in local farmland preservation plans. Only municipalities or counties that have farmland preservation plans in place that are funded by local farmland preservation programs are eligible for the incentive grants. Finally, the committee provides up to 50 percent matching grants to nonprofit groups that purchase farmland or easements. Separately, landowners can voluntarily restrict development on the property for eight years, in return for becoming eligible for cost-share grants for soil and water conservation projects.

New Jersey Environmental Infrastructure Financing Program

In the last few years, New Jersey municipalities have had access to a new source of land acquisition funding—the New Jersey Environmental Infrastructure Financing Program.[5] The program, the first of its kind in the nation when introduced in 1985, uses federal clean water funds and the proceeds from bonds sold by the New Jersey Environmental Infrastructure Trust to award low-interest loans to cities and authorities to improve wastewater treatment systems. To address nonpoint source water pollution, the program in 2001 began financing the acquisition of open space to protect water quality and provide watershed and aquifer recharge protection. Passive recreational uses, such as hiking, cross-country skiing, horseback riding, rowboating, canoeing, fishing, and hunting, are allowed on the land. In the first two years of program funding for land acquisition, sixteen communities borrowed $30 million to preserve more than 1,100 acres.

Maryland

Maryland makes a claim that no other state has dared to match. It has preserved more open space than was lost to development in seven of the last ten years. Thanks to the introduction of two land conservation programs in recent years—GreenPrint and Rural Legacy—that have bolstered three decades-old programs—Program Open Space, the Agricultural Land Preservation Program, and the Maryland Environmental

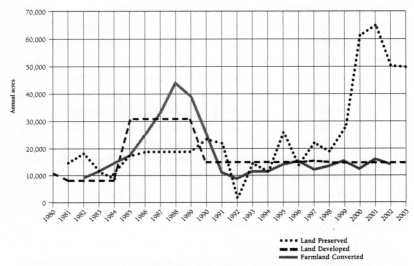

FIGURE 2.1 Land preserved and developed, state of Maryland, 1980–2003. *Source: Grant Dehart/Maryland Department of Natural Resources.* Figure by Sue Dodge.

Trust—the state now boasts perhaps the most effective, comprehensive land conservation and growth management program in the country. Together, the five programs have helped protect more than 1 million acres and 19 percent of the total land area in a state that is dominated geographically by the largest estuary in the nation—the Chesapeake Bay (see Figure 2.1). Physically bisecting the state, the bay also wields a hefty economic punch, generating more than $30 billion in tourism, fishing, and other commercial activity each year. But concern about the bay's health prompted Maryland, and neighboring Virginia, Pennsylvania, and Washington, D.C., to sign the Chesapeake Bay Agreement in June 2000, pledging to protect 20 percent of the bay's watershed lands by 2010 while reducing the rate of sprawling development by 30 percent by 2012.

PROGRAM OPEN SPACE

Maryland legislators created the state's nationally recognized Program Open Space in 1968, making it the second oldest open space program in the country, behind New Jersey's Green Acres Program.[6] State law-makers appropriate money each year to fund the program, derived mostly from the state's real estate transfer tax and supplemented occasionally by state general obligation bonds. By 2003, the program had helped acquire about 250,000 acres of state parks, wildlife habitat, and natural areas, and had awarded more than 4,000 grants to purchase and develop 36,000 acres of local parks. For FY 2000 through FY 2003 alone, the program received $230.5 million, which was split roughly fifty-fifty, with half devoted to state acquisitions and half allocated to the state's twenty-three counties and the city of Baltimore for local projects. The program also manages the Heritage Conservation Fund, which receives roughly $2 million each year in real estate transfer taxes to buy and protect important natural areas harboring habitats for rare species or unique natural communities.

As part of the state's Smart Growth Initiative, Program Open Space manages a new Community Parks and Playgrounds Initiative, which focuses on restoring existing parks and creating new park and green-space systems in municipalities. Using funding from general obligation bonds and general revenue, the program in its first two years awarded 109 grants totaling $10.6 million to local governments to rehabilitate, expand, or improve existing parks; create new parks; or purchase and install playground equipment in older neighborhoods.

RURAL LEGACY PROGRAM

Much of the credit for Maryland's leadership in the land conservation arena belongs to former governor Parris Glendening, who ushered in a statewide strategic approach to smart growth during his eight-year tenure, which ended in 2003. One of his accomplishments was the creation of the Rural Legacy Program in 1997, which broke new ground in the state's efforts to manage growth.[7]

Five years earlier, the general assembly had passed the Economic Growth, Resource Protection, and Planning Act, which required cities and counties to develop growth management plans. The Smart Growth Act of 1997 aimed to encourage compact development and control sprawl by prohibiting the state from funding growth-related projects, such as roads and sewers, that were not located within locally designated "priority funding areas."

As a complement to that effort, the Rural Legacy Program offered grants to local governments and land trusts to conserve significant, locally designated areas of open space, including large greenbelts around existing growth areas. Legislators appropriate bond funds each year to pay for the bulk of the program. A smaller percentage is drawn from Program Open Space money that is derived from the state's real estate transfer tax, in combination with general obligation bonds from the state's capital budget.

The early results have been encouraging. Around the state, twenty-five rural legacy areas have been created, with participation of twenty-one of Maryland's twenty-three counties and twenty-one land trusts. The results: from FY 1998 through FY 2003, nearly $132 million in grants have been awarded and $92.5 million in acquisitions have been completed, which have protected 39,000 acres of large contiguous areas of farmland, woodland, environmentally sensitive areas, and open space.

GreenPrint

Maryland's most recently created land conservation program—Green-Print—puts the state at the forefront of modern land conservation.[8] The program, created in 2001, provides an overarching plan to help coordinate ongoing public and private sector land protection activities in Maryland aimed at preserving a statewide network of green infrastructure that links protected lands of high environmental value. Legislators provided $51 million over the first two years of the program (FY 2002 and 2003), derived from general obligation bonds, with the intention of boosting the state's land conservation capacity by 10,000 acres per year. One-fourth of the funding is devoted each year to the acquisition of easements in agricultural districts created under the Agricultural Land Preservation Program, discussed below (see Maryland Agricultural Land Preservation Foundation).

Using satellite imaging technology and input from scientists, local governments, and conservation organizations, Maryland has mapped 1.5 million acres of important unprotected natural lands. The state envisions protecting much of this remaining green infrastructure through a combination of public acquisitions and easements and private stewardship efforts that will link large protected areas—sites of several hundred acres or more called green hubs—through a web of "green links." The connectors will form habitat highways—stream valleys and mountain ridges that allow safe passage for wildlife through natural habitat, facilitate seed and pollen transport to help plants thrive, and keep streams and wetlands healthy by protecting adjacent vegetation. Collateral program benefits include improving the state's air and water quality and protecting a land base upon which tourism and the forest products and seafood industries depend to flourish.

Maryland Agricultural Land Preservation Foundation

Maryland boasts one of the oldest and most successful farmland preservation programs in the country, with 228,854 acres under conservation easements since its creation in 1977. Annual appropriations that allow the state's twenty-six-year-old Maryland Agricultural Land Preservation Foundation (MALPF) to purchase the development rights comes from three sources: a portion of the state real estate transfer taxes; an agricultural land transfer tax, which is assessed on all agricultural land converted to other uses; and GreenPrint bond funds.[9] Most of the program's funding comes from a 14.5 percent share of the real estate transfer tax that also funds Program Open Space. MALPF also has been receiving one-fourth of the funds from the GreenPrint Program, which resulted in $8.75 million in bond funds in FY 2002 and $4 million in FY 2003 spent on MALPF/GreenPrint easements. These easement purchases use bond funds from the state Department of Natural Resources. MALPF also receives some matching funds from the county participants in the program and the Federal Farmland Protection Program.

Legislators had been appropriating about $19 million to the program until the budget crunch of FY 2003, which resulted in a cutback to $10 million. Half the money goes equally to all twenty-three counties; the other half is used by the state to obtain easements.

To become eligible for state purchase of development rights, landowners first must establish an agricultural land preservation district of 50 acres or more. If the property meets the minimum criteria, the landowners sign a voluntary agreement that the land will be maintained in agricultural use for five years or more. Landowners must agree not to subdivide the land for residential, commercial, or industrial use while under district status. Participating landowners then may apply to sell their development rights to the foundation. About 400,000 acres of farmland are now enrolled in the districts, a little more than half of which also has conservation easements on it.

State legislators are considering whether to expand the program. A legislative task force reported in 2001 that 371,000 acres of Maryland farmland had been lost in the preceding two decades, mostly to residential development. The task force recommended that the state set a goal of protecting 1.1 million acres of farmland by 2022, half the remaining privately owned farmland in the state. A joint legislative resolution during the 2002 legislative session set the goal for the protection of productive farmland at 1.03 million acres, protected by a combination of MALPF, Rural Legacy, GreenPrint, and county farmland preservation programs.

Maryland Environmental Trust

Even before Program Open Space was created, Maryland legislators in 1967 created the Maryland Environmental Trust (MET), a statewide land trust funded through the Department of Natural Resources budget.[10] The trust has helped landowners protect more than 85,000 acres through 676 conservation easements, several of which were purchased by Program Open Space on Civil War sites, or by the Rural Legacy Program, and held by the MET for stewardship.

In 1988, the trust created a land trust assistance program with federal funding from the Coastal Zone Management Program that has helped create fifty-two local land trusts. The trust also oversees a revolving Land Trust Grant Fund that has provided $2.5 million in zero-interest loans to local land trusts for land and easement acquisitions.

In May 2001, Maryland joined a growing list of states that allow state income tax credits for donations of conservation easements to the Maryland Environmental Trust and the Maryland Agricultural Preservation Foundation. Donors can deduct up to $5,000 in state taxes each year, and carry forward any unused credit for fifteen years. In the mid-1980s, state legislators approved a full property tax credit on the unimproved portion of conservation easements donated to the MET.

Florida

Arguably, Florida's land conservation program is the most ambitious in the world. Since 1989, the state has committed more than $6 billion in bonds to its land acquisition programs, the first $3 billion of which had by 2002 protected more than 1.7 million acres. The second $3 billion, expected to be spent by 2012, could preserve another 1.5 million to 2 million acres in the fourth fastest-growing state in the nation. Although the state's land acquisition efforts began in earnest in 1972 with a $240 million bond, it put real muscle behind land preservation during the 1990s when 3 million new residents pushed Florida's population over the 16 million mark.

And there's no slowdown in sight. The state added 400,000 residents from 2000 to 2001, nearly equivalent to the entire population of Wyoming. New residents mean new land development—to the tune of 165,000 acres each year in the Sunshine State. Florida's real estate market has been so hot for three decades that the state was forced to turn to the huge bond referenda as a land acquisition vehicle, said David Buchanan, a twenty-nine-year veteran of land acquisitions in the state's Division of Recreation and Parks. After seeing land double in value in a year, "you couldn't wait for a trust fund to accumulate money," he said.

As more Floridians cram onto the low-lying peninsula, they are sharing space with one of the nation's richest arrays of wildlife. The state ranks fourth among the lower forty-eight states in overall species richness, with more species than any other state east of the Mississippi River. More than 425 bird species are found in Florida, along with 184 species of amphibians and reptiles, 126 fishes, and 75 mammals.

The wildlife, warm weather, beaches, and vacation magnets like Disney World have created a $46 billion tourism and recreation industry that attracts more than 65 million visitors to Florida each year. Its state park system is one of the largest and most heavily used in the nation, with more than 150 parks covering 575,000 acres. The parks alone generate $528 million each year for local economies, create 9,900 jobs, and bring in $36.9 million in state sales tax revenue, according to the Florida State Park System Economic Impact Assessment for FY 2001/2002.[11]

The most glaring environmental casualty among all this bustle is the Everglades. The slow-moving sheet of water that has drained south Florida for ages was reengineered in the 1920s to regulate flooding and open up land to agriculture and development. What was perceived as an engineering marvel has caused widespread damage to the rich Everglades ecosystem, a miscalculation that the state and federal government now are trying to rectify with billions of dollars of restoration work over the next thirty years.

With the massive Everglades restoration as a backdrop, the state has created three major land conservation programs and a handful of small but vitally important programs to address a variety of recreation, environmental, and open space needs. The financial underpinnings for most of these programs have been the two $3 billion bond programs—Preservation 2000 and Florida Forever—approved by voters and the state legislature in 1989 and 1999, respectively.[12] The bonds are paid off by a documentary stamp tax—an excise tax for recording documents—mostly of real estate transactions, costing 70 cents of each $100 of value, along with annual appropriations. Legislators authorize spending each year for the various programs that derive their funding from the bonds.

Recent tight budget times in Florida made the land conservation accounts a tempting target for legislators. In 2001 the legislature appropriated $75 million from unspent, unobligated Preservation 2000 cash balances in various agency allocations to the Save Our Everglades Trust Fund. Governor Jeb Bush, running for reelection in 2002, vetoed a second attempt in 2002 to divert $100 million to pay for other state programs.

CONSERVATION AND RECREATION LANDS/FLORIDA FOREVER PROGRAM

Most of Florida's land conservation money over the past few decades has been devoted to the Conservation and Recreation Lands Program (CARL).[13] State legislators created the CARL Program in 1979 to fund large conservation and recreation projects of statewide significance. From its inception through 2001, the program acquired and protected 996,000 acres of environmentally endangered areas and other land for recreation, water management, and the preservation of historical and archaeological sites. The acreage includes Environmentally Endangered Lands funds spent since 1980, CARL funds from 1980 to 2001, and Preservation 2000 funds allocated to the CARL Program through 2002.

Legislators initially funded the program by transferring $27 million in bond funds left over from the Environmentally Endangered Lands Program. They added $15 million to $35 million annually in recurring revenues from state severance taxes on solid minerals and liquid fuels. Because of economic difficulties in the phosphate industry that resulted in reduced severance tax revenues, lawmakers reconfigured program funding in 1987 by dropping all severance taxes except the $10 million from phosphate minerals and adding a portion of state excise taxes on documents, mostly from real estate sales.

The program received a huge financial shot in the arm beginning in 1990, as passage of the Preservation 2000 bond package tripled funding. Throughout the 1990s, the CARL Program received $150 million a year from legislators. With the passage of Florida Forever in 1999, the program's funding was trimmed to a still substantial $105 million a year, which is expected to be available until 2010.

The Acquisition and Restoration Council meets twice a year to evaluate and select acquisition projects, which can be nominated by any private or public person or group. The council consists of nine members who represent the state Departments of Community Affairs and Environmental Protection, the Division of Forestry, the Florida Fish and Wildlife Conservation Commission, and the Division of Historical Resources. The governor also appoints four members with backgrounds in land, water, or environmental science. The projects are grouped in three lists: full-fee projects, less-than-fee projects, and small-parcel projects. After projects are approved and grouped, the council sends the list to the governor and cabinet for selection. Once selected, the Division of State Lands negotiates the purchase and buys the land. Despite the huge increase in program spending, demand continues to outstrip available funding, with more than $1 billion in property on the program's acquisition list.

FLORIDA COMMUNITIES TRUST

The second key component of Florida's land conservation effort—the Florida Communities Trust (FCT)—represents a $1 billion financial commitment to local land preservation. The trust, created by legislators in 1989 and funded by bonds approved by voters, provides grants to nonprofit groups and local governments to preserve parks, greenspace, open space, beaches, and natural areas.[14] In furtherance of the legislative directives to tie the grants to the implementation of local growth management plans, the FCT grants are ranked according to criteria that are linked to furthering a local government's growth management plan. The program received $300 million during the 1990s ($30 million a year) in Preservation 2000 bond funding, and is slated to receive an additional $660 million ($66 million a year) in Florida Forever bond funding from FY 2001 through FY 2010.

The results are impressive. Between 1993 and mid-2001, the trust and its local partners acquired and preserved more than 40,000 acres using $242 million in state grants that leveraged $175 million in local funding. By 2003, 25 local governments had approved bonds or identified dedicated funding sources for land acquisition to meet the trust grant program's requirement for a cash match to receive funding. Between 1991 and 2001 the program awarded 470 grants to 47 counties and 145 cities (see Map 2.2). Because of the ability for local governments to leverage their local land acquisition dollars, many communities have submitted land acquisition grants year after year to acquire additional park lands and open space.

The state funding has spurred local governments to formulate and implement a long-range vision of their recreation and open space needs. State legislators passed a statewide growth management law in 1985 that requires local governments to develop comprehensive plans that include "a recreation and open space element indicating a comprehensive system of public and private sites for recreation, including, but not limited to, natural reservations, parks and playgrounds, parkways, beaches and public access to beaches, open spaces, and other recreational facilities."[15]

As with the CARL/Florida Forever state program, demand easily outpaces the $66 million in annual grants available through the Florida Communities Trust/Florida Forever program. In 2001, when two years of funding was awarded in one grant cycle, applicants asked for funding to acquire property worth more than $400 million, with 75 projects receiving $122 million. The trust received 114 applications in 2002, requesting $185 million in grants backed up by $118 million in local matching funds.

SAVE OUR RIVERS PROGRAM

Florida's five water management districts, which cover the entire state, have provided the biggest boost to land conservation in the state.[16] Since their creation in 1972, the districts have purchased land and easements on nearly 2 million acres through funding from bond money,

MAP 2.2. The Florida Communities Trust has awarded $242 million in grants from 1991 to 2001 to protect more than 40,000 acres in cities and counties throughout the state. *Map courtesy of the Florida Communities Trust.*

documentary stamp taxes, and general revenue from state legislators. Under the landmark Save Our Rivers Program, which legislators created in 1981, the Water Management Lands Trust Fund has generated between $60 million and $70 million each year from the state docu-

PHOTO 2.1. Flagler County received grants from the Florida Communities Trust, Preservation 2000, and the St. Johns River Water Management District to preserve the Princess Place Lodge (pictured here) and 1,435 surrounding acres. *Photo courtesy of the Florida Communities Trust.*

mentary stamp taxes on real estate transactions for acquisitions of environmentally sensitive land. The program allows the districts to acquire fee or "less-than-fee" interests in lands needed for water management, water supply, or conservation and protection of water resources.

In addition to the trust fund, the districts received a total of $90 million each year during the 1990s exclusively for land acquisitions under the old Preservation 2000 bond program. In 1999 legislators boosted the districts' annual share to $105 million under the new Florida Forever program, although the districts no longer have to spend all their allotment on land acquisition. But most districts still plan to.

Some districts supplement the above acquisition funding with their own land acquisition bonds, such as in the South Florida Water Management District (WMD), which issued $36 million in bonds in 1996. Finally, under a Cash Mitigation Program, districts, such as the South Florida WMD, receive from $3 million to $5 million a year from environmental resource permit applicants in lieu of such applicants providing mitigation for wetland impacts themselves. These funds are then used by the district for the acquisition, enhancement, and long-term management of environmentally sensitive lands in accordance with the conditions of the permits.

In addition to protecting the land for water quality purposes, the districts also allow various activities on some of the lands they own, including hiking, canoeing, horseback riding, backpacking, camping, and picnicking, along with grazing and logging.

South Florida WMD also taps a special fund as part of its work to restore the Everglades. The Everglades Trust Fund was created in 1994 to implement the Everglades Forever Act. Funding comes from multiple sources, including the state and federal governments, as well as highway toll revenue, property taxes, and agricultural privilege taxes.

FLORIDA RECREATION DEVELOPMENT ASSISTANCE PROGRAM

The Florida Recreation Development Assistance Program (FRDAP) provides grants to local governments to acquire and develop land for public outdoor recreation and to construct or renovate recreational trails.[17] The program was established in 1972 as the successor to what was known as the "15 percent fund." The latter began in 1963, with passage of the Outdoor Recreation and Conservation Act, which created the $20 million Land Acquisition Trust Fund. The Florida Department of Environmental Protection administers the program. The Bureau of Design and Recreation Services of the department's Division of Recreation and Parks has direct responsibility for it.

The program is authorized to receive 5 percent of receipts from the state's Land Acquisition Trust Fund and 2 percent of Florida Forever bond proceeds. But legislators in recent years have been generous in funding the local park and recreation projects. Since FY 1990–1991, legislators have appropriated $146.7 million to fund 1,402 local projects, including 99 land acquisitions. In FY 2002–2003 alone, FRDAP funded 218 projects with $27.1 million in grants. Grant applications are accepted once a year, usually in the fall. Matching funds are required for projects costing $50,000 or more. In 2003, program staff oversaw almost 800 projects worth $90 million.

FLORIDA GREENWAYS AND TRAILS ACQUISITION PROGRAM

Florida is considered a national leader for its development of a comprehensive, statewide greenways and trails program. Its Office of

Greenways and Trails, created by state lawmakers in 1995, purchases greenway and trails land with the $4.5 million it receives annually in Florida Forever bond proceeds.[18] Local governments, nonprofit organizations, developers, and others can apply to the office to fund a greenway or trail acquisition.

To receive funding, successful projects must be recommended by the staff, selected by the twenty-one-member Florida Greenways and Trails Council, and approved by the secretary of the Department of Environmental Protection. Separately, the office awards $1.1 million in grants each year from the federal Recreational Trails Program for motorized and nonmotorized trails. Including acquisitions by its predecessor organization—the Rails-to-Trails Program—the office has acquired 18,000 acres of greenways and trails around the state with $46 million in funding from Preservation 2000 and Florida Forever bond proceeds.

As a key component of its approach to greenway and trail development, the land acquisition program contributes to the implementation of a comprehensive statewide Greenways and Trails Plan that has become a model for other states around the country. Regional greenways and trails consultants within the Office of Greenways and Trails work directly with local governments, developers, private landowners, and state and federal agencies to help establish the greenways and trails system. The Office of Greenways and Trails also administers a greenways and trails designation program that formally defines the statewide system through designation of public and private lands. The public outreach program maintains an online greenways and trails guide, publishes a quarterly newsletter, and offers an environmental education program.

The office was originally established to manage the Marjorie Harris Carr Cross Florida Greenway State Recreation and Conservation Area, a 110-mile greenway corridor that runs across the state. The federal government had planned to dig a ship canal along this corridor stretching across the northcentral section of the state from Inglis-Yankeetown on the Gulf of Mexico to the St. Johns River on the east coast. The canal project was deauthorized, and the lands were transferred to the state for development as a multiple-use recreational corridor.

PHOTO 2.2. The Marshall Swamp Trail in Marion County is located on the Marjorie Harris Carr Cross Florida Greenway. *Photo courtesy of the Florida Department of Environmental Protection, Office of Greenways and Trails.*

Minnesota

Minnesota has embraced a unique blend of funding sources to support its land conservation efforts: lottery revenue, cigarette taxes, general obligation bonds, and fees from environmental license plates.

The bulk of the state's spending on land conservation programs comes from general obligation bonds, from which the Minnesota Legislature funds capital projects for a variety of environmental projects on a biennial basis. In 2000, the state ranked thirteenth in general fund spending on parks and recreation, at $120.1 million, which was 46 percent above the national average of $16.68 per capita (see Table 2.3).

Environment and Natural Resources Trust Fund

To supplement the general fund spending, voters in 1988 approved a constitutional amendment that created the Environment and Natural Resources Trust Fund, a permanent fund to be used for the long-term benefit of the state's environment and natural resources.[19] Minnesota funnels 40 percent of yearly net proceeds from its state lottery, or about 6 cents for every dollar spent on lottery tickets, to the trust fund. In 1998, voters agreed to extend use of the lottery funds for the trust fund

TABLE 2.3

Minnesota general expenditure spending on parks and recreation, 2000

Rank	State	General Expenditures, Parks and Recreation (in thousands of dollars)	Per capita spending (in dollars)
1	Delaware	50,735	64.71
2	Louisiana	193,040	43.20
3	Maryland	216,920	40.96
4	New Jersey	324,078	38.52
5	Hawaii	45,851	37.83
6	West Virginia	54,581	30.19
7	South Dakota	22,311	29.55
8	Arkansas	78,074	29.21
9	Kentucky	115,380	28.55
10	Connecticut	93,919	27.57
11	New York	519,724	27.39
12	Massachusetts	156,498	24.65
13	Minnesota	120,100	24.42
14	New Mexico	44,297	24.35
15	Wyoming	11,504	23.29
16	Illinois	280,448	22.58
17	Tennessee	119,325	20.97
18	Oklahoma	66,784	19.35
19	North Carolina	153,330	19.05
20	Idaho	24,606	19.02
21	Mississippi	50,249	17.66
National average	**United States**	**4,684,669**	**16.68**
22	Georgia	134,272	16.40
23	Nebraska	27,469	16.05
24	Colorado	67,588	15.71
25	South Carolina	62,649	15.62
26	Montana	13,975	15.49
27	Alaska	9,055	14.44
28	North Dakota	9,180	14.30
29	Washington	81,125	13.76
30	Ohio	154,570	13.61
31	Utah	29,809	13.35
32	Michigan	131,894	13.27
33	Indiana	80,118	13.18
34	Oregon	43,648	12.76
35	Rhode Island	12,639	12.06
36	Wisconsin	64,490	12.02
37	Pennsylvania	139,898	11.39
38	Arizona	57,828	11.27
39	Vermont	6,776	11.13
40	California	374,415	11.05

TABLE 2.3. (*Continued*)

Minnesota general expenditure spending on parks and recreation, 2000

Rank	State	General Expenditures, Parks and Recreation (in thousands of dollars)	Per capita spending (in dollars)
41	Virginia	76,528	10.81
42	Florida	167,229	10.46
43	Nevada	19,013	9.52
44	Iowa	25,716	8.79
45	Maine	10,426	8.18
46	Missouri	42,521	7.60
47	New Hampshire	8,646	7.00
48	Texas	72,557	3.48
49	Kansas	7,555	2.81
50	Alabama	11,326	2.55

Source: *U.S. Census*; www.census.gov/govs/www/state00.html.

through 2024, a $700 million commitment. The trust fund, which invests in stocks and bonds, totaled about $300 million as of late 2002, with about $25 million in lottery proceeds added each year. By law, only 5.5 percent of the fund can be allocated for environmental projects annually.

Legislative Commission on Minnesota Resources

All projects that are funded by the state's Environment and Natural Resources Trust Fund first must be submitted to the Legislative Commission on Minnesota Resources, a bipartisan joint legislative commission that makes funding recommendations to the Minnesota Legislature for special natural resource projects.[20] Anyone can apply for an appropriation from the fund. Recipients have included state agencies, local governments, colleges and universities, school districts, and nonprofit organizations. The commission, and its predecessor, which dated to 1963, have recommended 1,214 projects over four decades, for which legislators have appropriated $525 million.

Every two years, the commission draws up a strategic plan that identifies the state's key environmental problems. The commission then selects projects for recommendation to state legislators, based on how well they meet the objectives outlined in the strategic plan. The lawmakers, in turn, appropriate money from the trust fund to finance the projects they approve, which then must be approved by the governor. Between 1991 and 2003, the legislature appropriated $142 million from the fund to finance 241 projects.

The legislature, through the commission, also recommends funding of projects through the Minnesota Future Resources Fund, which is financed through a 2-cents-per-pack tax on cigarettes, and the Great Lakes Protection Fund. The cigarette tax generates about $7 million per year for a variety of natural resource projects.

DEPARTMENT OF NATURAL RESOURCES

State bonding supports a number of state and local land acquisition grant programs managed by the Department of Natural Resources: the Reinvest in Minnesota Critical Habitat Match Program, the Critical Habitat Conservation License Plate Program, the Native Prairie Bank Conservation Easement Program, the Native Prairie Tax Exemption Program, the Metro Greenways Planning Grants Program, the Natural and Scenic Areas Grant Program, and several outdoor recreation and park grant programs.[21]

Reinvest in Minnesota Critical Habitat Match Program/Critical Habitat Conservation License Plate Program

Minnesota's Critical Habitat Match Program was established in 1986 based on a recommendation by the Citizens Commission to Promote Hunting and Fishing in Minnesota. Under the program, individuals or groups who donate land, easements, or cash to protect or enhance critical fish and wildlife habitat have their donations matched dollar for dollar for conservation projects. Since 1986, state legislators have appropriated $24 million to this program.

In 1996, Minnesota initiated the Critical Habitat Conservation License Plate Program, which also is used to match private donations. To date, the license plates have generated over $5 million for acquisition and enhancement of critical habitat to match the $26 million in land and cash donated by private donors. The state has received over $27 million in private donations that have been matched by the two critical habitat programs.

Native Prairie Bank Conservation Easement Program/Prairie Tax Exemption Program

Before Europeans settled Minnesota, the state was home to 18 million acres of native prairie. Today, less than 1 percent (150,000 acres) is left—mostly on private land. The state has two programs to encourage landowners to preserve their prairie land: the Minnesota Native Prairie Bank Conservation Easement Program and the Minnesota Native Prairie Tax Exemption Program. The Minnesota Prairie Bank was created in 1987 as part of its Reinvest in Minnesota initiative. Under the program, landowners may sell permanent easements to the state Department of Natural Resources. Payments are based on a percentage of the average assessed value of cropland. In some cases, landowners retain certain rights to continue selected agricultural uses, such as haying, grazing, or seed harvest. This reduces their payment rate. By late 2002, the state had spent $1,970,000 to purchase fifty-one prairie easements totaling 4,400 acres. Funding comes from general obligation bonds approved by the state legislature.

The Prairie Tax Exemption Program was established in 1980. Approximately 450 landowners enroll more than 12,000 acres annually under the program in return for complete exemption of local property taxes. Landowners receive the exemption in return for agreeing to leave the prairie in its natural state for the year. Annual haying is allowed, but grazing is not.

Metro Greenways Planning Grants Program

Owing to a rapid increase in development during the 1990s, the Metro region of the Minnesota Department of Natural Resources developed a collaborative in 1996 to define a vision for a regional greenways network in the Twin Cities metropolitan area. The Metro Greenways Program was created in 1998 with an appropriation from the state legislature. Approximately $200,000 in department matching grants has been awarded annually since 1999 to local implementing agencies. The grant program has awarded over $900,000 to local communities in four years, which has resulted in the generation of detailed land cover information as well as greenway plans and improved park management plans.

Outdoor Recreation, Regional Park, and Natural and Scenic
Area Grant Programs

Since 1965, state legislators have devoted $66 million in state funds to three programs in the Department of Natural Resources, which have generated $78 million in local matching funding, not including in-kind matches.

Under the Outdoor Recreation Grant Program, the department offers small matching grants to counties and municipalities in conjunction with the federal Land and Water Conservation Fund state grant program to acquire and develop local parks and recreation facilities. Since 1998, legislators have devoted $5.3 million to the program, using funding from bonds, the Minnesota Future Resources Fund, and the Environment and Natural Resources Trust Fund.

A separate Regional Grant Program begun in 2000 offers similar matching grants to regional park organizations outside the Minneapolis–St. Paul metro area. The program received $1.2 million in funding between 2000 and 2002, helping to acquire almost 600 acres.

Legislators created the Natural and Scenic Area Grant Program in 1994 to stimulate acquisition and protection of natural and scenic areas of local or regional interest. Under the program, counties, municipalities, and school districts may apply for up to $500,000 in grants to pay for 50 percent of the cost of acquiring land or easements that contain species or plant communities that are endangered, threatened, of special concern, or rare and unique; land that provides high-quality scenic viewscapes; and other lands that contain outstanding natural resource value.

Legislators appropriated $3.4 million for the program from 1998 to 2002, using funding from bonds, the Minnesota Future Resources Fund, and the Environment and Natural Resources Trust Fund. Between 1995, when the first grants were made, and 2003, the program helped local governments acquire more than 1,400 acres with forty-three grants totaling $5.5 million.

BOARD OF WATER AND SOIL RESOURCES

In addition to the land conservation programs managed by the state Department of Natural Resources, the state Board of Water and Soil

Resources manages several land conservation programs, two of which are described below.[22]

Reinvest in Minnesota Reserve Program

In 1986 in one of the first such programs of its kind in the nation, the state created the Reinvest in Minnesota Reserve Program. The program uses state bonds to buy conservation easements from willing landowners who agree to stop grazing or cropping the land to improve water quality, reduce soil erosion, and enhance fish and wildlife habitat. Owners also must institute conservation practices, such as planting grass or trees or restoring drained wetlands on the property, with the costs partially offset by state payments. The program is implemented locally by soil and water conservation districts with funding from state bonds and the state general fund.

After the U.S. Congress created the federal Conservation Reserve Enhancement Program in 1996, the state program has worked together with the U.S. Department of Agriculture program to concentrate their efforts on the thirty-seven-county Minnesota River Basin. Together, between 1998 and 2003, the programs have retired more than 100,000 acres of environmentally sensitive farmland in the river basin, using $81 million in state bonds, which leveraged $187 million in federal funding. The state money pays an up-front bonus to landowners, while the federal program follows up with annual payments for fifteen years.

The state Board of Water and Soil Resources also manages a wetland preservation program that pays landowners for permanent conservation easements on certain existing wetlands. The program, which operates in much the same way as the Reinvest in Minnesota Reserve Program, was created in 1991 with enactment of the Wetland Conservation Act.

MINNESOTA METROPOLITAN AGRICULTURAL PRESERVE/ AGRICULTURAL LAND PRESERVATION PROGRAMS

Legislators in 1980 created the Metropolitan Agricultural Preserve Program, which as of 2001 was preserving nearly 200,000 acres of farmland in the seven-county Minneapolis–St. Paul area. Through the program, local governments identify areas where agriculture is to be preserved, where nonfarm growth will be permitted, and what standards apply to each area. Farmers receive property tax credits and additional benefits.

Using the metro program as a model, legislators in 1984 created a similar program for the rest of the state, called the Agricultural Land Preservation Program. Counties adopting agricultural land preservation plans and implementing controls may offer agricultural preserves (an agricultural preserve is a restrictive covenant on qualifying land, limiting its use to agriculture or forestry). In return, farmers receive property tax credits, protection for normal agricultural practices, and other benefits. As of 2001, 156,429 acres in three counties were enrolled in the program.[23]

Illinois

Illinois joined many other states in the 1980s that created a parks and open space grant program funded by the state's real estate transfer tax. The Open Space Lands Acquisition and Development Program aimed to replace federal funding for outdoor recreation from state grants under the Land and Water Conservation Fund program, which had all but dried up.[24] The grant program, created in 1985, is funded by 35 percent of the state real estate transfer tax. As of 2003, it had provided more than $161 million in matching grants for 900 projects in counties, townships, municipalities, park districts, conservation districts, and forest preserve districts for the acquisition, development, and rehabilitation of land for public outdoor recreation.

The state Department of Natural Resources runs the program, which provides up to 50 percent matching grants up to $750,000 for acquisition costs and $400,000 for development costs for localities under 2 million residents. Counties and cities with over 2 million residents may receive up to $1.15 million and $2.3 million, respectively, for acquisition and development projects. Eligible projects include not only public park acquisition and development but also open space acquisitions to protect floodplains, wetlands, natural areas, wildlife habitat, and unique geologic or biologic features. Projects are judged on how well they address state and local recreation and conservation issues identified in Illinois's Statewide Comprehensive Outdoor Recreation Plan.

State legislators in 2002, trying to close a FY 2003 budget deficit, cut the dedicated funding to 20 percent of real estate transfer tax revenue, resulting in a $9 million cut in the program. But then Governor George Ryan signed legislation in January 2003 that restored the original formula for the next fiscal year, effective July 1, 2003.

ILLINOIS OPEN LANDS TRUST

During the 1990s, evidence mounted that Illinois was consuming land much faster than its population was increasing. In Springfield, land consumption increased 89 percent over thirty years while the population increased 12 percent, according to the Illinois Association of Park Districts.[25] In Peoria, a 34 percent population increase required 159 percent more land over the same time period. A study conducted by the Openlands Project predicted that the amount of developed land in the thirteen-county Chicago metropolitan area could double in the next thirty years.[26]

In response, the state created the Open Lands Trust in 1998, the largest open space acquisition and development program in the state's history.[27] The program authorized $160 million in state general obligation bonds over four years to step up land acquisition to protect more open space and wildlife habitat. It provides funding for state land acquisitions as well as loans and matching grants up to $2 million for local governments. Nonprofit land conservation groups also are eligible.

CONSERVATION 2000

In 1995, the Illinois General Assembly unanimously approved a six-year, $100 million program, called the Conservation 2000 Initiative, that takes an ecosystem approach to an array of local environmental problems that were hard to address—in part because Illinois is 90 percent privately owned and 75 percent farmland. In August of 1999, legislators extended the program until 2009 with $268 million in new funding. Conservation 2000 consists of nine programs at the Department of Natural Resources, the Department of Agriculture, and the Environmental Protection Agency. These programs focus on monitoring and preserving the state's natural lands and waters, funding outdoor recreational activities, and promoting sustainable agriculture. Individuals, nonprofit organizations, and local governments can apply for grants through one of the nine programs.

One of the nine, the Ecosystems Program, had created thirty-nine local partnership councils by late 2002, covering 82 percent of the state and 98 percent of its population. The partnerships are broad-based, locally organized efforts incorporating local communities and private, public, and corporate landowners. General appropriation and general obligation bonding provide grants to the partnerships to acquire land and easements. By late 2002, the partnerships had protected 5,000 acres through conservation easements or simple acquisition and restored more than 50,000 acres of habitat. And between 1996 and late 2002, the program had awarded more than $23 million in grants, leveraging $32 million in matching funds from local partners, for a total of $55 million for 580 habitat restoration and land protection projects.

Trail Grant Programs

Since 1990, Illinois has tapped a percentage of its title transfer fees for motor vehicles to help acquire, develop, and renovate bicycle path projects in local communities. From 1998 through 2001, the state provided $15.8 million in funding. The grants, which range up to $200,000 to cover half of project costs, have helped add hundreds of miles of locally managed trails throughout the state. The state also created a Snowmobile Trail Grant Program with registration fees from snowmobiles that funds trail corridor land acquisition and development at a level of $120,000 annually. Illinois also has a separate Off-Highway Vehicle (OHV) Trails Fund, financed through all-terrain-vehicle titling and registration fees, that provides grants to acquire and build OHV trails and to repair damage from their unauthorized use. This program has an annual budget of approximately $600,000.

Natural Areas Acquisition Fund

The state's Natural Areas Acquisition Fund (NAAF) has provided approximately $9 million yearly from the dedication of 15 percent of the state's real estate transfer tax to the acquisition and stewardship of lands that are of statewide significance because of high-quality habitat or the presence of endangered or threatened species. In 2002, the Illinois General Assembly reduced the dedicated percentage to 5 percent, reducing NAAF revenue to about $3 million. In early January 2003,

Illinois governor George Ryan signed legislation just before leaving office that restored the 15 percent allocation effective July 1, 2003.

Colorado

Colorado is a state that thinks open space is a "good bet." Perhaps this is why Colorado uses its lottery proceeds to finance a statewide land protection program known as GOCO, short for Great Outdoors Colorado. As originally approved by voters in 1980, and state lawmakers two years later, lottery proceeds were split three ways: 40 percent for the Conservation Trust Fund for distribution to local governments and park and recreation districts on a per capita basis for parks, recreation, and open space; 10 percent for Colorado State Parks for state parks and outdoor recreation projects; and the remaining 50 percent for the state Capital Construction Fund to pay for state prisons and other buildings.

In 1992 voters approved an amendment to the Colorado Constitution (Article XXVII) to create the Great Outdoors Colorado (GOCO) Trust Fund to fund projects that preserve Colorado's wildlife, parks, rivers, trails, and open spaces.[28] From 1993 through 1998, 15 percent of the lottery proceeds originally spent on prisons and state buildings was redirected to the new trust fund. Beginning in 1999, when lottery proceeds for the Capital Construction Fund were phased out, fully half the lottery proceeds went to GOCO. In FY 2002, the lottery generated $46.5 million for the trust fund, based on a formula that designates half the annual proceeds from the lottery ($105 million in FY 2002) for the fund, with a cap of $35 million adjusted for inflation.

The lottery money comes none too soon for the Centennial State. Colorado had 4.4 million residents in July 2001, a 34 percent increase since 1990, making it the third fastest-growing state in the nation, behind Nevada and Arizona. The population of Douglas County, sandwiched between the sprawling Denver and Colorado Springs metro areas, grew 11.1 percent a year from 1990 to 2001 (from 61,559 to 200,385), making it the fastest-growing county in the nation.

Despite the growth, Colorado has built up an impressive network of parks and wildlife areas to protect its natural areas. The Colorado Division of Parks and Outdoor Recreation, known as Colorado State Parks, manages more than 215,000 acres in 40 parks, which attract more than

PHOTO 2.3. GOCO funding helped The Nature Conservancy purchase the Carpenter Ranch in Routt County, Colorado. *Photo courtesy of The Nature Conservancy.*

11 million visitors each year. And the state Division of Wildlife manages more than 240 wildlife areas and 960 wildlife species.

With the addition of the GOCO program, the state has taken its land protection efforts to a new level, strengthening state-level acquisition programs while giving local citizens a new tool to preserve land in cities and counties around the state. Between 1994, when it first began awarding grants, and April 2003, GOCO awarded $338 million for more than 1,800 projects across Colorado. As of mid-2002, the grants, which have been matched on a three-to-one basis in cash and in-kind services, have preserved 361,145 acres of open space, acquired 47,041 acres for parks and wildlife areas, and built or restored 569 miles of trails. The money also helped build or improve 162 sporting fields, improve or expand campgrounds at ten state parks, and protect forty-three threatened or endangered wildlife species. The enormously successful program planned to award $55 million in grants during FY 2002, up dramatically from $25 million the year before, thanks to a boost in lottery proceeds from the arrival of the multistate Powerball lottery.

To further expand the program's financial clout (demand for grants is triple available funding), Colorado voters approved a referendum by a 58 percent to 42 percent margin in November 2001 to give GOCO bonding authority of up to $115 million for urgent land preservation projects. Governor Bill Owens followed up in 2002 by signing legislation to extend the sunset date of the lottery to 2024 to ensure that GOCO has an adequate revenue stream.

The lottery money is channeled into seven GOCO grant programs. The staff reviews project applications and makes recommendations to a seventeen-member board, which is appointed by the governor and confirmed by the state senate. The grant programs require up to 50 percent cash and in-kind matches, depending on the grant, to meet objectives for outdoor recreation, wildlife, open space and local government involvement:

- Legacy initiative grants, 19 of which, totaling $118.3 million, had been awarded as of mid-2002, are large-scale, multiyear projects of regional or statewide significance that meet multiple program objectives for outdoor recreation, wildlife, open space, and local government involvement.
- Open space grants, 147 totaling $36.4 million as of mid-2002, are awarded twice a year competitively to nonprofit land conservation groups, local governments, Colorado State Parks, and the Colorado Division of Wildlife to protect land and natural areas such as urban open space, riparian corridors, wildlife habitat, agricultural land, and community separators.
- Local government grants, 605 totaling $27.2 million as of mid-2002, also are awarded competitively twice a year to counties, municipalities, and special districts to acquire, establish, expand, and enhance park, outdoor recreation, and environmental education facilities.
- State park grants, 519 totaling $44.3 million as of mid-2002, to Colorado State Parks to build, maintain, or improve state parks. Projects include land acquisitions, enhancements such as campgrounds and visitor centers, and education and interpretation programs.
- Wildlife grants, 186 totaling $53 million as of mid-2002, to the Colorado Division of Wildlife for wildlife education programs, wildlife viewing programs, and efforts that will help keep species off the federal threatened and endangered species list through recovery efforts and the protection and restoration of critical wildlife habitats.

- Trail grants, 262 as of mid-2002 totaling $7.4 million, which GOCO funds once a year through the Colorado State Parks Trails Program, a partnership between GOCO and Colorado State Parks, to build, enhance, maintain, or expand trails around the state.
- Planning and capacity building grants, 231 totaling $8.6 million as of mid-2002, which GOCO gives once a year to local governments, non-profit land conservation organizations, the Colorado Division of Wildlife, and Colorado State Parks to develop plans to preserve or enhance parks, open space, and outdoor recreation, or to help build the capacity of organizations to do so.

The GOCO program stands out from many other land conservation programs for several reasons, said John Hereford, the executive director: "I'm not aware of any other state program like GOCO. We have a locked-in yearly revenue source that's not dependent on year-to-year appropriations from the legislature. It's such a huge advantage for Colorado. We can take a strategic, long-term, multiyear view of land conservation and recreation." Although establishing a GOCO program might not be possible in many other states, Hereford said, he advised others to try: "People here saw that the elements that make this a special place were threatened. The natural assets and the outdoor lifestyle are central to why people live here and move here."

As with many state land conservation grant programs that require local matching funds, GOCO has helped spark a movement among local governments to create their own land conservation funding through bonds or dedicated sales taxes. Since 1992, when GOCO was created, twenty-four communities have approved open space tax or bond measures. "Counties saw what others were doing with their GOCO dollars," Hereford said. "Success begets success. It's absolutely been a driver for instigating local land conservation programs. And it makes our dollars go further."

Conservation Trust Fund

The second beneficiary of Colorado's lottery proceeds is the Conservation Trust Fund, which receives 40 percent of the revenue ($471 million between 1983 and 2002, $44 million in FY 2002) for local park and recreation projects. The state Department of Local Affairs distributes money from this fund to more than 400 local and county governments or special recreation districts based on population.[29] Projects include open space and land acquisitions, equipment and facility purchases, park maintenance, and renovation or restoration of local facilities.

COLORADO STATE PARKS

The third piece of the lottery pie goes to Colorado's forty state parks, which receive 10 percent of the proceeds ($118 million between 1983 and 2002, $11 million in FY 2002) for open space and land acquisitions, trail system construction and maintenance, equipment and facility purchases, and maintenance and renovation of state parks facilities. The Colorado State Parks Trails Program,[30] started in 1971, also uses lottery proceeds to award $2.6 million in grants each year to construct, improve, plan, or acquire trails.

CONSERVATION EASEMENT TAX CREDIT

Beyond the GOCO program, Colorado lawmakers approved bills in 1999, 2000, and 2001 that boost incentives for the donation of conservation easements to government agencies or nonprofit groups. Beginning in 2000, such donors could claim a state income tax credit of up to $100,000 for the donation of conservation easements. Unused credit can be carried forward up to twenty years.

A year after approving the tax credit, state lawmakers expanded the tax break by allowing donors to claim a refund or to transfer the $100,000 income tax credit to a third party. The refunds are allowed only when the state is running a surplus. If a refund is claimed, the combination of the refund and tax credit is capped at $20,000 per year. Donors may also elect to sell their tax credit to third parties, who can use it to lower their state income taxes. No refunds are allowed with transferred tax credits.

In another expansion of the tax credit in 2001, lawmakers raised the maximum tax credit for the donation of a conservation easement to $260,000 and increased the annual tax refund a landowner who donates an easement can claim to $50,000, beginning in 2003.[31]

In 2001, the first year that the trading of state tax credits was allowed, an estimated twenty-eight easement tax credits were sold, worth $1.5 million, said Mike Strugar, whose group, the Conservation Resource Center in Boulder, Colorado, brokered two-thirds of the trades. Strugar expected the number of trades to double in 2002 to about sixty, worth between $4 million and $5 million. The volume could double again in 2003, Strugar predicted, with $10 million in trading. Although it is too early to tell what effect the expanded tax breaks are having on the popularity of conservation easements, the conservation easement tax credits have given "real farmers and ranchers" access to funding that was reserved for the wealthy, Strugar said.

California

Everything about California is big, including its approach to financing land conservation. From 2000 through 2002, state voters approved $10.1 billion in natural resource bonds, including $4.7 billion for parks and open space and $5.4 billion for water projects. That's twice what voters approved in bonds between 1970 through 1999 for parks, clean water, and wildlife habitat combined. Since 1970 Californians have approved twenty-seven of thirty-seven natural resource bond measures to fund $15.3 billion in park and water-related programs, an overall 73 percent approval rate. Although more than 90 percent of bond referenda were approved in the 1970s and 1980s, not one park bond and only one water bond measure passed in the 1990s as the state worked through its worst recession since the 1930s. The trend reversed itself with the dawn of the new century as voters embraced spending billions of dollars to improve access to parks and recreation, preserve vital open space, and enhance water quality and fish and wildlife habitat.

For many conservationists in California, the resurgence came none too soon. In 1999, the California Environmental Dialogue (CED), a collaborative of corporate, environmental, and government leaders, commissioned a study, "Land Conservation in California: Needs for the Next Decade," that found the state will need to spend $12.3 billion by 2010 to preserve 5.4 million acres marked for protection by government agencies and nonprofit groups.[32] The study came while the state was losing more than 100,000 acres of farmland to urban development every year, according to the American Farmland Trust, while an additional 240,000 acres a year were being converted from rangeland to more intensive agricultural practices.

Wildlife habitat also was under attack. California has more threatened and endangered species than any other state. Thirty-six species have been driven to extinction in California in recent times. And another 1,088 are listed as rare, endangered, or threatened by state and federal fish and wildlife agencies.

LAND OWNERSHIP

Before getting into the specifics of the state's complex array of land conservation activities, let's look at some numbers to put the state in context. The state's population passed the 35 million mark in late 2001, by far the most of any state in the nation. One in eight Americans now calls California home. At least 15 million more Californians are expected by 2025. It is the most ethnically diverse state in the nation. It is the seventh largest economy in the world.

Geographically, the state of California encompasses roughly 100 million acres. About 75 million acres are classified as wildlands, defined as all undeveloped and noncultivated property. Agriculture takes up 24 million acres. The remainder—1 million acres—is urbanized or otherwise developed.

Ownership of California's 75 million acres of wildlands is divided primarily among federal, state, and private entities. The federal government owns 60 percent, 37 percent is privately held, and most of the remainder—about 2.3 million acres—is owned by the state, primarily by the Departments of Fish and Game, Parks and Recreation, and Forestry and Fire Protection. Local governments own less than 0.5 percent of the state's land. About 18 percent of California is protected as open space, natural habitat, or for other conservation purposes, according to the 1999 CED study.

FINANCING

State policy declares that "California's land is an exhaustible resource, not just a commodity, and is essential to the economy, environment, and general well-being of the people of California."[33] To protect the resource, the state has established numerous programs and agencies to achieve the state's key conservation goals: to preserve agricultural land, maintain natural habitat for wildlife, provide outdoor recreational opportunities, and promote the environmental quality of watersheds. Following are descriptions of some of the bonds, special resource funds, and programs that serve a variety of land conservation needs spread among more than a dozen state agencies.

Park Bonds

In 1928, California voters approved the California State Park Bonds Act, the state's first park bond ($6 million) and one of the first of its kind in the nation, by an overwhelming three-to-one margin.[34] State officials used the money to expand the state park system, which is now the nation's largest. The park system, run by the state Department of Parks and Recreation, comprises more than 270 park sites, 280 miles of coastline, 625 miles of lake and river frontage, nearly 18,000 campsites, and 3,000 miles of hiking, biking, and equestrian trails, all on 1.4 million acres of state land.

Since that early effort to fund park acquisitions with bond money, voters have gone to the polls numerous times to bolster California's parks, recreation, fish and wildlife habitat, and coastal protection. In 1964, they approved a $150 million State Beach, Park, Recreational, and Historical Facilities Bond Act—by a 62 percent to 38 percent margin. The act funded the acquisition and development of state and local parks, beaches, recreational and historical facilities, and wildlife management areas. In November 1970, voters approved a $60 million measure called the Recreation and Fish and Wildlife Enhancement (Proposition 20) by a 57 percent to 43 percent margin. Two much larger park bonds followed in the mid-1970s: Proposition 1—a $250 million successor to the 1964 State Beach, Park, Recreational, and Historical Facilities Bond Act—approved by a 60 percent to 40 percent margin in June 1974; and the Nejedly-Hart State, Urban, and Coastal Park Bond Act (Proposition 2), a $280 million measure approved by a 52 percent to 48 percent margin in November 1976.

After a four-year lull, the 1980s saw a flurry of park bonds—eight in all—that devoted more than $2.6 billion to state and local parks and wildlife:

- The California Parklands Act of 1980, passed in November 1980, provided $285 million for acquisition and development of state and local parks, recreation areas, and beaches.
- The Lake Tahoe Protection Act, passed in November 1982 as Proposition 4 by a 53 percent to 47 percent margin, devoted $85 million in bonds for land acquisition and restoration at the lake.
- The California Park and Recreational Facilities Act, approved in June 1984 as Proposition 18 and approved by a 63 percent to 37 percent margin,

devoted $370 million to state and local parks and recreational facilities, wildlife management areas, and coastal conservation.

- The Fish and Wildlife Habitat Enhancement Act, approved in June 1984 as Proposition 19 by a 64 percent to 36 percent margin, devoted $85 million to acquisition, enhancement, and development of habitat for fish and wildlife.
- The Community Parklands Act of 1986, passed in June 1986 as Proposition 43 by a 67 percent to 33 percent margin, devoted $100 million in grants for localities to acquire, develop, or rehabilitate park and recreational facilities.
- The California Wildlife, Coastal and Park Land Conservation Bond Act, passed in June 1988 as Proposition 70 with 65 percent approving, devoted $776 million to state and local parks, wetlands, fish and wildlife habitat, and coastal areas.
- In November 1988, 58 percent of voters approved Proposition 99, the Tobacco Tax and Health Protection Act. It raised the state tobacco tax by 25 cents per pack, and dedicated $30 million a year to park and wildlife programs, including programs for wetlands and fisheries.
- In June 1990, voters approved Proposition 117, the California Wildlife Protection Act, by a 52 percent to 48 percent margin. It prohibited sport hunting of mountain lions and dedicated a minimum of $30 million a year for thirty years for habitat purposes. These funds have proved vital in sustaining habitation preservation efforts during the lean funding years that followed in the 1990s.

After June of 1990, state park funding from bonds dried up until 2000. Voters defeated Proposition 149, the California Park, Recreation and Wildlife Act, a $437 million parks bond, in November 1990 by a 53 percent to 47 percent vote, and a $2 billion Park Lands, Historic Sites, Wildlife and Forest Conservation Bond Act in June 1994, which lost 57 percent to 43 percent, along with every other bond measure on the ballot. The 1990 bond was thought to have narrowly lost owing to a long list of bonds on the ballot, several of which were controversial, according to the Planning and Conservation League (PCL).[35] Belt tightening during the state's recession, low voter turnout, and too many bonds on the ballot were blamed for all the bonds failing four years later, said Jerry Meral, the former executive director of PCL, whose organization has been active in the park and water bond arena since 1972.

The lack of new park bond money at the state level was compounded by a state constitution provision that requires a two-thirds vote to approve general obligation bonds for local land preservation or any other local purpose. Despite the high hurdle, voters in the Los Angeles and San Francisco metropolitan areas approved significant local funding for parks while the state bond funding was scarce. In 1988, the East Bay Regional Park District, covering Alameda and Contra Costa Counties along the eastern side of San Francisco Bay, approved Measure AA, which provided $225 million to expand their park system. And in Los Angeles County, voters in 1992 and again in 1996 approved benefit assessment districts that provided $1 billion for park and habitat purposes.

But on March 7, 2000, the state dry spell ended.[36] By a 63 percent to 37 percent margin, voters approved a $2.1 billion bond measure (Proposition 12), the Safe Neighborhood Parks, Clean Water, and Coastal Protection Bond Act of 2000, to protect open space and coastal resources, upgrade parks, and improve water quality. The money was split between funding for the state—$1.16 billion to acquire and develop recreational facilities, natural areas, and fish and wildlife habitat—and grants to local governments and nonprofit organizations—$940 million geared toward recreation projects, particularly in cities.

Two years later, in March 2002, voters returned to the polls to approve an even larger park bond, the California Clean Water, Clean Air, Safe Neighborhood Parks, and Coastal Protection Act of 2002 (Proposition 40), by a 57 percent to 43 percent margin. The $2.6 billion bond, the largest conservation bond in U.S. history, devoted $1.275 billion to a range of air, land, and water conservation projects, including $445 million for state conservancies to acquire and protect land, $300 million to acquire and restore wildlife habitat, $300 million for water quality projects, and $75 million each for farmland protection and urban parkways. Another $1.058 billion was earmarked for urban parks and recreation ($460 million), regional and local parks ($372.5 million), and state parks ($225 million). The remaining $267.5 million is aimed to help acquire, develop, and preserve historical and cultural resources. (See Table 2.4.)

TABLE 2.4.
Allocations of California's Proposition 40 funds by recipient agency—2002 (in millions of dollars)

Recipient	Purpose	Amount (millions of dollars)
State Departments (total)		1,915.0
State Parks and Recreation		1,015.0
	Acquisition and development of state parks	225.0
	Local assistance	790.0
State Conservancies		445.0
State Coastal Conservancy	Land/water resource acquisition/restoration	200.0
Baldwin Hills Conservancy	Land/water resource acquisition/restoration	40.0
California Tahoe Conservancy	Land/water resource acquisition/restoration	40.0
San Francisco Bay Area Conservancy Program (Coastal Conservancy)	Land/water resource acquisition/restoration	40.0
San Gabriel and Lower Los Angeles Rivers and Mountains Conservancy	Land/water resource acquisition/restoration	40.0
Santa Monica Mountains Conservancy	Land/water resource acquisition/restoration	40.0
San Joaquin River Conservancy	Land/water resource acquisition/restoration	25.0
Coachella Valley Mountains Conservancy	Land/water resource acquisition/restoration	20.0
Wildlife Conservation Board	Habitat acquisition and restoration	300.0
Resources Agency	Grants for development and acquisition of river parkways	70.0
	Grants for urban streams program	5.0
Air Resources Board	Grants to local air districts	50.0
California Conservation Corps	Grants to local conservation corps	15.0
	Resource conservation activities	5.0
Department of Forestry and Fire Protection	Grants for urban forestry	10.0
Local Recipients to be Allocated Funds Directly (total)		80.0
City of Los Angeles	Local parks, per capita	12.5
City of Los Angeles	Hansen Dam and Sepulveda Basin recreational areas	10.0
City of Rancho Cucamonga	Development of Central Park	10.0
City of San Francisco	Golden Gate Park	35.0
County of Los Angeles	Local parks, per capita	10.0
County of Los Angeles	El Pueblo Cultural and Performing Arts Center	2.5

TABLE 2.4. (*Continued*)

Allocations of California's Proposition 40 funds by recipient agency—2002
(in millions of dollars)

Unspecified (total)		605.0
	Grants for water quality protection and restoration	300.0
	Historical and cultural resources	230.0
	Grants for agricultural land preservation	75.0
Total		$2,600.0

Adapted from Mark Newton, *Enhancing Implementation and Oversight: Proposition 40 Resources Bond* (Sacramento: California Legislative Analyst's Office, May 7, 2002); www.lao.ca.gov.

Water Bonds

Californians have approved billions of dollars of bonds over the years to improve water quality, expand water supply, control floods, and provide safe drinking water. In recent years, the scope of these water bonds has broadened to include projects that protect watersheds, restore habitat, and acquire river parkway land.

In November 1996, voters approved the first such bond, Proposition 204—the Safe, Clean, Reliable Water Supply Act of 1996. The measure provided $995 million for various water-related purposes, including $583 million for various projects to restore fish and wildlife habitat in the ecosystem of the San Francisco Bay/Sacramento–San Joaquin Delta Estuary. The estuary plays a critical role in the state, providing a substantial amount of the water used for domestic, industrial, agricultural, and environmental purposes. In a related state–federal project, California has joined CALFED, a cooperative effort of more than twenty state and federal agencies working with local communities to improve the management of water resources in the bay-delta, a thirty-year project expected to cost as much as $10 billion.

Proposition 204 also created the Central Valley Project Improvement Subaccount to provide $93 million to pay the state's share of the federal Central Valley Project Improvement Act (CVPIA) of 1992, a federal law that required the secretary of the interior to restore fish and wildlife in the Central Valley, including the development of a program to double the production of anadromous fish (steelhead, salmon, and sturgeon) in Central Valley rivers and streams. Proposition 204 also included $27 million that was earmarked for river parkway acquisition and riparian habitat restoration.

In March 2000, two-thirds of voters approved the Safe Drinking Water, Clean Water, Watershed Protection and Flood Protection Act (Proposition 13). Proposition 13 authorized $1.97 billion in bonds to support safe drinking water, flood control, bay-delta restoration, watershed protection, and water quality and supply projects. Besides the $250 million to fund various CALFED bay-delta projects, $95 million was earmarked to acquire and restore riparian habitat, riverine aquatic habitat, and other land along waterways, mostly in urban areas. Grants to local agencies totaling $70 million were included to acquire, restore, enhance, and protect land property for flood protection, agricultural land preservation, and wildlife habitat protection. Another $25 million will protect, restore, acquire, and enhance salmon habitat.

Capping off an incredible resurgence in natural resource bonds, voters in November 2002 approved a $3.44 billion water bond (Proposition 50), which included $950 million to purchase stretches of land next to rivers, lakes, and the Pacific Ocean. Proposition 50 also provides funding to buy land next to rivers and streams that are sources of clean drinking water, and land that is home to endangered fish and wildlife. (See Table 2.5.)

Special Funds

Until the recent influx of bond funding for natural resources in California, special funds in which revenues other than general fund revenue are maintained for particular environmental purposes had become an increasingly important source of support for natural resource programs. In 1979, approximately 51 percent of the state funding for natural resource programs came from the general fund and 15 percent from special funds.[37] Twenty-three years later, the general fund accounted for 35 percent of the total and special funds financed close to 58 percent. Below are descriptions of a handful of more than 50 environmentally related special funds in the state.

Environmental License Plate Fund. The Environmental License Plate Fund, created in 1970, derives its funding from the sale of personalized motor license plates by the Department of Motor Vehicles. Personalized license plates cost $90, yielding about $25 million each year for the state. The money may be used to control and reduce air pollution; acquire, preserve, and restore natural areas and ecological reserves; pro-

TABLE 2.5.

Use of bond funds in Proposition 50 (in millions of dollars), 2002

Purpose	Amount (millions of dollars)
Coastal Protection	$950
Wetlands acquisition, protection, and restoration	750
Watershed protection	200
CALFED Bay-Delta Program	$825
Water use efficiency and conservation	180
Water supply reliability	180
Ecosystem restoration	180
Watershed protection	90
Water conveyance	75
Delta levee restoration	70
Water storage planning and studies	50
Integrated regional water management	$640
Various water supply, pollution, water treatment, flood management, and wetlands restoration projects	500
Land and water acquisitions to improve and protect water quality, water supply reliability, and fish and wildlife habitat	140
Safe drinking water	$435
Small community drinking water system upgrades, contaminant removal and treatment, water quality monitoring, and drinking water protection	
Clean water and water quality	$370
Water pollution prevention, water recycling, and water quality improvements	100
River parkway projects	100
Coastal nonpoint source pollution control	100
Lake Tahoe water quality improvements	40
Land and water acquisitions to protect water quality in the Sierra Nevada-Cascade Mountain region	30
Desalination and water treatment project	$100
Desalination projects, treatment and removal of specified contaminants, and drinking water disinfecting projects	
Colorado River management	$70
Ecosystem restoration	50
Canal lining	20
Water security	$50
Protection of drinking water systems form terrorist attacks and other deliberate acts of destruction or degradation	

From *Proposition 50: Water Quality, Supply and Safe Drinking Water Projects. Coastal Wetlands Purchase and Protection. Bonds. Initiative Statute* (Sacramento: California Legislative Analyst's Office, July 23, 2002); http://www.lao.ca.gov/initiatives/2002/50_11_2002.htm.

vide environmental education; protect nongame species and threatened and endangered plants and animals; protect, enhance, and restore fish and wildlife habitat and related water quality; buy sensitive natural areas for state, local, or regional park systems; and reduce the effects of soil erosion and the discharge of sediment into the waters of the Lake Tahoe region. Legislators have used the license plate funding in recent years mostly to support programs of the Department of Fish and Game.

Public Resources Account/Cigarette and Tobacco Products Surtax Fund. In 1988, California voters raised the state tax on tobacco products by approving Proposition 99, which raised the levy on cigarettes to 35 cents per pack from a dime. Of the $600 million the tax originally raised annually, 5 percent ($30 million) went into a Public Resources Account, where it is divided each year between state Department of Fish and Game programs that protect, restore, enhance, or maintain fish, waterfowl, and other wildlife habitat areas; and Department of Parks and Recreation programs that improve state and local park and recreation resources. Revenues have declined as cigarette consumption has dropped, leaving about $20 million available each year now, with about three-fourths going to programs of the Department of Parks and Recreation.

Habitat Conservation Fund. In 1990, two years after creating the tobacco tax fund, voters approved Proposition 117, the California Wildlife Protection Act, by a 52 percent to 48 percent margin, to create a Habitat Conservation Fund. The proposition requires that the fund receive annual revenues of $30 million for thirty years from the unallocated account created in the Cigarette and Tobacco Products Surtax Fund and the state's general fund. In the first few years, money from the fund went to three state land conservancies and the Department of Parks and Recreation for land acquisition, but now most of the money goes to the Wildlife Conservation Board, primarily to acquire lands for the protection of deer and mountain lions, rare and endangered animals and plant life, and wetlands, as well as for park purposes.

The Wildlife Conservation Board is the key state agency that acquires wildlife habitat. It has acquired 500,000 acres and easements on several hundred thousand more acres. Most of the lands acquired by the board are managed by the Department of Fish and Game, while the remainder are managed by local and nonprofit agencies.

Fish and Game Preservation Fund. The Fish and Game Preservation Fund derives most of its revenues from fishing and hunting licenses, tags, and permits. In recent years, the legislature has approved about $90 million in spending each year for the Department of Fish and Game, which uses the money to protect fish and wildlife. Most of the money is restricted for specific purposes or species.

Resources Trust Fund. The Resources Trust Fund, created in 1997, helps preserve and protect natural and recreational resources in the state. The fund receives a portion of the state revenue derived from oil, gas, and other minerals extracted from the state's tidelands. The trust fund is split into two separate accounts: the Salmon and Steelhead Trout Restoration Account and the Natural Resources Infrastructure Fund. The first $8 million from the fund is deposited into the restoration account for grants from the Department of Fish and Game to recover salmon and steelhead trout. The grants are to be awarded for activities that improve fish habitat in coastal water utilized by salmon and anadromous trout, and are to emphasize the development of coordinated watershed improvement activities.

In 1998, two additional accounts were created within the trust fund, the Marine Life and Marine Reserve Management Account, which will receive $2.2 million annually through 2005–2006 for marine life management programs in the Department of Fish and Game; and the State Parks System Deferred Maintenance Account, which is to receive $10 million annually through 2005–2006 for the Department of Parks and Recreation for deferred maintenance expenses.

Whatever money remains is to be deposited in the Natural Resources Infrastructure Fund to preserve and protect natural and recreational resources. Priorities are environmental review and monitoring by the Department of Fish and Game, Natural Community Conservation Plan acquisitions, Habitat Conservation Fund funding requirements, and expenditures for nonpoint source pollution control programs. Funds not appropriated to these priorities will be spent on natural and recreational resources.

Uncertainties over tideland oil revenues have made it difficult for the legislature to fund the above programs, which have caused lawmakers to use other funding sources instead, including the Environmental License Plate Fund and the general fund.

FARMLAND PRESERVATION PROGRAM

California has 87,500 farms, which constitute about 4 percent of the nation's total. However, these farms account for 13 percent of the national gross cash receipts from farming. Agriculture cash receipts in California topped $25.5 billion in 2002, nearly twice as much as second-place Texas. One in five glasses of milk in the nation comes for California, 92 percent of the grapes, and more than half the nation's fruits, nuts, and vegetables.[38] While the nation is heavily dependent on the state for food, about 109,231 acres of California farmland was converted to nonagricultural uses between 1996 and 1998, according to the state Department of Conservation figures.

WILLIAMSON ACT

In 1965 California legislators approved the Williamson Act (California Land Conservation Act), which offered tax breaks to owners of agricultural land and open space in return for restricting use of their land to farming and ranching for ten years. The program got off to a slow start in its first two years, enrolling only 200,000 acres, owing to uncertainty over the legality of preferential tax treatment of the land. As a remedy, state legislators placed Proposition 3 on the ballot in November 1966, which passed with 56 percent in favor. The measure amended the state constitution (Article 28 then, now Article 13) by authorizing the legislature to define open space lands and restrict their use for recreation, scenic beauty, natural resources, or production of food or fiber, while reducing their value for property tax purposes.[39]

Lawmakers also provided another shot in the arm in 1971 through the Open Space Subvention Act, which partially reimbursed local governments for the lost tax revenue based on acreage enrolled in the program. In 1998, lawmakers created farmland security zones as part of the Williamson Act Program, which gave landowners a further 35 percent tax break in return for twenty-year contracts.

By 2002 all but four of the state's fifty-eight counties had signed up for the program, with about 16.5 million acres (two-thirds of the agriculture land in the state) enrolled in the program. In FY 2001–2002, the state used general fund money to make $37 million in subvention payments to counties. But the state's fiscal crisis in 2003 threatened the program, as Governor Gray Davis proposed to abolish the subvention program.

California Farmland Conservancy Program

The California Farmland Conservancy Program (CFCP), created by the state legislature in 1995 to augment the state's thirty-year-old farmland preservation tax break program under the Williamson Act, provides grants to local governments, nonprofit groups, and resource conservation districts to conserve farmland through the voluntary acquisition of conservation easements.[40] The program also provides grants for policy planning purposes—mostly for the targeting of future agricultural easement work. A 2000 park bond measure (Proposition 12) provided the CFCP with $25 million in funding. A subsequent 2002 park bond measure (Proposition 40) made an additional $75 million available for conservation easements on agricultural land, grazing land, and oak woodlands. The CFCP anticipates receiving a large portion of this funding for agricultural conservation easement grants. The legislature budgeted $11.7 million for the program in FY 2002–2003. To date, the program has obtained seventy-four agricultural easements on 21,000 acres in fifteen counties.

Environmental Enhancement and Mitigation Program

The Environmental Enhancement and Mitigation Program was established by the state legislature in 1989 with funding from state gas taxes.[41] It offers a total of $10 million each year for grants to local, state, and federal governmental agencies and to nonprofit organizations for projects to mitigate the environmental impacts caused by new or modified state transportation facilities. Grants are awarded for air quality improvement through the planting of trees and other suitable plants, acquisition, restoration, or enhancement of watersheds, wildlife habitat, wetlands, forests, or other natural areas; and acquisition and/or development of roadside recreational opportunities. The state Resources Agency administers the grant applications and recommends projects to the state Transportation Commission. The state Department of Transportation administers the approved grant agreements.

Governor Gray Davis proposed cutting funding for the program to $3.5 million for FY 2002–2003 and eliminating funding for FY 2003–2004.

STATE CONSERVANCIES

In order to promote the conservation of its land resources, the state has created eight state "conservancies" that acquire and protect undeveloped lands in specific regions of the state.[42] Proposition 40, which voters passed in 2002, included $445 million for the conservancies, which receive their money through appropriations from the legislature for land acquisition and other capital outlay purposes. The state's conservancies seek to acquire property within their own defined geographic areas. Unlike the Wildlife Conservation Board, the conservancies do not focus primarily on acquiring wildlife habitat. Instead, they pursue a mix of objectives, generally reflecting aspects of the four land conservation goals discussed earlier.

In general, state conservancies further the acquisition of public lands either by direct purchase themselves, or by facilitating purchases by other entities. Funding for these acquisitions comes from a variety of sources, including state general funds and special funds, bond proceeds, and private contributions. Also, conservancies sometimes participate in real estate transactions that involve the trading or consolidation of parcels. Conservancies can also accept donated lands.

The 2000–2001 budget appropriated about $300 million for the conservancies. About two-thirds of this money came from state general obligation bonds authorized by Proposition 12.

NATURAL HERITAGE PRESERVATION TAX CREDIT PROGRAM

In 2000, California enacted the Natural Heritage Preservation Tax Credit Act, which allows private landowners to donate land or water rights to state or local agencies or nonprofit organizations for land conservation purposes and receive a tax credit for 55 percent of the value of the donation.[43] The Wildlife Conservation Board awarded more than $40 million in credits in the first few years of the program, which was suspended for the budget year ending June 30, 2003, as part of the state's efforts to tackle its massive budget shortfall.

Conclusion

The success of the land conservation programs profiled in this chapter illustrates the great progress states have made in financing open space preservation. Voters and legislators in California, Florida, and New

TABLE 2.6.

Population growth versus land development in the
United States, 1982–1997

U.S. Regions	Increase in Population (%)	Increase in Urbanized Land (%)
Midwest	7.06%	32.23%
Northeast	6.91%	39.10%
South	22.23%	59.61%
West	32.21%	48.94%
United States	17.02%	47.14%

Source: Mark A. Benedict and Edward T. McMahon, "Green Infrastructure: Smart Conservation for the 21st Century," (The Conservation Fund), Sprawl Watch Clearinghouse, Monograph Series, May 2002, p. 10. www.greeninfrastructure.net.

Jersey in particular have voted to spend billions of dollars to protect their undeveloped land. Coloradans, with their rich outdoor heritage at stake, also have stepped forward to devote hundreds of millions to preserve their vital resources.

While the increase in state funding for land conservation is impressive, the pace of development continues to outstrip land preservation (see Table 2.6). And the nation's economic downturn since 2000 is beginning to take its toll in many state land conservation programs, particularly in those states that don't have dedicated sources of funding for these programs. Colorado's GOCO program is largely insulated from the state's budget deficit because its funding comes from state lottery proceeds without an annual appropriation from state legislators. But in many other states, including Florida, Illinois, and New York, attempts have been made, with some success, to divert land conservation money to other programs. More are likely to follow until state budgets regain their equilibrium.

The lesson here is that lawmakers and voters alike need to elevate funding for land conservation to the same level of seriousness as funding for roads, water and sewer systems, and other infrastructure so that these land preservation programs survive during economic downturns. While funding for a new bridge or a widened highway can be delayed a year or two without major disruptions, once a tract of land is bought, subdivided, and developed, it's gone for good.

CHAPTER THREE

FINANCING LOCAL LAND CONSERVATION PROGRAMS

Although the preservation of huge tracts of woodlands or wetlands is undeniably a great achievement, sometimes it's the protection of a small pond, family ranch, or scenic view that drives home the real benefit of a successful land conservation program. The recent explosion of interest in the preservation of open space at the county and municipal level bears testimony to the old adage that all politics is local, or, in this case, all open space preservation is local.

When the preservation of a treasured piece of land might suddenly occupy center stage in a community's public desires, many times in the past there was no local funding mechanism to save it from development. With local means of preservation inadequate or nonexistent, appeals for funding would have to be made to the state or federal government, with little chance of success. But in county after county and city after city in this country, that is no longer the case. Often with the spur of additional state funding, hundreds of communities throughout the United States have dedicated revenue to create local land conservation programs, giving residents and local officials an important locally controlled instrument to shape their future.

It's no coincidence that state programs with local matching grant components (e.g., in Colorado, Florida, Massachusetts, and New Jersey) have helped spark the revolution in open space funding among local communities. In New Jersey alone, 20 counties and 187 municipalities have approved funding for local open space and recreation plans to match the new state funding voters approved statewide in 1998. In Florida, 23 of the state's 67 counties, representing much of the state's population, have created local financing for open space to help attract state grants under the Florida Communities Trust Program. And in Massachusetts, 58 towns have raised property taxes to acquire open space, provide affordable housing, and preserve historic sites and buildings, prompted by access to $26 million in new state grant money.

Whether or not there's a strong financial incentive coming from the state level, local politicians often lead the drive for local land conservation funding. A mayor, city councilor, county commissioner, or state representative is in a good position to sense the need for public funding for open space and begin building public support for it. A case in point is Jacksonville, Florida, where former mayor John Delaney made it his personal mission to greatly expand the city's park system.

In other cases, local land trusts, local environmental advocacy groups, or even progressive chambers of commerce or realtor associations take the initiative to create land conservation programs. Or citizens themselves can get the ball rolling, as in Lancaster County, Pennsylvania, where residents and farmers petitioned the county commissioners to protect valuable farmland from development.

This chapter profiles eight communities from Cape Cod, Massachusetts, to Marin County, California, that have done just that. Using sales, property, and cigarette taxes, general obligation bonds, state and federal funding, and donations from private individuals, corporations, and foundations, these communities have protected tens of thousands of acres of farm and ranch land, scenic viewsheds, and wetlands, while expanding park and recreation areas for their residents. None of these programs came into being without great vision by their community leaders, a tremendous amount of work by the public and private sectors, and in the end, the support of voters.

Cape Cod, Massachusetts

If you've ever been to Cape Cod in Massachusetts, you know the slender, 65-mile-long arm of land is a unique and very special place. Central to its preservation was the protection of Cape Cod National Seashore, a 40-mile-long stretch of federally owned shoreline, uplands, and ponds comprising 43,570 acres designated by Congress as National Park Service land in 1961.

Increasingly, the Cape's fifteen towns face great challenges as development gobbles up dwindling open space, new residents and millions of tourists bring more traffic, housing becomes less affordable, and water supply and wastewater problems grow. But the area's 222,000 year-round residents, who see their numbers grow to 600,000 during the summer, haven't stood still as these problems have mounted.

In fact, the Cape Cod Commission, a regional planning and regulatory agency created in 1990 after a growth boom in the 1980s, has made preservation of half the remaining open space on Cape Cod—40,000 acres—one of its key goals. Considering that nearly one-third of the sandy peninsula already is protected, that's an impressive ambition. A key goal behind the effort is to protect the recharge zone for the underground aquifer, the sole source of drinking water for the area.

To help achieve the goal, voters in all fifteen towns in Barnstable County agreed in November 1998 to create the Cape Cod Land Bank, funded by a 3 percent surcharge on property taxes. Based on 2003 estimates, the towns may generate $250 million over twenty years to protect open space.[1] The state of Massachusetts sweetened the deal by making available $15 million in matching grants to encourage the towns to participate. By early 2003, the Cape's fifteen towns had committed more than $75 million to protect 2,871 acres of vitally important natural land. Passage of the Cape Cod Land Bank also laid the groundwork for creation of the statewide Community Preservation Act program profiled in Chapter 2, which enabled communities across the state to raise property taxes to protect open space, provide affordable housing, and preserve historic sites and buildings.

Creation of the land bank didn't occur overnight. In fact, it took years of stop-and-start efforts by conservationists before the state legislature approved the necessary legislation. Cape Cod voters first

PHOTO 3.1. The Harwick Land Bank partnered with the Harwick Conservation Trust to purchase 23.8 acres of wetlands and uplands bordering Coy's Brook (pictured here) with $360,000 in land bank funds and $140,000 from the trust. The parcel connects with other protected open space in the town of Harwich, which hopes to link the land to the 25-mile Cape Cod Rail Trail. *Photo courtesy of the Cape Cod Commission.*

approved a regional open space program in 1996, fueled by a 3 percent tax on property transfers, to be paid by buyers. State legislators took up the issue and, at the urging of real estate interests, made the transfer tax payable by sellers instead. The new proposal then went back to Cape Cod voters for approval, but they rejected it in January 1998 after a successful media campaign paid for by the real estate community.

Conservationists, this time in partnership with real estate interests, went back to the drawing board and came up with the 3 percent property tax as a funding mechanism, which spread the costs of open space among all landowners, rather than only those who were buying or selling real estate. Having found the right formula, the real estate community and conservationists backed the Cape Cod Land Bank proposal, which passed in all fifteen Cape Cod towns, receiving an overall 58 percent approval in November 1998.

The state legislation that creates the Cape Cod Land Bank allows towns to use the property taxes to acquire land, conservation easements, and development rights to protect public drinking water supplies, open space, and conservation land, and to create walking and bicycle trails and recreational areas. The surcharge money is held by each town in a special fund, which was matched on a 50 percent basis by the state during the first three years of the program, a $14.2 million contribution.

Each town was required to create or designate an open space committee that recommends projects to be funded by its land bank. Town meetings (or, in Barnstable, a meeting of the town council) are required for final approval of projects. Eligible projects include the acquisition of existing and future wellfields, aquifers, and recharge areas; agricultural lands; forest lands; fresh and salt water marshes and other wetlands; ocean and pond frontage, beaches, dunes, and other coastal lands; scenic vistas; nature or wildlife preserves; land and easements for trails; and land for recreational use. Only 3 percent of land bank funds may be spent on maintenance and improvements. Towns can issue bonds based on future land bank revenue and use land bank funds to purchase land in another town. All purchased land is owned by the town that bought it, although management can be turned over to a qualified nonprofit group, or a water or fire district.

"After a decade with little or no municipal spending on land protection," said Heather McElroy, natural resources and open space specialist with the Cape Cod Commission, "the land bank tax has allowed Cape Cod towns to begin preserving open space again, without the funding battles at town meetings. With the dedicated funding source of the land bank in place, communities can now focus the discussion on 'What are the important lands to protect?' rather than 'How are we going to pay for it?'"

Lancaster County, Pennsylvania

Countless communities in America have stood by idly while the features that made them unique and attractive places to live were destroyed. Lancaster County, Pennsylvania, is not among them. In 1980, its visionary community leaders created one of the earliest, most comprehensive, and successful farmland conservation programs in the country.[2] Local officials now use zoning, preferential tax assessment,

PHOTO 3.2. Working farm protected with conservation easement held by the Lancaster Farmland Trust in Lancaster County, Pennsylvania.
Photo courtesy of Lancaster Farmland Trust; www.savelancasterfarms.org.

the purchase of development rights and donation of easements, as well as agricultural districts and urban growth boundaries, to protect the farming industry in the county, which is considered to possess the most productive, nonirrigated farmland in the nation.

Farming is a key ingredient of Lancaster County's economy. Agriculture provides one in five jobs in the community. More than 3,380 people consider farming to be their primary occupation. And Lancaster County is home to 4,556 farms with an average size of 85 acres and a total economic impact of $5.5 billion annually.

By early 2003, the county had preserved 55,000 acres of farmland through the purchase and donation of 460 easements, an investment of $80 million in state, county, and federal funding. In addition, the Lancaster Farmland Trust has protected 148 farms on 9,584 acres through donations and bargain sale easement purchases.[3] The trust was created to provide an alternative means of protecting agricultural land for Amish and Mennonite farmers whose beliefs discourage the acceptance of public money from the county for selling development rights.

The county also has zoned more than 350,000 acres—nearly 60 percent of the county—for agriculture. Of the total, 130,000 acres of farmland have been enrolled in agricultural security zones, which provide an umbrella of protective benefits for farmers.

Funding for the county's land conservation efforts has come from a variety of local, state, and federal sources, derived primarily from the county's general fund, general obligation bonds, dedicated cigarette tax revenue, and funding associated with Growing Greener legislation, signed into law in early 2000 by then-governor Thomas Ridge. Lancaster County took a bold step in 2000 by issuing a $25 million bond specifically for farmland conservation that allowed the county's annual rate of preservation to jump from approximately twenty-three farms (2,000 acres) to seventy farms (6,000 acres). With the 2000 bond fund now exhausted, the county currently contributes about $3 million to $4 million a year for the program, mostly from county bond money, which has been bolstered since 2000 by $3 million to $4 million each year from the state's Growing Greener Initiative, as well as ongoing state funding from a dedicated two-cents-per-pack cigarette tax.

The effort to preserve the county's farmland began with a grassroots effort by local farmers and residents. In the late 1970s, they petitioned the county commissioners to protect agricultural land from development. In 1980, the commissioners appointed a nine-member Agricultural Preserve Board to devise ways to protect the county's agricultural lands. The board became a county department in 1983, when it first began purchasing development rights to preserve land for farming. In 1989, the Preserve Board began to participate in Pennsylvania's statewide purchase of development rights program, which opened up new sources of funding, specifically a $100 million bond issue passed by voter referendum. In addition, in 1999 the state legislature, as part of the budget approval process, approved a line item for farmland preservation, which made available substantial supplemental funding for a specified period. The county now receives about $3.7 million a year from the state in return for following guidelines from the state's hugely successful farmland protection program, which recently surpassed neighboring Maryland to protect the most farmland acreage in the country through the purchase of development rights.

Under the program, landowners apply to sell development rights to the Preserve Board, which then ranks the applications, hires appraisers to estimate the value of development rights, and makes a formal offer to the landowner. Landowners who sell their development rights must maintain the land in farming.

To beef up its other farmland preservation efforts, the county started giving major property tax breaks to farmers in 1997 by taxing farmland at its agricultural value rather than its market value. More than 353,000 acres were enrolled in the program in 2002, half the land in the county and nearly all its farmland, yielding an annual property tax break of $20 million a year for farmers and forestland owners.

Twenty years after the county began its preservation efforts, farmland protection remains a key concern among local residents. Throughout the county are adopted growth areas as well as substantial acreage that is zoned agricultural, which has been increasing over the past few years. These tools have helped to slow the loss of farmland; however, roughly 2,500 acres of farmland are converted to some type of nonagricultural use each year. The county is preserving about as much agricultural land as is developed each year, but with a population projected to double within the next fifty years, the value of farmland preservation is still a number one issue among the citizens of the county.

A 2001 survey by the local Hourglass Foundation found that 92 percent of the people polled felt something should be done to stop or slow down the loss of farmland, 96 percent felt that continued loss of farmland is a problem, with 77 percent feeling it is a serious problem. More than 90 percent of respondents felt there should be restrictions or limits placed on growth in the county, with an additional 4 percent advocating no additional growth.

"Preserving farmland is a means to preserve one of Lancaster's best natural resources, which is farmland," said June Mengel, director of the Agricultural Preserve Board. "It is an investment in the future. In a nutshell, preserving this resource is good fiscal policy, good economic development policy, and a sound land use policy."

DeKalb County, Georgia

Residents of DeKalb County, which is home to part of Atlanta and Georgia's second largest county, took a giant step forward in March 2001 to link and preserve its dwindling green space while giving a shot in the arm to the county's park system. Voters in the majority black county (population 665,133) approved a small property tax increase to fund a $125 million parks bond, with strong support from the county's new chief executive officer, Vernon Jones, and the county commissioners. At least 70 percent of the bond money is dedicated to land acquisition for parks and green space and up to 30 percent to park improvements and new facilities.[4]

County officials wasted no time putting the money to work. By late 2002, DeKalb County had acquired 1,175 acres of new park and open space land, and committed $9.3 million to renovate athletic fields, swimming pools, tennis courts, and lakes at the county's parks.

DeKalb's efforts come none too soon. The Atlanta region had been losing 500 acres each week to development, according to a 1998 Sierra Club report.[5] DeKalb County currently owns 6 acres of parks and green space per 1,000 residents, roughly one-third the average for the nation's largest fifty-five urban areas, according to "Inside City Parks," a Trust for Public Land report.[6]

Responding to the challenges faced by the Atlanta area, the Georgia General Assembly and former governor Roy Barnes approved legislation in April 2000 to create the Georgia Community Greenspace Initiative. Under the program, the state Department of Natural Resources can provide up to $30 million in grants annually, subject to annual appropriations by the state legislature, to fast-growing or urbanized communities that develop and implement greenspace plans that protect 20 percent of their land in order to further water quality, preserve resources, and achieve recreation goals of the program. The state-appropriated funds, to be disbursed to local governments on a per capita basis, are available to offset costs of obtaining real property and conservation easements that qualify as permanently protected greenspace under the state's guidelines.

To qualify for the state funds, DeKalb County worked with its nine municipalities to create the Joint DeKalb County/Municipal Greenspace Program, which outlines their plans for preserving 22 percent of their land (nearly 38,000 acres) as greenspace. The county commissioners then created advisory committees and a county Office of Parks Bond and Greenspace to oversee and implement the greenspace program.

Passage of the bond referendum had helped attract more than $13 million in additional funding for open space by late 2002. Because of the county's fiscal health, DeKalb was able to obtain a $5.2 million pre-

PHOTO 3.3. DeKalb County, Georgia, is focusing on the Davidson–Arabia Mountain Nature Preserve (pictured here) in its effort to protect dwindling open space in the fast-growing Atlanta region. *Photo by Craig M. Tanner.*

mium when it sold its bond in the fall of 2001, yielding a total of $130.2 million in open space and park funding. The new state Greenspace Grant Program awarded $5.5 million to DeKalb County and nearly $900,000 to its nine municipalities in 2001 and 2002. The Arthur M. Blank Family Foundation donated nearly $1.6 million to the county in the first cycle of its three-year commitment to donate at least $20 million to boost park and open space opportunities in the Atlanta region. And the Richard King Mellon Foundation stepped forward in late 2001 to purchase and donate 100 acres valued at more than $1 million for addition to the county's premier greenspace area—the 2,000-acre Davidson–Arabia Mountain Nature Preserve. The county itself has spent more than $18 million in bond money to acquire more than 1,000 acres to expand the preserve.

Popularity of the county's greenspace program has extended well beyond the ballot box. More than 600 properties have been nominated for inclusion in the county's park and greenspace system in the program's first year of operation. The county commission selects the properties for protection based on recommendations from county staff and a greenspace advisory council based on criteria in the county's Parks and Recreation Comprehensive Strategic Plan and its Initiative for a Green DeKalb Program.

By late 2002, the county had protected 1,175 acres using $22.8 million of its parks and greenspace funding. The county hopes to protect up to another 2,825 acres of greenspace with the remaining bond money. Another 3,055 acres of open space already is owned and permanently protected by the county, with perhaps another 2,000 acres of county-owned land that may qualify as protected greenspace under the state's guidelines. The 9,055-acre total put the county about one-fourth of the way toward its long-term land preservation goal. To make further progress toward its goal of 38,000 acres of greenspace, said Tina Arbes, who heads the county's parks and greenspace office, the county is actively leveraging its funding, seeking partnerships with other governments and organizations, and looking for open space and partnerships with developers who are seeking approval of new subdivisions in the county.

Jacksonville, Florida

Geographically the largest city in the continental United States, Jacksonville, Florida, until recently sported one of the smallest urban park systems in the nation—2,600 acres as recently as 1992. All that changed during the second term of former mayor John Delaney, who ran the city from 1995 until 2003. As Delaney tells it, the idea to embark on a major land preservation initiative occurred during a fishing trip with a friend at the Timucuan Ecological and Historic Preserve. That day, he noticed that much of the federal park, located within city borders, was privately owned and likely to sprout condos and shopping malls unless someone took action to protect the land.

So Delaney began his search for funding to do just that. His staff tracked how much money Jacksonville's 735,617 residents were contributing to Florida's impressive suite of land conservation programs through their payments of documentary tax stamps, which fuels the ten-year, $3 billion Florida Forever program. The answer: more than they were getting back.

PHOTO 3.4. Man kayaks on the St. Johns River at Reddie Point in Arlington, a 101-acre acquisition funded by the city of Jacksonville's Preservation Project and the Florida Communities Trust. *Photo courtesy of Wes Lester/City of Jacksonville.*

So in January 1999, the mayor announced a bold, five-year plan called Preservation Project Jacksonville that has propelled the city's park system into one of the largest parks systems in the nation—in just five years.[7] The program's original goal: to protect 10 to 20 square miles of the remaining open space in the huge 840-square-mile city. The result: the city and its partners greatly exceeded its goal by protecting more than 62 square miles. It did so by raising $150 million, less than half the money that city officials thought they would need to accomplish their goal.

So how did they do it? First, in 1999, the city appropriated $21 million in a combination of a bond refunding and general revenue funding. A year later, voters in September 2000 agreed to devote $50 million of a one-half-cent sales tax increase over ten years for land acquisition and recreation. The state contributed $32 million through two programs: the Florida Forever program and the Florida Communities Trust Program, which gives matching grants to local governments for conservation and recreation projects. The St. Johns River Water Management District contributed $19.2 million as part of a statewide effort by the state's five water districts to protect Florida's fragile water resources. And JEA, the local electric, water, and sewer utility, invested $25 million over a five-year period to purchase land to buffer its properties. Donations of land and money totaled more than $11 million. And a court settlement over a local cogeneration power plant yielded $300,000 for local land acquisitions.

To set the stage for the acquisition program, city officials inventoried more than 300,000 parcels of land to see what was protected, what was undeveloped, and what was already developed. That review led to a proposal to create five corridors running through the city—the Southeastern, Intracoastal Waterway, Timucuan Preserve, Western Greenbelt, and St. Johns River corridors—which would link existing recreational lands and, significantly, help manage the city's growth.

While the city bought much of the land to protect environmentally sensitive areas, said Mark Middlebrook, executive director for the Preservation Project, other tracts were acquired strictly to prevent development in unwanted areas and enhance public access to beaches, fishing spots, and other waterways. Middlebrook credited the program with blocking a golf course, shopping center, septic sludge farm, and subdivisions that would have spawned 2,000 homes in areas the city of Jacksonville felt were best left undeveloped.

Preservation Project Jacksonville also has sparked two new partnerships for the city. Jacksonville signed an agreement with the National Park Service and the Florida Park Service to cooperatively manage its conservation and park lands as one park, the first such arrangement in the nation. The city also is working with the U.S. Army Corps of Engineers, the St. Johns River Water Management District, and a private wetland mitigation banker to use wetland mitigation funds from highway and other construction projects to protect and restore the local ecosystem.

Lake County, Illinois

Illinois has adopted a unique approach to saving its natural lands and providing recreational and open space opportunities for its residents. The state's thirteen active forest preserve districts and six active conservation districts have independent special district governing commissions that raise revenue through their property taxing power to acquire and protect important environmental and recreational land.

Although forest preserve districts in Chicago's Cook County and DuPage County are the oldest in the state, dating to the 1920s, another collar county of Chicago—Lake County—has shown great leadership in land preservation since voters created the Lake County Forest Preserve District in 1958.[8]

Particularly impressive is the public and political support for the forest preserve's activities that has gathered steam since the early 1990s. The district has conducted several surveys to identify major critical issues of residents. Overdevelopment and preservation of open space emerged as two key concerns. The elected board of commissioners placed three referenda on the ballot, which voters approved, on average, by a two-to-one margin. In 1993, voters passed a $30 million bond referendum, followed by a $55 million measure in 1999, and an $85 million in 2000, for a total of $170 million in spending for land acquisition, trails, maintenance, and habitat restoration.

As a result, the district now boasts nearly 25,000 acres of holdings, which brings the district within 2,000 acres of its goal of providing 40 acres of parks and open space for every 1,000 residents, by far the most per resident of any forest preserve in the state. And the district still had $40 million in remaining bond money in early 2003, which will help acquire an estimated 1,700 acres within the next two years, bringing the district very close to its long-term goal, said executive director Steven Messerli.

The bonds are paid off with property taxes assessed on landowners in the county of 660,000 residents. The combined tax rate, as of early 2003 and including debt service for the voter-approved bonds, was 22.4 cents per $100 of assessed valuation, or $141.49 per year for the owner of a $200,000 home. Since the passage of the 1993 referenda, the district has acquired about 7,000 acres (a 25 percent increase) and provided miles of new trails and other public access to its lands. The expansion prompted the commissioners to ask voters in the fall of 2002 for new funding to maintain and restore the new properties they hold. Voters approved the measure, which will support more than 30 miles of new hiking and biking trails that have been created since 1999, bringing the trail system to more than 115 miles.

Counting all four referenda, roughly 3 percent of the county's property taxes are devoted to supporting the forest district. The flurry of

PHOTO 3.5. The central section of the Des Plaines River Trail connects here with 7 miles of trail at Independence Grove in Libertyville. Both are part of the Lake County Forest Preserves' 115-mile trail system. *Photo courtesy of Lake County Forest Preserves, Illinois*

recent bond activity hasn't hurt its ratings in the financial markets, either. Its solid tax base growth and strong financial operations recently earned a AAA rating from Standard and Poor's, the highest available.

The program also has attracted significant state support from the new Open Lands Trust Act, a four-year program begun in 1998 that set aside $40 million for local land protection efforts. Of the $40 million, the Lake County district managed to receive $12 million, including a $4.6 million grant awarded in late 2002.

Lands acquired for the forest preserves must meet requirements set by the twenty-three-member board of commissioners. The requirements include protecting natural areas for wildlife habitat; preserving wetlands, prairies, and forests; providing trails, greenways, river and lake access; protecting against flooding; expanding existing preserves; and creating new sites. The district also has an ongoing habitat restoration program, with its army of 1,300 conservation volunteers who donate 4,000 hours annually to clear hundreds of acres of brush and other invasive plants to make room for native grasses, wildflowers, and trees.

The impressive volunteer force underlies the growing popularity of the preserve district. A recent survey found that 72 percent of Lake County households visited the preserves an average of seven times per year. Hiking, bicycling, and other trail activities were among the most popular activities, along with picnicking, attending educational programs and exhibits, fishing, and watching nature.

St. Louis, Missouri

St. Louis is among many cities that have taken a comprehensive look at themselves and developed ambitious plans to reinvigorate city life from top to bottom. In 1996, a broad-based, public-private effort began a multiyear planning process to revitalize the urban area by 2004, the bicentennial of the Lewis and Clark Expedition and the one hundredth anniversary of the St. Louis World's Fair.

Community leaders developed eleven initiatives for the St. Louis 2004 renaissance effort, including a plan to create the nation's first bi-state multicounty park district.[9] The plan envisioned spending more than $400 million over twenty years to develop greenways, parks, and trails for hiking, biking, and other recreational activities throughout the St. Louis region.

What began as a unique idea has grown into a substantial success. Residents of the city of St. Louis, as well as St. Louis and St. Charles Counties in Missouri and St. Clair and Madison Counties in neighboring Illinois, approved a one-tenth-cent increase in sales taxes in November 2000 to fund the initiative. The proceeds are split evenly between county parks and the two new regional park districts—the Metropolitan Park and Recreation District (MPRD, in Missouri) and the Metro East Park and Recreation District (in Illinois). The two new regional park districts plan to work closely to ensure maximum regional benefit.

In late 2001, MPRD appointed David Fisher to be its first executive director. Fisher will help develop an interconnected greenways, parks, and trails system that proponents foresee as a boon to economic development, community stability, and an improved quality of life. In December 2002, MPRD launched a process to develop a collaborative plan for regional the parks system. MPRD appointed representatives from St. Louis City, St. Louis County, and St. Charles County to serve on a Citizen Advisory Committee, which includes up to forty members. The committee will help facilitate communication between local citizens and MPRD to meet regional objectives and local community desires.

While MPRD's key focus is the development of the collaborative regional plan, the organization has started working on a number of projects. MPRD is currently collaborating with the municipalities of Bridgeton, Florissant, Hazelwood, Maryland Heights, and St. Louis County to develop a 34-mile greenway along the Missouri River in north St. Louis County. MPRD also is helping the city of Fenton in the construction of a 1-mile trail along the Meramec River Greenway to connect St. Louis County's Unger Park and Fenton City Park. The Meramec River Greenway consists of a 108-mile-long corridor that parallels the course of the Meramec River, extending from the confluence of the Meramec and Mississippi Rivers to Meramec State Park and Forest in Sullivan, Missouri. The district and Bike St. Louis, a group of neighborhood, bicycle, government, and business representatives, are developing a system of on-street bicycle lanes and directional signage in the city of St. Louis.

MPRD also provided funding for year-round public access to the Old Chain of Rocks Bridge, an abandoned section of the fabled Route 66 that reopened in 1999 as the longest pedestrian and bicycle bridge in the world, crossing the Mississippi River and linking Missouri with Illinois. Prior to MPRD's funding, bridge access was limited to weekends and major holidays between April and November. A local trail group, TrailNet, Inc., raised $4 million for the restoration, with $2 million coming from a federal Transportation Enhancement grant; $500,000 from the McKnight Foundation of Minneapolis; $400,000 from the Gateway Foundation; and the remainder from more than two hundred individuals, corporations, and foundations.

In June 2001, the MPRD board voted unanimously to commit $36 million to develop the Confluence Greenway Project. The proposed $87 million Confluence Greenway, a 40-mile riverside park and trail, will extend from the Gateway Arch on both sides of the Mississippi River to its confluence with the Illinois River at Pere Marquette State Park near Grafton, Illinois. Nearly 3,000 acres had been acquired for the Confluence Greenway, including 2,000 acres by the Illinois Department of Natural Resources; 200 acres by the Missouri Department of Natural Resources, with funding assistance from the Danforth Foundation; and 634 acres by the Metropolitan Park and Recreation District.

Douglas County, Colorado

Not so long ago, Douglas County, Colorado, was a sparsely populated, politically conservative ranch community beyond Denver's suburban reach. While still politically conservative, the county, which had just 8,407 residents in 1970, has shed some of its natural quiet to become the fastest-growing county in the nation. More than 200,000 people lived in the county in 2002, with an estimated 320,000 expected by 2010.

The secret is out that Douglas County is a beautiful place to live. The county boasts expansive vistas and cattle ranches that give way to the forests and snow-capped mountains of Colorado's Front Range. But years ago, many in Douglas County foresaw what could happen to their home. Spillover growth creeping south down Interstate 25 from Denver and north from Colorado Springs could transform the I-25 corridor that bisects the county into an uninterrupted 70-mile stretch of development.

Douglas County residents weren't alone in their concerns. As droves of newcomers flocked to the county and the rest of Colorado, state voters in 1992 approved a constitutional amendment to create the Great Outdoors Colorado Trust Fund. State lottery revenue fuels the fund, which pays for land acquisition projects around the state that preserve Colorado's rich natural heritage—its rivers, wildlife, scenic vistas, and open spaces.

Just one year later, in 1993, Douglas County voters soundly rejected a bond referendum backed by the county commission that would have raised the county's sales and use tax to acquire open space, build roads, and boost services for senior citizens. County open space supporters regrouped over the next year and collected enough signatures to put a straight open space proposal on the November ballot funded by a one-sixth-cent increase in the sales and use tax. The result: county voters approved the Open Space, Trails, and Parks Sales and Use Tax by a 58 percent to 42 percent margin, which yielded $2.5 million annually, two-thirds for open space acquisition, the rest for parks.[10]

Two years later, in 1996, residents authorized the issuance of bonds for twenty-five years to put the program on solid financial footing. In 1998, 54 percent of voters approved a fifteen-year extension of the sales tax for open space, allowing the county to issue $25 million in open space bonds, all of which was allocated for acquisitions within three years. And in 2001, an overwhelming 70 percent of voters approved the issuance of $43 million in bonds, with $29 million earmarked for open space acquisition and $14 million for parks.

The county sales and use tax now generates over $6 million annually to preserve wildlife habitat; protect the county's rural landscape and agricultural heritage; create community buffers; protect scenic views, historic properties, and archaeological resources; and enhance passive recreational opportunities. The county receives approximately 88 percent of the one-sixth-cent sales tax proceeds for parks, trails, and open space, and the remainder is split on the basis of license plate registrations among three towns—Parker, Castle Rock, and Larkspur—for their local park, trail, and open space programs.

By late 2002, the county had spent $34 million in sales tax proceeds to preserve more than 41,200 acres, including the 21,000-acre Greenland Ranch, a 12-mile stretch along the I-25 corridor that has been protected in perpetuity through a public–private partnership. Every dollar spent by Douglas County for land acquisition has been matched by nearly three dollars in partner contributions, including $22 million in state GOCO money.

Marin County, California

Located across the Golden Gate Bridge from San Francisco, Marin County's ocean views, rolling hills, farms, and ranchland have helped create its reputation as one of the more desirable places to live in the nation. Less well known is the remarkable complement of public and private land conservation programs that have protected well over half the county's 333,000 acres despite tremendous development pressures.

Anchoring the multipronged land preservation effort are federal holdings totaling 78,551 acres at Point Reyes National Seashore, Golden Gate National Recreation Area, and Muir Woods National Monument. State, county, and local parks total 14,721 acres. And the Marin Municipal and North Marin water districts also hold 21,802 acres in public trust to protect the area's water supply.

MARIN COUNTY OPEN SPACE DISTRICT

Marin County's proximity to San Francisco and its 70 miles of open coastline and 40 miles of bay frontage have made it hot property for developers. Rather than accepting whatever development came their way and seeing their valued open space and farmland disappear, county residents voted in 1972 to create the Marin County Open Space District, funded by a property tax.[11]

Since its founding more than thirty years ago, the district has acquired more than 14,000 acres of natural lands in thirty-three separate preserves, primarily for hiking, biking, horseback riding, and other low-impact recreational uses. Besides tapping property tax revenue, the district has boosted the size of the preserve system by obtaining grants from the Marin Community Foundation and other private sources, as well as state bond money that is distributed on a per capita basis, and revenue from local assessment districts and community services districts.

More recently, nonprofit organizations such as the Marin Audubon Society have partnered with the district to acquire important open space. While most of the land the district acquires is purchased, it also obtains land through donations and by transfer from other land management agencies. Increasingly, the district has obtained open space through the dedication of property as a condition for the subdivision of land and approval of new development, including 800 acres from the filmmaker George Lucas for the approval of a major office building, said David Hansen, open space and park planner with the district.

MARIN AGRICULTURAL LAND TRUST

Marin County's farms and ranches occupy some of most attractive undeveloped real estate in the San Francisco Bay Area. They also contribute more than $50 million to the local economy, and produce 20 percent of the milk supply for the area, along with livestock and poultry, feed crops, and fruits and vegetables. The same development pressure spilling over the Golden Gate Bridge that led to creation of the county Open Space District also drove ranchers and farmers in 1980 to team up with environmentalists to create the nation's first land trust dedicated to farmland preservation. Twenty-three years later, the Marin Agricultural Land Trust (MALT) had acquired conservation easements on forty-seven family farms and ranches totaling 32,000

PHOTO 3.6. Marin Agricultural Land Trust purchased an easement on the 1,192-acre Nobmann Ranch in Point Reyes Station in 1993, permanently protecting the beef cattle ranch and Black Mountain (pictured here), a prominent West Marin landmark. *Photo courtesy of Elisabeth Ptak/Marin Agricultural Land Trust.*

acres, or about one-fifth of the farmland in the county.[12] Now considered a model for agricultural land trusts in the nation, MALT started with a shoestring budget and gradually attracted $1 million grants from the San Francisco Foundation and the State Coastal Conservancy. In 1988, the land trust received a major shot in the arm financially with statewide passage of Proposition 70—the California Wildlife, Coastal and Parkland Conservation Bond Act. It included $15 million to preserve agricultural land in the county, which MALT spent over the next nine years to acquire twenty-five easements, permanently protecting 15,000 acres.

By the late 1990s, the $15 million in bond funding was spent, and MALT hired a full-time campaign director to run a three-year, $10 million fundraiser, said Robert Berner, MALT's executive director. The land trust raised $5 million from individual donors, $2.5 million from the Marin Community Foundation from a matching grant, and the remainder from the California State Coastal Conservancy and other public agencies. As of 2003, MALT's 4,600 members and donors contribute $500,000 annually to support its operating budget.

MARIN COMMUNITY FOUNDATION

The Marin Community Foundation has played a critical role in the county's land conservation efforts since it was established in 1986 with the assets of a trust created by long-time Marin residents Leonard and Beryl H. Buck.[13] Since 1988 the foundation's Beryl Buck Open Space Fund has provided $5.8 million in challenge grants to assist twenty land acquisition projects totaling 3,556 acres. The grants have leveraged $7.3 million from the county open space district and more than twice that amount from other public agencies and private donors, said Sallyanne Wilson, who oversees the foundation's environmental program. Besides managing the open space fund, Wilson also oversees the foundation's work to promote land conservation efforts that preserve agriculture, open space, and sensitive habitats, such as the $2.5 million challenge grant to MALT.

Although open space funding might seem plentiful in Marin County, the real estate prices are easily keeping pace, Berner said. In the 1980s, MALT purchased farmland easements for an average $460 an acre. Easement prices cracked the $1,000-an-acre level during the 1990s, and two easements in 2002 cost $1,700 an acre. With $10 million of easements under negotiation in early 2003, MALT plans to raise up to $60 million over the next ten years to continue its farmland preservation work in the county. Perhaps a third of the total could come from public agencies, particularly watershed and rangeland protection programs funded through the state's recently passed multibillion-dollar bond referenda.

One way to measure how successful the county's land preservation efforts is how well it has stemmed the onslaught of development foreseen back in the early 1970s. While the state of California as a whole has grown more than 70 percent in population between 1970 and 2001, Marin County has increased just 20 percent.

"What we've learned," said MALT co-founder Phyllis Faber, "is that you can have a vision of what you want the future to look like, and you can make it happen."

Conclusion

As this chapter's profiles demonstrate, local land conservation efforts are sprouting up across the country. Farmland preservation efforts are growing in communities as diverse as Lancaster County, Pennsylvania, and Marin County, California. Major urban areas such as DeKalb County, Georgia; Jacksonville, Florida; and St. Louis, Missouri, are making strides in providing their citizens with safe parks while protecting open space and developing greenway and trail systems. And communities such as Douglas County, Colorado, and Lake County, Illinois, are showing that suburban sprawl doesn't have to consume all remaining undeveloped land in its path. Even the long-time tourist destination of Cape Cod, Massachusetts, has generated funding to preserve thousands of acres of its dwindling undeveloped lands.

Finding the right funding mechanism can be a challenge, as residents of Cape Cod found when they attempted to raise land conservation money from taxes on real estate transfers. But they teamed up with real estate interests who had opposed the transfer tax to find a more acceptable source of open space funding. Flexibility and perseverance are key ingredients of any grassroots effort to create funding for local open space preservation, along with raising and spending money wisely on a professionally run ballot measure campaign.

CHAPTER FOUR

CREATING LOCAL CONSERVATION FUNDING

As many states in recent years have created financing programs to create parks and protect open space, hundreds of communities across the United States have established land protection programs with funding from general revenues, bond referenda, sales and property taxes, or other dedicated sources of revenue (see Table 4.1). In most of these cities and counties, a long process of planning and preparation ended successfully at the polls when voters approved a ballot measure to create a locally funded program to preserve land.

A handful of states have stood out since the early 1990s as national leaders in locally approved land conservation programs. New Jersey leads the nation, but Massachusetts, Colorado, New York, and Pennsylvania also have experienced significant progress in the creation of these programs. The link is clear: the number of locally funded land conservation programs increases significantly if state leaders create a statewide program that provides local grants to communities that have their own funding sources to leverage the state money. But other communities outside of these states have funded new land conservation programs as well, including counties that want to protect their farm and ranch land or cities that seek funding to expand their park and greenway systems to improve their quality of life.

TABLE 4.1.

Number of approved county and municipal land conservation measures in selected states, 1998–2002

State	1998	1999	2000	2001	2002	Total
1. New Jersey	52	48	48	45	25	218
2. Massachusetts	18	1	2	36	22	79
3. Colorado	4	12	14	9	10	49
4. New York	8	3	11	5	12	39
5. Pennsylvania	2	7	7	4	15	35
6. Illinois	1	5	10	3	5	24
7. Florida	2	3	10	4	4	23
8. Rhode Island	4	1	14	—	3	22
9. Connecticut	3	5	5	2	2	17
10. Ohio	2	4	4	4	1	15
11. Texas	3	—	3	7	2	15
12. New Hampshire	—	1	—	2	9	12
13. California	1	1	3	2	4	11
14. North Carolina	1	2	5	1	—	9
15. Maine	—	—	6	1	1	8
16. Michigan	1	1	2	2	2	8
17. Arizona	1	3	1	1	1	7
18. Virginia	3	—	2	—	2	7
19. Georgia	—	1	3	2	—	6
20. New Mexico	2	—	3	—	1	6
21. Utah	1	1	1	1	2	6
22. Missouri	—	—	4	1	—	5
23. Oregon	3	—	1	—	1	5
24. South Carolina	1	—	3	—	1	5
25. Washington	—	1	1	1	2	5
26. Minnesota	—	—	1	1	1	3
27. Oklahoma	—	—	1	—	2	3
28. Hawaii	—	—	—	—	2	2
29. Maryland	2	—	—	—	—	2
30. Wisconsin	—	1	1	—	—	2
31. Delaware	—	1	—	—	—	1
32. Idaho	—	—	—	1	—	1
33. Iowa	—	—	—	1	—	1
34. Montana	—	—	1	—	—	1
35. Nevada	—	—	1	—	—	1
36. Wyoming	—	—	—	1	—	1

Sources: Adapted from Land Trust Alliance, 1998, 1999, and 2000 *Referenda Results;* and Trust for Public Land and Land Trust Alliance, *LandVote 2001* and *LandVote 2002.*

This land conservation money, which runs in the hundreds of millions of dollars nationwide, didn't show up by magic. There's no simple formula to create local funding for land preservation. But the groundswell of support for such financing has proved that both small towns and big cities can develop successful land conservation programs backed by voter-approved ballot measures. This chapter discusses some key elements of conservation funding campaigns, followed by case studies in California and the St. Louis area.

To Campaign or Not to Campaign

Anyone seeking funding for land conservation from legislators or the public must answer a basic question: Why do you need the money? It helps to have a well-researched open space plan in hand along with a thorough knowledge of existing federal, state, and local funding sources. At the local level, county or municipal planning departments and local environmental advocacy groups may be a good resource in researching how much work on open space planning has been completed. For funding assistance, the Sonoran Institute in Tucson, Arizona, hosts a web site (Conservation Assistance Tools, at http://cat. sonoran.org) that lists nearly 1,000 organizations and agencies that provide financial and technical assistance for natural resource conservation projects across the United States. Appendix A at the end of this book also lists major land conservation programs and funding sources in all fifty states.

The remainder of this chapter assumes that feasibility research has been completed, and that community leaders have decided to ask state legislators, county commissioners, or city councilors to create a new—and preferably dedicated—funding source for land conservation by placing an open space measure on the ballot. While many states and some localities allow citizens to bypass their elected bodies (state legislatures or local governing councils) and place bond initiatives directly on the ballot by obtaining enough signatures on a petition, the following discussion assumes that the funding effort will require authorizing legislation from a state legislature or local governing body for referral to the ballot. Although the focus here is on key aspects of conducting a campaign to win a ballot measure for open space funding, the process we describe is not meant to be a step-by-step description of how a campaign is run from start to finish.[1]

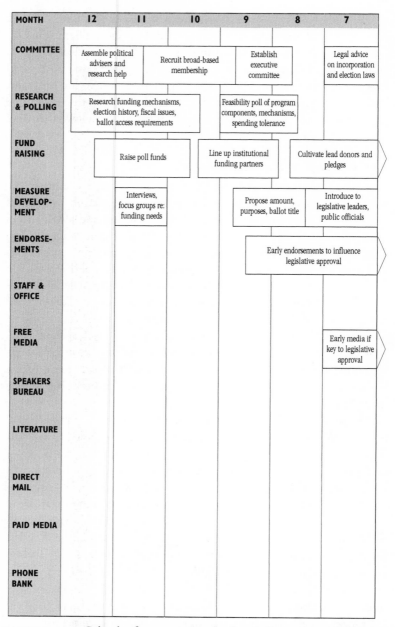

FIGURE 4.I. Calendar for open space funding ballot measure (legislative referral). *Source:* Trust for Public Land. Figure by Sue Dodge.

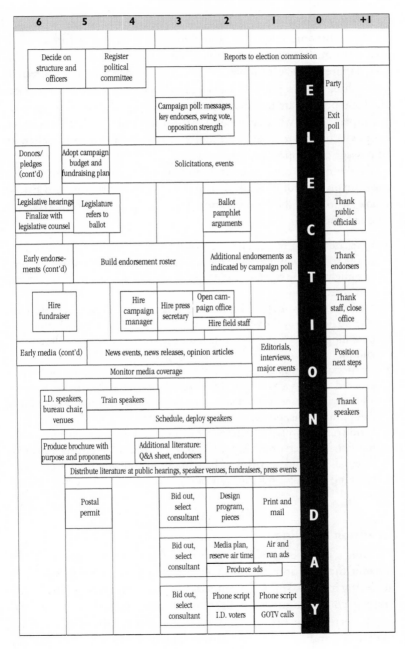

6	5	4	3	2	1	0	+1

Decide on structure and officers | Register political committee | Reports to election commission

Campaign poll: messages, key endorsers, swing vote, opposition strength

E L E C T I O N

Party

Exit poll

Donors/pledges (cont'd) | Adopt campaign budget and fundraising plan | Solicitations, events

Legislative hearings | Legislature refers to ballot | Ballot pamphlet arguments | Thank public officials
Finalize with legislative counsel

Early endorsements (cont'd) | Build endorsement roster | Additional endorsements as indicated by campaign poll | Thank endorsers

Hire fundraiser | Hire campaign manager | Hire press secretary | Open campaign office | Thank staff, close office
Hire field staff

Early media (cont'd) | News events, news releases, opinion articles | Editorials, interviews, major events | Position next steps
Monitor media coverage

I.D. speakers, bureau chair, venues | Train speakers | Thank speakers
Schedule, deploy speakers

Produce brochure with purpose and proponents | Additional literature: Q&A sheet, endorsers
Distribute literature at public hearings, speaker venues, fundraisers, press events

D A Y

Postal permit | Bid out, select consultant | Design program, pieces | Print and mail

Bid out, select consultant | Media plan, reserve air time | Air and run ads
Produce ads

Bid out, select consultant | Phone script | Phone script
I.D. voters | GOTV calls

Getting Started

In the embryonic stage of a campaign, perhaps a year before election day, a committee should assemble political advisers and research help (see Figure 4.1). A number of basic issues need to be addressed: researching funding mechanisms and ballot access requirements, what the local politics are like, how much funding can be raised to support a campaign, and whether other issues on the ballot (other tax and fee proposals or controversial candidates or issues) may hurt the chances of passage of an open space proposal.

At the outset, anyone considering an effort to get an open space measure on the ballot needs to keep in mind several points, said Ernest Cook, who runs the Conservation Finance Program at the Trust for Public Land:

- One size doesn't fit all. There is a right measure for the right time done in the right way. But a ballot measure can be poorly structured, the timing might not be right, or campaign methods might turn off supporters and voters.
- Do your homework first. Know your terrain and what is achievable. Getting 60 percent of the vote for a $20 million bond measure is better than obtaining a losing 45 percent share of the vote for an $80 million referendum.
- Don't expect immediate and easy answers about what to do or how to proceed. It takes a variety of skills, techniques, and expertise to organize a successful conservation finance campaign, involving public education, communications, public policy, campaign expertise, and fundraising.
- Land trusts can play a leadership role in a campaign to generate public funding to preserve open space (see Box 4.1). Many land trusts think that Internal Revenue Service law bars nonprofit organizations from campaigning for ballot questions or taking stands on public issues. It's not true.

Coalition Building

Building a broad base of support for a ballot measure is essential. The broader the coalition, the stronger and more persuasive it will be in achieving its goal—more funding for land conservation—with the city council, county commission, or state legislature and in convincing voters on election day. Because land trusts often occupy the political center in their communities, they are natural leaders in creating a constituency

BOX 4.1.

*Top 10 things land trusts can do to increase public funding
for open space*

10. Know that your land trust can take positions on public issues,
    lobby your elected representatives, and campaign for ballot ques-
    tions, just as the Red Cross, the Girl Scouts, and thousands of
    other 501(c)(3) charitable nonprofits do every day.

9. Know the Internal Revenue Service and state rules on lobbying
   and campaign finance, and make sure that you follow them.

8. Know your legislators and other elected officials, and inform them
   of the benefits your land trust brings to the community and of the
   importance of protecting land.

7. Have an up-to-date strategy to support new and increased public
   funding for land conservation. Ballot campaigns and lobbying are
   rarely one-time or short-term pursuits. Be in the conservation
   finance game for the long run.

6. Formally endorse open space ballot questions in your jurisdiction
   or state.

5. Be public, visible, and tangible in your support of ballot campaigns for open space funding. Publicize your support, collect signatures, organize phone banks. The leadership and credibility of
   your land trust can influence many voters.

4. Donate organizational resources—such as office space, copiers,
   and computer—to open space campaigns.

3. Encourage your board members and other volunteers to participate actively in lobbying and ballot campaigns. They can do a
   great deal of good.

2. Help financially, and encourage land trust members to contribute
   financially, to ballot question campaigns for open space funding.

1. Get involved and stay involved in public issues. Land trusts and
   their supporters are important, respected members of their communities. Land trusts should lead on public funding, just as they
   do in private conservation, stewardship, and other land trust roles.
   You can and should be involved—in a responsible, accountable
   manner—in the issues of importance to land protection in your
   region.

Source: Trust for Public Land Conservation Finance Program; see www.tpl.org.

to back an open space referendum. From the center, it is easier for a land trust or campaign organizers to reach out to potential allies on the political left and right: political leaders; environmental groups; the business and agricultural communities; civic, ethnic, and labor groups; minorities; health and safety organizations; and ultimately to the all citizens of the community to form a coalition to back an open space referendum.

The broader the coalition, the less likely organized opposition will surface. Getting potential opponents to at least stay neutral in a campaign can save a lot of time, effort, and money as election day approaches.

Polling

Polling is a critical tool in any campaign, small or large, as is hiring a professional pollster. Using outdated polls, or polls on park usage or other seemingly related subjects, or polls that aren't well-designed for your specific purpose are deadly mistakes. A well-designed poll will ask the key questions that help determine whether or how to proceed on an open space ballot question. These polls often comprise eight components:

1. Introductory questions that ask how likely it is that the respondent will vote in the election, how the respondent thinks about whether his or her city or county is headed in the right direction, and how the respondent rates the performance of local officials.
2. Political landscape questions that determine the relative importance of issues such as jobs, crime, schools, taxes, growth, the environment, drinking water, and transportation.
3. Ballot option questions that ask what the most popular funding source is for parks and open space preservation—property taxes, sales taxes, bonds, or some other mechanism.
4. Purpose questions that reveal what the most popular use of the funds would be—protecting wildlife habitat, enhancing water quality, creating parks, building a trail system, or other activities.
5. Argument and persuasion questions that test which reasons for funding open space draw the strongest and weakest responses.
6. A re-test section that repeats the ballot option questions mentioned above to see whether any change in the earlier response has occurred.
7. An endorsement section to determine how backing by different local officials or groups might help or hurt a ballot measure's chances of passage.

8. A demographics section on the respondent's age, education, income, political affiliation, and number of children, which will uncover how popular a ballot measure might be among these potential target groups.

Once the initial polling is completed, the question becomes, "Is there enough support to go forward?" said Steven Glazer of Glazer & Associates, a political consultant based in Orinda, California, who is on contract with the Trust for Public Land to develop open space initiatives. Some of the factors that Glazer examines in a poll to gauge the likelihood of success are voter support and level of intensity for and against a draft ballot question; the level of concern for the programmatic improvements being proposed by the measure; the degree of tax sensitivity if the measure would increase taxes; and the popularity of the proponents and opponents. In addition, although determining if a proposed measure may have well-funded community opposition is difficult to interpret through a poll, it can also have a significant effect on the measure's prospects.

Demographics can be destiny with ballot measures, according to Glazer. Polls identify the demographics of the electorate that are your base of support or opposition. This base could be voters of a certain age, sex, political party, race, and even high likelihood or low likelihood of voting in any particular election. Once polling determines these demographic factors, you can then relate them to the types of people who, based on historical voting patterns, turn out in different types of elections—special, local, state, federal, primary, general, U.S. Senate, gubernatorial, or presidential. These same demographic patterns can be determined for other issues or candidates that are to appear on the ballot, and the analysis of being helped or hurt by these developments can be undertaken.

For example, if an open space measure receives high support from ethnic minorities and their turnout is higher in presidential general elections, then targeting that ballot for your measure may be desirable. But if a controversial ballot measure excites a demographic group that is primarily composed of opponents to a proposed open space measure, then it would be best to avoid the election when that measure is on the ballot. Examples of these could be matters relating to gun control, criminal justice, or issues affecting senior citizens, Glazer said.

Assuming minimal opposition, proposed measures that garner less than 50 percent support in early polling are very challenging to pass, according to Glazer. Propositions that earn 51 to 65 percent in early support have a moderately good chance of winning. Measures that exceed 65 percent in early support and which have voter support intensity levels that exceed 40 percent have a strong chance of passing. Voter intensity level is determined by asking voters if they feel strongly in favor of the proposed measure or only somewhat in favor.

These percentages are rough calculations based on Glazer's experience with more than a hundred surveys on land use and open space taxes. Individual community circumstances and a detailed review of a completed survey instrument can produce different conclusions, Glazer said.

Ballot Language

Once initial polling, an assessment of the political climate, and other research have been completed, picking the proper funding mechanism and choosing how and when the funds are used are major decisions that can help a campaign gain support rather than generate significant opposition. Once these issues are decided, another important consideration is how the funding mechanism is presented on the ballot. To the uninitiated, it may come as a surprise that the actual wording of a ballot and its title is critical. But Adam Eichberg of the Trust for Public Land states that "ballot language is the single most important thing that you have to do right. It will benefit you a hundred times over."

One can quickly see why. Which title seems more worthy of support: "General Obligation Bonds" or "Safe Drinking Water, Park Improvement, and Wildlife Habitat Protection Bonds"? That's why it's necessary to know the rules that govern ballot language. They vary. Some states require specific opening language and limit the numbers of words on the ballot after a certain point in the bond description. Colorado requires that the ballot language open with "Shall _____ County taxes be increased . . . ?" or "Shall _____ County debt be raised . . . ?" In one case, the ballot language that was used in polling wasn't close enough to what ended up appearing on the actual ballot. Despite strong backing in the polls, the measure failed on election day because voters didn't like what they read.

Much of the language that usually appears in a ballot measure is there because of precedent rather than law. If elected officials aren't familiar with the ballot language process, it may help if campaign organizers have examples of ballot language from similar counties or states. At the local level, the county attorney usually ends up devising the ballot language or at least having the final say in its wording, which can result in legally defensible language that make the measure's benefits less apparent than its costs.

The best ballot language emphasizes the purpose of the ballot referendum rather than the mechanism by which the funds are collected, stored, or spent. A case in point: in 1997, 61 percent of voters in Adams County, Colorado, defeated an open space measure that would have raised $75 million over fifteen years through a one-fifth-cent sales tax increase. The ballot language totaled 156 words, with just 13 words describing how the money would be spent (see Box 4.2)

Two years later, Adams County faced new open space ballot language that supporters slimmed down to 120 words. Much of the process language was dropped in favor of more description, which totaled 29 words, of how the money would be spent. Polling also showed that adding farmland preservation was key to political support. The result: a huge turnaround, as 60 percent approved the same one-fifth-cent sales tax to raise $37.5 million over seven years. Adams County joined more than twenty other cities and counties in Colorado that have approved local funding programs since 1992 to help attract state grants available under the Great Outdoors Colorado program (Map 4.1) (see Chapter 2 for profile of the Colorado program).

Running a Campaign

To manage a campaign, organizers often form a committee rather than operate the campaign under the banner of one coalition member. In many cases, depending on legal implications and reporting issues, organizers may be required to set up a political action committee to run a campaign, depending on the state and local campaign regulations. It's advantageous to give the committee a name, such as "Clean Water, Safe Parks Committee," that incorporates the most compelling benefits of a campaign and encourages broad participation. Once the committee is in place, the individual members then may advocate the

BOX 4.2.
Comparison of open space ballot language from Adams County,
Colorado, in 1997 and 1999

1997 Open Space Measure (lost 61 percent to 39 percent)
Shall Adams County taxes be increased $5,000,000 (first full year dollar increase) by a countywide sales tax of one-fifth of one percent (one-fifth of one cent per dollar) for fifteen years (terminating December 31, 2013) for the purpose of acquiring, constructing, equipping, operating and maintaining open space and parks and recreational facilities (the "Open Space Tax"); and shall all or a portion of the revenues from such tax be deposited into a special fund to be known as the "Adams County Open Space Sales Tax Capital Improvement Fund" and utilized solely to provide the capital improvements authorized in Adams County Resolution No. 92-2 or for repayment of bonds; and shall all revenues from such tax and any earnings on such revenues (regardless of amount) constitute a voter-approved revenue change; and shall such tax be imposed, collected, administered and enforced as provided in Adams County Resolution No. 93-1, as amended by Adams County Resolution No. 97-2?

1999 Open Space Measure (approved 60 percent to 40 percent)
Shall Adams County taxes be increased $5.5 million, and whatever amounts are raised annually thereafter, by a countywide sales tax of one-fifth of one percent (20 cents on a $100 purchase), effective January 1, 2000, and automatically expiring after 7 years, with the proceeds to be used solely to preserve open space in order to limit sprawl, to preserve farmland, to protect wildlife areas, wetlands, rivers and streams, and for creating, improving and maintaining parks and recreation facilities, in accordance with Resolution 99-1, with all expenditures based on recommendations of a citizen advisory commission and subject to an annual independent audit and shall all revenues from such tax and any earnings thereon, constitute a voter approved revenue change.

Source: Trust for Public Land; Adams County, Colorado.

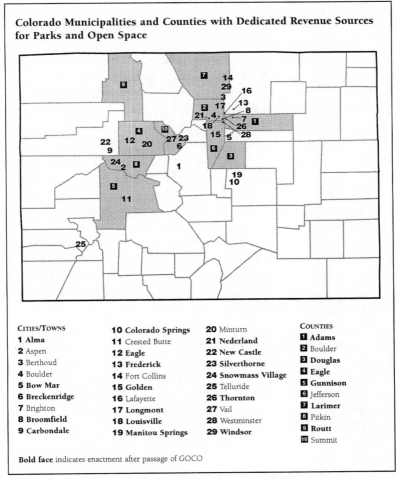

Colorado Municipalities and Counties with Dedicated Revenue Sources for Parks and Open Space

CITIES/TOWNS			COUNTIES
1 Alma	**10 Colorado Springs**	20 Minturn	**1 Adams**
2 Aspen	11 Crested Butte	**21 Nederland**	**2 Boulder**
3 Berthoud	**12 Eagle**	22 New Castle	**3 Douglas**
4 Boulder	**13 Frederick**	23 Silverthorne	**4 Eagle**
5 Bow Mar	14 Fort Collins	24 Snowmass Village	**5 Gunnison**
6 Breckenridge	**15 Golden**	25 Telluride	6 Jefferson
7 Brighton	16 Lafayette	**26 Thornton**	**7 Larimer**
8 Broomfield	**17 Longmont**	27 Vail	8 Pitkin
9 Carbondale	**18 Louisville**	28 Westminster	**9 Routt**
	19 Manitou Springs	**29 Windsor**	10 Summit

Bold face indicates enactment after passage of GOCO

MAP 4.1. Colorado voters created the Great Outdoors Colorado (GOCO) Trust Fund in 1992 to finance projects that preserve wildlife, parks, rivers, trails, and open spaces. To help attract GOCO grants, eighteen municipalities and six counties have dedicated revenue sources for parks and open space since the creation of the program. *Information courtesy of Great Outdoors Colorado. Map by Sue Dodge.*

measure separately and as part of the committee to broaden the reach and impact of the coalition. And, as mentioned earlier, there is nothing in Internal Revenue Service law regarding 501(c)(3) charitable nonprofit groups that precludes them from supporting a campaign, although individual nonprofit groups may have bylaws that do.

Funding is a key factor in how a campaign is run. An $8,000 campaign budget requires a different approach than a $200,000 budget, or, in the case of California's Proposition 40 referendum in March 2002— $7.8 million. Advertising in large urban media markets requires lots of money compared with voter outreach in small towns. If resources are tight, the campaign committee faces tough allocation issues, said Bill Lee of the Trust for Public Land.

One approach to media coverage—the news conference—is rarely used, according to Glazer. Why? In big media markets, the coverage will include the pros and cons of the ballot measure. There's no reason to give free media exposure to your opponents. But in some campaigns, free media and press events can be a good idea, especially when campaign organizers don't have the money to carry out a more sophisticated media strategy.

One of the goals of any campaign strategy is ensuring that your hard-core supporters turn out to vote. Polling may show that this base of support is of sufficient size that these voters will carry the referendum to victory—as long as they vote. In a special election, targeting your base voters with mailings may be wise. But more often, it's the undecided swing group that must be identified through polling and targeted with advertising and campaign literature.

The myriad decisions required in running a campaign include how to raise money and how best to spend valuable time and resources on television, radio, newspapers, press conferences, brochures, mailings, and speakers. Following are case studies that show how some of these decisions were made in two recent ballot referenda—a statewide contest in California in 2002 and a two-state, multijurisdictional vote in the St. Louis area in 2000.

Winning Proposition 40 in California

Conservationists achieved their biggest ballot box victory in history in March 2002, when 57 percent of California voters approved the $2.6

billion California Clean Water, Clean Air, Safe Neighborhood Parks, and Coastal Protection Act of 2002. Backers of the referendum raised $7.8 million in their successful campaign effort.

Early polling in California showed that water quality, air quality, and quality-of-life issues drew the highest positive ratings from voters, according to The Nature Conservancy, which backed the campaign. Underlying this support were two factors. First, Californians were becoming increasingly concerned about the state's population growth, which had jumped nearly 5 million since 1990, and its effect on land development. Second, the state had just emerged in 2000 from a decade-long absence of bond funding for parks, open space, and wildlife habitat after approving more than $2.6 billion in similar funding during the 1980s. Although voters approved a $2.1 billion parks bond in 2000 (Proposition 12), the money was quickly allocated to address the huge backlog of unmet demand.

Campaign organizers also faced a deteriorating economy and an energy crisis in the state as they went to state legislators to seek authorizing legislation for the measure. As the new bond measure took shape in the state legislature in August and September of 2001, legislative support remained high because polling in August had showed that support for the measure was strong even after a summer of rolling electricity blackouts. The final vote on legislation that placed the bond measure on the ballot occurred in the early morning hours of September 15, less than four days after the terrorist attacks in New York City and Washington, D.C. The state assembly voted 60 to 8 in favor, and the senate followed suit with a 29 to 4 vote.

In authorizing legislation for Proposition 40, state legislators developed a funding package that included $1.325 billion for park and historic resource projects and $1.275 billion for land, air, and water protection projects. The park and historic resources allotment included $225 million for state parks and $832.5 million for local parks, with the remaining $267.5 million for historic and cultural resources. Legislators divided the money for the bond measure among a number of state agencies, rather that directing it toward specific "pork" projects, which made Proposition 40 an unusually "clean" measure, supporters said.

After the legislative victory, The Nature Conservancy and other proposition backers created an executive committee whose members were chosen because of their fundraising ability, reputation, diversity, and their geographic sphere of influence. The size of the group—which ranged between thirty and fifty people—reflected the complexity of California's politics. A smaller core group ran the campaign on a day-to-day basis.

Organizers sought a consultant to manage the campaign and help decide what it would take to win in March 2002. They wanted someone who had experience in California and who had worked on ballot measures, rather than someone who had only managed candidate campaigns, and someone who had "full-service" media experience rather than knowledge of one medium of communication. The leaders also hired an attorney to ensure that it complied with state and federal reporting guidelines.

To raise $7.8 million to fuel the campaign, organizers developed talking points and obtained a lead gift and attracted other smaller donations by leveraging larger contributions from major donors. Although raising millions of dollars for a ballot drive isn't typical for most measures, in California it was necessary because of the cost of television airtime in multiple and expensive media markets. In the end, the campaign spent 84 percent of the $7.8 million on voter education and persuasion, exceeding an unwritten guideline in campaign planning that calls for devoting at least three-fourths of available funding to voter contact. The campaign's polling and research were essential in determining where funds would best be spent. Developing the right messages required thorough knowledge of what polled well with which groups.

Knowing voter trends and voting patterns is key to success in any campaign. As an example, the rise in absentee balloting has made it more important to assess voting trends among this group. Organizers pegged some of the direct mailing and television advertising to the time when absentee ballots arrived in voters' mailboxes, which occurred about one month before the March 5 vote. Organizers wanted to make sure they were getting their message to this key group of voters as they were making up their minds on the referendum. Not only was timing key with absentee voters, but they required specialized mailings as well. Polling had shown that absentee voters, as a group, tended to read more than average voters. In response, mailings to them included more written detail about the referendum.

The campaign also knew that focusing on California's ethnic and cultural diversity was important because polling has consistently found that communities of color provide some of the strongest support for park and open space measures. Organizers addressed the state's diversity, beginning with the composition of the executive committee that ran the campaign to community outreach and the development of campaign materials.

To reach the state's Hispanic, Latino, Asian, and African American populations, the campaign manager and the executive committee created a special working group to develop campaign materials that recognized the culture, traditions, and heritages of the communities.

RESULTS

Initial polling found that 28 percent of voters definitely planned to vote for Proposition 40, with 17 percent probably voting yes, and 7 percent that were considering it—a potential 52 percent victory, or basically no room to spare. By finding and communicating positive arguments in favor of the bond measure, the campaign pushed the yes vote to 57 percent on election day. Exit polling by the *Los Angeles Times* found that while an impressive 56 percent of white voters said yes to Proposition 40, 77 percent of blacks, 74 percent of Latinos, and 60 percent of Asians did.[2]

Creating Regional Park Districts in the St. Louis Area

The St. Louis region hosted one of the most politically ambitious park ballot referenda in recent memory—spanning two states (Missouri and Illinois), six counties, and the city of St. Louis. In November 2000, voters in St. Louis and four counties along the Mississippi River approved a one-tenth-cent sales tax increase to raise more than $400 million over twenty years to fund an interconnected park and open space system.

Work on Proposition C developed out of St. Louis 2004, a broad-based public–private effort begun in 1996. Organizers want to revitalize the urban area by 2004, the bicentennial of the Lewis and Clark Expedition, which started there, and the one hundredth anniversary of the St. Louis World's Fair. Extensive polling and public meetings found support for a regional park system and trail network, as well as a need to bolster funding for the existing park and recreation districts within the cities and counties in the St. Louis region. A committee of citizens, community leaders, and park professionals called the 2004 Parks and Open Space Task Force conceived legislation to accomplish these goals and helped form Gateway Parks and Trails 2004, a nonprofit group charged with producing a regional parks and open space plan.

Before any trail network that extended outside a county could be organized, funded, and built, state legislation was required, said Steven Glazer, who did much of the polling for Proposition C. Among his findings: (1) a modest sales tax was the most popular means to fund a regional park district, (2) parks and trails were, in fact, only a medium priority, and (3) improving water quality and making parks safer were the most popular public desires. In the end, a blend of these projects went forward to the ballot.

To create a regional park district in two states, the Trust for Public Land and other supporters helped draft legislation, which St. Louis 2004 helped move through the Missouri and Illinois Legislatures in 1999. One requirement: the city of St. Louis and all six counties that voted on the measure (St. Louis and St. Charles Counties in Missouri, and Clinton, Madison, Monroe, and St. Clair Counties in Illinois) had to use the same ballot title and summary language. That stipulation worked in the campaign's favor. It greatly simplified efforts to advertise Proposition C—the Clean Water, Safe Parks, and Community Trails Initiative.

Former Missouri senator John Danforth chaired the $1 million ballot campaign, and Olympian Jackie Joyner-Kersee and sports broadcaster Bob Costas served as co-chairs. Although there were community-level concerns about the regional parks draining local parks of money, that fear was overcome by a revenue sharing plan that sent half of the new sales tax money back to the counties and municipalities that generated it. The other half would go to the two new regional park districts—$10 million a year to the Metropolitan Park and Recreation District in Missouri and $1.5 million to the Metro East Park and Recreation District in Illinois.

Three years of planning and hard work paid off in November 2000. Proposition C passed in five of seven jurisdictions, failing only in sparsely populated Clinton and Monroe Counties in Illinois, two counties that represented just 1 percent of projected revenue for the park districts. An overwhelming 77 percent of voters in the city of St. Louis and 70 percent in St. Louis County approved the measure.

Conclusion

The California and St. Louis conservation ballot campaigns illustrate how different one ballot drive can be from another. The challenges of California's size, diversity, and media markets put that campaign, which spent $7.8 million to pass $2.6 billion in bonds, in a league by itself. The St. Louis measure required legislation in two state legislatures and cooperation among seven local jurisdictions, but it yielded more than $400 million in new park and open space revenue over twenty years.

Supporters of the St. Louis effort came away with a number of lessons that can help conservationists who are considering large statewide campaigns or much smaller campaigns confined to just one county or municipality.

First, organizers in St. Louis found that an early driving force for the regional park system—an interconnected trail system—needed to be looked at more broadly to incorporate its potential benefits as a vegetative buffer to protect waterways, as a wildlife corridor, and as a means of access to rivers and streams. Conservationists often begin campaign planning with a preconceived goal, but polling and research may indicate that a change in focus may be necessary to improve chances of passing a ballot measure.

Second, having a nontraditional leader for the campaign—former Republican senator and attorney John Danforth, who was not known as an environmentalist—proved to be enormously helpful because of his solid political reputation, connections to the St. Louis business community, and fundraising prowess. Coalition building is critical.

Third, aiming high sometimes works. Many skeptics thought that the attempt to create a two-state, multijurisdictional park district was doomed to failure because of the inherent political complexities. In this case, they were wrong.

Finally, organizers succeeded in demonstrating to the voters what Glazer considers the key components of any winning land conservation measure: (1) that the creation of the new districts would fulfill a compelling public need; (2) that the tax was affordable; and (3) that the money would be spent correctly. Finally, successful campaigns must be well conducted, they must build broad support among community leaders and organizations, and they should communicate the measure's key benefits to undecided voters.

In California, organizers credited the win to a disciplined, aggressive, and well-organized campaign. Californians' concerns about the rate of population growth and land development proved to be a powerful force underlying voters' support for conservation. Another factor that helped build support for the measure was the bond's impact on essential quality-of-life issues—cleaner air, cleaner water, and safer parks. Finally, the positive, upbeat tone of the campaign helped to build voter support in the final days before the election, organizers said.

CHAPTER FIVE

CONSERVING LAND WITH PRIVATE-SECTOR FUNDING

In the 1990s, land conservation stood out among the many beneficiaries of a mushrooming stock market and the resultant boom in giving by foundations in the United States. Assets of more than 56,000 grant-making foundations, which totaled $176.8 billion in 1992, had jumped 175 percent to $486.1 billion by 2000, according to the Foundation Center.[1] In response, giving by these foundations jumped from $10.2 billion to $27.6 billion over the same time period, a 170 percent increase.

Based on grants awarded by more than 1,000 of the largest U.S. foundations (which accounted for over half of all grant dollars), giving for the environment, of which land conservation is a significant part, topped $886.3 million in 2001, the third fastest growth in grant dollars since 1999 among the major grant categories tracked by the center. Impressive as those numbers are, grant giving for the environment nearly quadrupled between 1992 and 2001 (from $204.5 million to $886.3 million), jumping from 3.8 percent to 5.3 percent of all giving by the 1,000 foundations in the center's sample (see Table 5.1). While breakout figures are unavailable, land conservation grants represented a significant portion of total foundation support of the environment

TABLE 5.1

Top 50 U.S. foundations awarding grants for the environment,
ca. 2001*

Foundation	State	Grant Amount (dollars)	Number of Grants
1. Foundation for Deep Ecology	Calif.	$102,784,074	102
2. David and Lucile Packard Foundation	Calif.	79,630,248	288
3. Ford Foundation	N.Y.	48,103,790	246
4. John D. and Catherine T. MacArthur Foundation	Ill.	39,223,000	63
5. Pew Charitable Trusts	Pa.	38,665,400	38
6. William and Flora Hewlett Foundation	Calif.	32,863,000	112
7. Turner Foundation, Inc.	Ga.	30,396,028	308
8. Charles Stewart Mott Foundation	Mich.	22,559,070	103
9. Energy Foundation	Calif.	20,125,032	208
10. Andrew W. Mellon Foundation	N.Y.	18,507,000	60
11. Doris Duke Charitable Foundation	N.Y.	18,436,727	15
12. Robert W. Woodruff Foundation, Inc.	Ga.	17,145,985	7
13. Richard & Rhoda Goldman Fund	Calif.	16,279,635	164
14. Rockefeller Foundation	N.Y.	15,289,924	34
15. Ford Motor Company Fund	Mich.	14,576,234	55
16. Longwood Foundation, Inc.	Del.	14,500,000	3
17. Kresge Foundation	Mich.	14,330,000	18
18. Surdna Foundation, Inc.	N.Y.	12,385,000	77
19. Richard King Mellon Foundation	Pa.	10,290,000	23
20. Henry Luce Foundation, Inc.	N.Y.	9,785,000	20
21. Joyce Foundation	Ill.	9,783,991	50
22. Meijer Foundation	Mich.	9,472,836	2
23. Educational Foundation of America	Conn.	9,454,547	75
24. William Penn Foundation	Pa.	9,452,770	36
25. Beldon Fund	N.Y.	9,288,000	76
26. James Irvine Foundation	Calif.	8,970,000	17
27. Howard Heinz Endowment	Pa.	7,447,150	36
28. Paul G. Allen Forest Protection Foundation	Wash.	6,835,800	13
29. McKnight Foundation	Minn.	6,791,000	48
30. Peninsula Community Foundation	Calif.	6,738,000	53
31. Summit Charitable Foundation, Inc.	D.C.	6,734,348	50
32. Barbara Delano Foundation, Inc.	Calif.	6,539,564	7
33. Danforth Foundation	Mo.	6,507,353	9
34. Rockefeller Brothers Fund, Inc.	N.Y.	6,222,683	57
35. Moore Family Foundation	Calif.	5,784,000	13

TABLE 5.1 (Continued)

Top 50 U.S. foundations awarding grants for the environment, ca. 2001*

Foundation	State	Grant Amount (dollars)	Number of Grants
36. Houston Endowment Inc.	Tex..	5,760,500	27
37. Geraldine R. Dodge Foundation, Inc.	N.J.	5,747,000	66
38. John S. and James L. Knight Foundation	Fla.	5,577,000	4
39. Sarah Scaife Foundation, Inc.	Pa.	5,350,000	4
40. New York Community Trust	N.Y.	5,118,800	107
41. Freeman Foundation	N.Y.	4,981,010	8
42. San Francisco Foundation	Calif.	4,911,014	96
43. James H. Clark Charitable Foundation	Nev.	4,660,000	1
44. Craig and Susan McCaw Foundation	Wash.	4,287,000	11
45. John Merck Fund	Mass.	4,033,000	81
46. Homeland Foundation	Calif.	3,930,000	94
47. Barr Foundation	Mass.	3,830,000	23
48. Wilburforce Foundation	Wash.	3,793,000	89
49. Alcoa Foundation	Pa.	3,786,180	33
50. Vira I. Heinz Endowment	Pa.	3,721,000	27
Total		$761,382,693	3,157

Source: The Foundation Center.
*Based on grants of $10,000 or more awarded by a national sample of 1,007 larger U.S. foundations (including 800 of the 1,000 largest ranked by total giving). For community foundations, only discretionary grants are included. Grants to individuals are not included. The search set includes all grants to recipient organizations classified in this topic area and grants to other recipient types for activities classified in this topic area. Grants may therefore be included in more than one topic table—e.g., a grant to a university for its arts program is included in Education, Higher Education, and Arts.

Environment grants comprise programs that focus on the preservation and protection of the environment, including pollution control and abatement programs, conservation and development of natural resources (land, plant, water, energy), control or elimination of hazardous wastes and toxic substances (including pesticides), solid waste management programs, botanical gardens and societies, urban beautification and open spaces programs, and environmental education. They do not include programs that focus primarily on the protection and preservation of wildlife or fisheries or programs that focus on the protection or preservation of farmlands or soil and water conservation for agricultural/food production purposes.

from 1992 to 2000, which is evidenced by the actions of six major foundation supporters of land preservation.

The six foundations—the Richard King Mellon Foundation, the David and Lucile Packard Foundation, the Turner Foundation, the Doris Duke Charitable Foundation, the Arthur M. Blank Family Foundation, and the Gordon I. and Betty E. Moore Foundation—

have donated hundreds of millions of dollars for open space preservation since the late 1980s. Chief among them is the Richard King Mellon Foundation, which in 1988 established the American Land Conservation Program, the boldest program of its kind in the foundation world. Fifteen years and $400 million later, the Pittsburgh-based foundation surpassed the 1-million-acre mark in gifts of land to local, state, and federal agencies spread throughout the fifty states.

In the West, the explosion of wealth in Silicon Valley paved the way for the David and Lucile Packard Foundation to donate more than $175 million between 1998 and 2003 to protect 500,000 acres in three target areas in California.

A key goal of these foundations was to demonstrate that private organizations could preserve land as a means to improve the quality of life in the United States.

When the breath got knocked out of the stock market beginning in 2000, foundations also felt the pain, some more than others. Assets of the Packard Foundation, whose stock portfolio consisted mostly of Hewlett-Packard Company stock, had mushroomed to $17 billion by 2000 but retracted to less than $5 billion by 2003. And the Turner Foundation, created by CNN founder Ted Turner, suffered a serious cutback when AOL Time Warner stock fell, precipitating a layoff of two-thirds of the foundation's staff in late 2002 and the suspension of all new grant making for 2003.

On the brighter side, the founders of two of the newest high-tech-related foundations—the Gordon I. and Betty E. Moore Foundation, created by Gordon Moore of Intel; and the William and Flora Hewlett Foundation, created by William Hewlett, co-founder of Hewlett-Packard—have transferred billions of dollars into the new foundations, instantly catapulting them to the top echelon of U.S. foundations. Both have made bold entrances in the U.S. land conservation arena, committing tens of millions of dollars for large projects in the San Francisco Bay Area.

In New York, the Doris Duke Charitable Foundation has awarded more than $96 million in grants for land and forest conservation and conservation leadership between 1996 and 2002. And in Atlanta, the Arthur M. Blank Foundation, created by the founder of the Home

Depot, announced in 2002 that it would launch a three-year initiative to invest at least $20 million in the Atlanta area to increase the city's greenspace.

Following are short profiles of some of the key foundations that helped make the 1990s a banner decade for land conservation, along with a few whose promise is forthcoming.

The Richard King Mellon Foundation

One of the great unsung land conservation stories rests inside the walls of the Richard King Mellon Foundation.[2] The American Land Conservation Program, which the foundation launched in 1988 with the encouragement of trustee Mason Walsh Jr., represents the greatest outpouring of foundation support for open space preservation in U.S. history. By 2002, the foundation's program reached a milestone—it had donated more than 1 million acres of wetlands, wildlife habitat, and historic land in all fifty states—an investment of $400 million.

The gifts comprise over 190 properties at 81 sites, including hundreds of thousand of acres in gifts to the U.S. Fish and Wildlife Service, the National Park Service, and the Bureau of Land Management, as well as state natural resource agencies and local nonprofit groups. The projects ranged from the acquisition of grazing rights on 374,000 acres of Nevada grasslands to the protection of a 0.5-acre nesting site for endangered turtles along a Florida beach. Other projects include the foundation's gift of 33,804 acres in Izembek National Wildlife Refuge, Alaska, that protects 40 miles of coastline near the tip of the Alaska Peninsula; and gifts of three tracts—the Cornfield, the West Woods, and the Sunken Road—to the National Park Service that permanently protect hallowed ground at Antietam National Battlefield in Maryland. The Conservation Fund provided guidance and assistance to the foundation on identification, purchase, and disposition of Mellon's conservation lands over the entire fifteen years of the program.

Closer to home, the Pittsburgh-based foundation has long supported land conservation in Pennsylvania, including a recent $2 million matching grant in 2002 to The Conservation Fund to complete a 12,000-acre acquisition in Sproul State Forest in central Pennsylvania, the largest acquisition of state forest land in decades.

The David and Lucile Packard Foundation

More than 400,000 acres along California's central coast, in the Central Valley, and in the Sierra Nevada have been protected since 1998, thanks to an ambitious effort by the David and Lucile Packard Foundation.[3] The foundation, created in 1964 by the co-founder of Hewlett-Packard Company, awarded more than $175 million in grants between 1998 and 2003 to preserve open space, farmland, and wildlife habitat as part of its Conserving California's Landscapes Initiative. The initiative, which leveraged over $300 million in public and private funds, capped a long-term commitment to land conservation by the foundation. This initiative continued the foundation's long-standing involvement in land acquisition and conservation projects in California that dates back to its early years in helping to create key land trusts in the state and assist in several real estate conservation transactions by them.

Flush with a $5 billion infusion of assets from the estate of David Packard, who died in 1996, the foundation launched the California Landscapes Initiative with the intention of protecting 250,000 acres over five years. To everyone's surprise, the foundation reached its goal in half the time, which prompted foundation officials to double the protected acreage goal to 500,000, which was expected to be reached in 2003.

Halfway through the land conservation initiative, the slumping stock market began to takes its toll on the foundation's assets, which were concentrated in Hewlett-Packard stock. The foundation's portfolio, which hit a peak of $17 billion in 2000, had drifted back to a still hefty $4.8 billion by year's end in 2002, which made it one of the fifteen largest foundations in the United States. The foundation also has diversified its portfolio, leaving roughly half its money in Hewlett-Packard stock.

The retrenchment caused the foundation to merge its conservation and science programs in 2002 and cut grant making for both programs to $83 million for 2003, down from $100 million the previous year. Officials decided to refocus the foundation's land conservation efforts, one of many parts of its overall conservation program, to help integrate key coastal land, stream, and marine protection priorities along the coast of California, with a particular emphasis on the watersheds and lands along the central coast of California.

The Resources Legacy Fund Foundation runs the new Conserving Coastal and Marine Initiative for the Packard Foundation.[4] While the overall grants budget for the new initiative will likely be in the $8 million range, the foundation will continue to make bridge financing through loans available as well as grants to help catalyze major land acquisition and habitat restoration projects. The passage of major land conservation bond measures in California since 2000 has made far more public money available for such projects than was the case when the foundation first announced its major landscapes initiative in 1998.

Despite the cutbacks in the larger land conservation program, the foundation maintains a separate "special opportunities fund" that can be tapped for unique land conservation projects. Two grants from the account totaled more than $60 million. In 2001, the foundation awarded the largest land conservation grant in its history—$50 million—to the Peninsula Open Space Trust to boost the group's effort to preserve more than 20,000 acres along the San Mateo County coast. In 2002, the foundation contributed more than $11 million as part of a $35 million partnership by four California foundations to help acquire and restore 16,500 acres of salt ponds in the San Francisco Bay Area. The foundation will continue to access the account when the need arises, said Chris DeCardy, communications director for the Packard Foundation.

The Gordon I. and Betty E. Moore Foundation

When Intel Corporation co-founder Gordon Moore turned his attention to philanthropy, he moved with the speed of a microchip. Since setting up the Gordon and Betty Moore Foundation in November 2000 in San Francisco, Moore transferred $5.2 billion to his new venture by 2003, making it one of the ten largest foundations in America.[5]

In the first eighteen months of grant making, the foundation committed $1.1 billion to its key focus areas—the environment, scientific research, higher education, and the San Francisco Bay Area. To maintain flexibility, the young foundation hasn't set budgets for each program. But funding for the environment and conservation science has been a major thrust in the foundation's short life, including a ten-year, $261 million grant to Conservation International for its biological diversity work around the world.

The foundation's San Francisco Bay Area program has made its presence known in the local land conservation arena. In 2001, the foundation approved a ten-year, $50 million grant to the Peninsula Open Space Trust, as did its partner in the venture, the David and Lucile Packard Foundation. The trust is using the $100 million, as well as an expected $100 million in matching funds, to protect 20,000 acres of open space and natural habitat in San Mateo County, south of San Francisco.

In 2002, the Moore Foundation contributed $6.33 million to a partnership involving the Hewlett, Packard, and Goldman Foundations to provide a total of $20 million in grants to acquire 16,500 acres of salt ponds in the San Francisco Bay Area that are owned by Cargill. The state of California agreed to contribute $72 million toward the $100 million acquisition, with the remainder coming from the U.S. Fish and Wildlife Service. The foundations also pledged $15 million in restoration and long-term stewardship funds, in keeping with the foundation's emphasis on long-term objectives aimed at ensuring that all its grant money is spent on projects that achieve measurable results, said Frank Jordan, who runs the foundation's San Francisco Bay Area program.

The foundation also agreed in late 2002 to devote up to $25 million in grants to its Wild Salmon Ecosystems Initiative, which seeks to preserve the North Pacific coastal ecosystems in Alaska and Russia. Another $40 million has been committed to the foundation's Andes-Amazon Initiative, a first step in its investigation to seek ways to help preserve the 2.7 million square miles of wilderness in South America.

Closer to home, the foundation spent $2 million to investigate the causes of sudden oak death in California, which has drawn the interest of the state of California as well as the forestry industry after initial research indicated that the disease could pose a threat to the state's renowned redwood forests as well as its logging industry.

The Arthur M. Blank Family Foundation

Atlanta has provided much of the economic muscle for the Southeast in recent decades. The city's go-go business environment attracted people and companies from around the nation. The city's population boomed. But with that upswing came less desirable byproducts, including the conversion of 500 acres of open space a week to development, violations of federal Clean Air standards stemming from an overwhelmed transportation system, and an expensive court settlement over the city's pollution of the Chattahoochee River, Atlanta's main water supply.[6] And in 2000, the Trust for Public Land and Urban Land Institute ranked Atlanta dead last among similar cities in the amount of park and open space land per 1,000 residents and second to last in the percentage of city land set aside for parks and open space.[7]

City leaders realized that what had been attracting people and business to Atlanta for decades—its quality of life—was in jeopardy. One prominent businessman took notice. Arthur Blank, who grew up in a working-class neighborhood in Queens, New York, moved to Atlanta, co-founded the Home Depot in 1978, and made a fortune over two decades. Since creating the Arthur M. Blank Family Foundation in 1995, he has transferred sufficient money to the foundation each year to fuel its grant making, which totaled $35 million in 2002, and more than $100 million in grants since its creation.[8]

Although the foundation focuses primarily on programs for young people, it became evident from the nature and size of unsolicited grant requests that land conservation had become a key concern in the Atlanta region, said Margaret Gray, environmental program officer with the foundation. After awarding its first few grants to fund specific land acquisitions, the foundation decided to take a more long-range approach to the metro region's parks and open space concerns. After a year's study, the Blank Foundation announced in December 2001 that it would award at least $20 million over three years to enhance the region's parks and greenspace within Interstate 285, the urban core of Atlanta. With at least a 60 percent match in funding required, the foundation's Environmental Initiative is expected to produce at least $50 million for park and open space projects in the Atlanta area.

The first round of grants, announced in July 2002, devoted $6.5 million to preserve 430 acres in metropolitan Atlanta. Two-thirds of the money was earmarked for specific land acquisition and capital projects, while the remaining $2.15 million was awarded to The Conservation Fund for a revolving loan fund. The foundation set up the

PHOTO 5.1. The Arthur M. Blank Family Foundation awarded a grant to purchase a 1.76-acre parcel to create a park in the Vine City neighborhood in Atlanta. "A park would be a beacon of hope that shows we can turn this neighborhood around if we work together," said Byron Amos (pictured here), the director of the Vine City Civic Association. *Photo courtesy of the Arthur M. Blank Family Foundation.*

loan fund so that worthy land conservation projects that arose between the foundation's annual grant announcements would have bridge funding until adequate long-term financing could be obtained.

Early projections showed that Atlanta needs to spend approximately $400 million to acquire 3,000 acres to double the city of Atlanta's park system and make it comparable in size to those of other large urban areas in the United States. Foundation officials thought their critical seed funding could help spark the regionwide commitment needed to make the goal achievable. Their private sector funding effort complements significant public sector funding for parks and open space that has appeared in recent years.

In April 2000, then-governor Roy Barnes signed legislation to create the Georgia Community Greenspace Initiative. Under the program, the state Department of Natural Resources can provide up to $30 million in grants annually, subject to annual appropriations by the state legislature, to fast-growing or urbanized communities that develop and implement greenspace plans to protect 20 percent of their land for the purpose of improving water quality, preserving natural resources, and achieving the recreation goals of the program. But Georgia's new governor, Sonny Perdue, proposed cutting the program funding to $15 million in early 2003, and some legislators were considering zeroing out funding for the initiative.

On the local level, Atlanta's next-door neighbor, DeKalb County, approved a $125 million bond referendum in 2001 to boost its parks and open space (see the profile of DeKalb County in Chapter 3). And in 2002, Shirley Franklin, the new mayor of Atlanta, created a Parks and Greenspace Task Force, which recommended that the city raise $400 million through general obligation bonds and donations from the business and philanthropic communities to acquire a 500-acre park and double the size of the city's 3,122-acre park and greenspace system within a decade.[9]

The Doris Duke Charitable Foundation

Doris Duke, the tobacco heiress who died in 1993, left more than 90 percent of her estate to the Doris Duke Charitable Foundation. Since its founding in 1996, the New York City foundation has quickly become a leader in land conservation. By the end of 2002, it had awarded eighty-eight grants totaling more than $96 million in its Environment Program to protect ecologically significant open space and forestland, improve land use planning, encourage sustainable forestry, and fund conservation fellowship programs at five universities.[10]

The foundation devoted most of the Environment Program money (eleven grants totaling $50.7 million) to four regions targeted in its Land Conservation Initiative program and two other regions in its Forest Conservation Initiative program. A seventh target region is to be announced in 2003.

The foundation's first foray into land conservation came in 1997, when it donated $5 million to the Trust for Public Land and the Open Space Institute to complete the acquisition of Sterling Forest, a 17,719-acre tract of undeveloped and environmentally sensitive land on the New Jersey–New York border that is now the Sterling Forest State Park.

In 1999, the foundation announced the first two focus regions for its Land Conservation Initiative—New Jersey and Rhode Island, two states where Doris Duke spent much of her time at her estate and summer home. The foundation awarded multiyear grants totaling $12.8 million to The Nature Conservancy and the Trust for Public Land to protect environmentally significant open space in the two states, funding that is expected to leverage $44 million in new public and private dollars for land conservation and help protect 15,000 acres. It provided complementary support to regional conservation organizations in both states to strengthen land trusts and improve land use planning.

The following year, the foundation conducted a national assessment of potential ecoregions and convened experts to review and rank them before selecting its third "sprawl" site—the eastern coastal plain along the Gulf of Mexico, including the Florida Panhandle and parts of southern Georgia and southern Alabama. In May of 2000, it awarded four grants totaling $10.9 million to help protect land in the Florida Panhandle and nearby sections of Georgia and Alabama and two grants to "smart growth" organizations working in Florida and Georgia.

Later in 2000, the foundation announced the first site under its new Forest Conservation Initiative. Four grants totaling $12.1 million were awarded to protect 200,000 acres of preserves, wildlife corridors, and working forests in the northern forests of upstate New York and upper New England. The multiyear grants included $10.55 million to the Beaverkill Conservancy and the Open Space Institute to acquire at least 200,000 acres of forest land and easements in the four states.

Based on its research and the recommendation of its expert advisors, the foundation in 2001 added a fourth focus region to its Land Conservation Initiative—the Greater Yellowstone ecosystem. Seven multiyear grants totaling $8.2 million were awarded to protect the 18-million-acre Yellowstone region in Wyoming, Montana, and Idaho. The Nature Conservancy, The Conservation Fund, and the Trust for Public Land received a total of $6.5 million to buy land and easements on 60,000 acres, in partnership with regional land trusts. The remaining grants went to four organizations to improve local land use planning and strengthen land trusts.

In September of 2001, following a review of forested ecoregions across the nation, the foundation picked its second focus area for its Forest Conservation Initiative—the southern Appalachian Mountains.

The foundation awarded a total of $6 million to The Conservation Fund and The Nature Conservancy to conserve forestland in focus areas in eastern Tennessee, northeastern Alabama, and western North Carolina. The Conservation Fund is also working with other partners to develop a conservation plan and support sustainable forestry projects in North Carolina.

In 2003, the foundation planned to pick a third focus site for its Forest Conservation Initiative from four prospective areas—Hawaii, Oregon, South Carolina, or the Pacific Northwest. The proposals were solicited using a Request for Proposal and were to be reviewed by an expert panel.

In 2001, the foundation commissioned an external midterm assessment of its grant making in New Jersey and Rhode Island. In early 2003, it was planning to conduct assessments of its grant making in other sites and was also considering consolidating its Land Conservation and Forest Conservation initiatives into one program, reducing the number of sites and sharpening its focus to conserving biodiversity.

The Turner Foundation

Ted Turner established the Turner Foundation in 1990 with a vision toward the preservation and conservation of the environment throughout the world.[11] To that end, the foundation developed a grant program to help protect biodiversity through habitat preservation. Between 1991 and 2003, the foundation has awarded more than 1,200 habitat grants totaling $51.5 million for an array of causes and organizations. Among the program priorities are the support of ecosystem-level habitat protection with an emphasis on locally developed strategies for private and public lands; funding of efforts that defend wild places from destructive practices such as mining, unsustainable logging, and over-grazing; and educational efforts that foster understanding of the relationship between wildlife, habitat protection, and long-term economic stability.

The foundation also supports habitat protection through its water and toxics program, which seeks to protect rivers, lakes, wetlands, aquifers, oceans, and other water systems from contamination and degradation. Among its priorities are efforts to halt the degradation of water-dependent habitats from new dams, diversions, and other large infrastructure projects; and to promote the allocation of water for environmental purposes, including habitat restoration and fish and wildlife protection.

More than 80 percent of the foundation's habitat-related grants are devoted to general operational support of groups involved in environmental advocacy, environmental justice, and regulatory reform and enforcement, as well as land trusts at both the national and local level.

On the national level, the foundation has supported the Land Trust Alliance ($400,000) for its work to strengthen the land trust movement, and the Mineral Policy Center ($190,000), which seeks to protect people and the environment from destructive mining practices. Locally, the foundation has supported land trusts around the country, with a focus on the states where Turner, one of the largest individual landowners in the country, owns property—Colorado, Florida, Georgia, Montana, Nebraska, New Mexico, and South Carolina. Among the local grant beneficiaries have been the Montana Land Reliance and the Gallatin Valley Land Trust in Montana, and the Lowcountry Open Land Trust in South Carolina, which received $45,000 to increase its protection of coastal lands through the acquisition of conservation easements. Water and toxic grants include $50,000 to the Altamaha Riverkeeper in Georgia, which monitors the health of the state's longest river.

On the international level, the foundation funds habitat protection work in Argentina, Brazil, British Columbia, Mexico, and Russia. As an example, the foundation has funded salmon protection efforts in the Kamchatka Peninsula, where one-third of the world's salmon spawn, through grants to the Wild Salmon Center in Portland, Oregon.

Because of the stock market crunch and its effect on Turner's holdings of stock in AOL Time Warner, the foundation's board of directors decided in 2002 to cut the foundation's staff by two-thirds and to suspend new grant making for 2003. It is fulfilling its prior-year commitments to multiyear grants, which will total $11.5 million for 2003, just below the foundation's 2002 grant-making total of $12.5 million. In 2004, when the foundation's multiyear grant commitments will be completed, the foundation will resume new grant making, but on an invitation-only basis, said Michael Finley, the foundation's president.

Conclusion

Although the double-digit growth in foundation giving is over, with giving likely to have remained flat in 2002 and possibly decreasing modestly over the next couple of years, the long-term prospects for growth in foundation giving remain strong. If the past is any guide, foundation assets will rebound, and foundations that were hurt by the post-1990s market bust will regroup and emerge as stronger operations with more diversified portfolios. And it's important to keep in mind that many of the foundations whose assets have shrunk in recent years still have portfolios that are much larger than they were a decade ago. For example, the Packard Foundation, whose assets totaled $4.8 billion at year's end in 2002, had just $718 million in holdings in 1991.

And two researchers at the Boston College Social Welfare Research Institute predicted in 1999 that at least $41 trillion in wealth will be transferred to succeeding generations between 1998 and 2052, with at least $6 trillion of the total going to charity.[12] They reaffirmed their belief in 2003 despite the recent market downturn. So, the foundation support for land conservation, which took off in the 1990s, has taken a breather in the early 2000s, but should recover.

CHAPTER SIX

FINANCING GREEN INFRASTRUCTURE: SMARTER, MORE COST-EFFECTIVE LAND CONSERVATION

The United States has seen an explosion of land conservation programs and policies since the early 1990s. Federal, state, and local governments have devoted billions of dollars to a wide variety of land acquisition and protection projects. Private foundations, national conservation organizations, and local land trusts have done even more, but a big question remains: How effective have their efforts been at shaping or directing growth, preserving essential ecological processes, or preserving large working landscapes?

Many people would argue that the funding has not been nearly as effective as it could be. Critics say that we're doing little more than throwing money at the land; that, with some notable exceptions, most of the recent land conservation efforts have been well intentioned but haphazard and narrowly focused—that they have done little to integrate land use planning and biodiversity, or to shape and direct growth.

This chapter argues that we need a more strategic approach to land conservation—that open space should be planned and developed as a system. It discusses green infrastructure as a critical concept for designing a strategic approach to land conservation in the twenty-first century and presents a series of case studies that illustrate how green infrastructure is being financed and applied at the local, regional, and state levels.[1]

From Ad Hoc to Comprehensive Land Conservation

Open space in the United States plays a much more complex role today than it did in 1964 when Congress passed the Land and Water Conservation Fund Act. During the congressional debate in the 1960s, lawmakers focused much of their discussion on financing new recreation: how to fund the acquisition of land and the development of facilities to meet rising demand for recreational opportunities.

Over the years, conservationists have taken an increasingly broader view of the functions of open space and how to finance it. By the dawn of the twenty-first century, parks, open space, greenways, and trails were making great contributions to modern American society by continuing to meet growing recreational demand, but also by preserving land and water habitat for plants and animals, protecting water quality, shaping and directing growth, reducing flood damage, preserving farm and forest land, combating global warming, and protecting historical and cultural areas.

What these many new roles for open space lack is an overall defining vision, a framework to guide land conservation. Across America, states, communities, private landowners, public agencies, and conservation organizations are working to develop such a framework, which conserves and restores our country's natural life support system. Although these projects are called different names (greenway planning, ecosystem management, watershed protection, conservation development, habitat restoration, greenprints, etc.), successful initiatives are based on a more systematic, strategic approach to open space preservation, with its roots in ecological protection, which we call green infrastructure.

Funding for green infrastructure should be included in a government's annual budget, as are roads, sewers, and other public works. Many states and communities have begun using conventional mechanisms to finance green infrastructure projects—including bond referenda, real estate transfer taxes, dedicated development fees, and direct budgetary line items.

Conservationists over the past several decades have expended much effort in protecting individual parcels of land as opportunities arose, without giving much thought to how these tracts fit into a larger ecological mosaic. In the future, successful land conservation will have to be more proactive and less reactive; more systematic and less haphazard; multifunctional, not single-purpose; large-scale, not small-scale; and better integrated with other efforts to manage growth and development.

The key to accomplishing this goal is green infrastructure, a framework that provides a strategic approach to land conservation. Green infrastructure is an interconnected network of greenspace that conserves natural ecosystem values and functions and provides associated benefits to human populations. It is the ecological framework needed for environmental, social, and economic sustainability—the nation's natural life support system.

Webster's New World Dictionary defines infrastructure as "the substructure or underlying foundation, especially the basic installations and facilities on which the continuance and growth of a community or state depends." Most people think of infrastructure as roads, sewers, and utility lines—gray infrastructure; or as schools, hospitals, and prisons—social infrastructure. Together they are often called built infrastructure. The concept of green infrastructure elevates the protection and management of ecological systems involving air, land, and water to an equal footing with built infrastructure and transforms open space from "nice to have" to "must have." At the same time, green infrastructure helps frame the most efficient location for development and growth—and related gray infrastructure—ensuring that developers, citizens, and communities capture the cost advantages of location and create and protect household and community amenities.

Green Infrastructure versus Traditional Land Conservation

Many people believe that green infrastructure represents the next generation of conservation action because it forges an important connection between land conservation and land use planning. Traditional land conservation and green infrastructure planning both focus on environmental restoration and preservation, but green infrastructure also concentrates on the pace, shape, and location of development and its relationship to important natural resources and amenities. Unlike more conventional conservation approaches, green infrastructure strategies actively seek to promote more efficient and sustainable land use and development patterns, as well as protect natural ecosystems. Green infrastructure differs from traditional conservation efforts in the following ways:

- It focuses on the protection of connected natural ecosystems as the framework for both conservation and development.
- It recognizes that physical linkage between greenspace elements is key to sustaining natural ecosystems and landscape processes.
- It emphasizes the importance of planning and protecting green infrastructure before development.
- It recognizes the need to connect greenspace elements across multiple jurisdictions, scales, and landscape types.
- It focuses on the creation of a greenspace vision that excites and engages people and guides implementation actions.
- It considers the needs of both nature *and* humans—addressing both the environmental effects of proposed development and the economic well-being of a community.

What Does Green Infrastructure Look Like?

Green infrastructure's components encompass a variety of natural and restored ecosystems and landscape features that make up a system of "hubs," "links," and "sites" (see Figure 6.1).

Hubs anchor green infrastructure networks, providing origins and destinations for wildlife and ecological processes moving to or through them. Hubs vary in size, shape, and ownership, including:

- Reserves—large protected areas, such as national and state parks and wildlife refuges
- Managed native landscapes—large publicly owned lands, such as national and state forests, managed for resource extraction as well as natural and recreational values
- Working lands—private farms, forests, and ranches that are managed for commodity production yet remain in a predominantly open and undeveloped state
- Regional parks and preserves—less extensive hubs of regional ecological significance

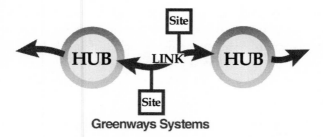

FIGURE 6.1. Green infrastructure networks comprise interconnections of hubs, links, and sites. *Source:* Florida Greenways Commission.

- Community parks and natural areas—smaller parks and other sites at the community level where natural features and ecological processes are protected and/or restored

Links are the connections that tie the system together and enable green infrastructure networks to work. They range in size, function, and ownership, including:

- Landscape linkages—large protected natural areas that connect existing parks, preserves, or natural areas and provide sufficient space for native plants and animals to flourish while serving as corridors connecting ecosystems and landscapes. Landscape linkages may also provide space for the protection of historic sites and opportunities for recreational use.
- Conservation corridors—less extensive linear protected areas, such as river and stream corridors that serve as biological conduits for wildlife and may provide recreational opportunities.
- Greenways—protected corridors of land managed for resource conservation and/or recreational use.
- Greenbelts—protected natural lands or working lands that serve as a framework for development while also preserving native ecosystems and/or farms or ranchland.
- Ecobelts—linear woody buffers that can ease the zone of tension between urban and rural land uses while providing ecological and social benefits for urban and rural residents.

Sites are smaller greenspace areas that can contribute ecological and social values even though they may not be attached to larger interconnected community and regional conservation systems. They include:

- Urban pocket parks
- Smaller natural heritage areas

A true green infrastructure network, with functioning ecological systems that provide benefits to nature and people, must have ecological hubs connected by ecological corridors (e.g., wetland hubs connected by river corridors). Though there is nothing "wrong" with designing greenspace or greenway systems that consist of ecological hubs connected by *recreational* corridors, these systems are not true green infrastructure networks, and they will not, therefore, provide the ecological system benefits that green infrastructure offers.

Principles and Strategies

Following are seven guiding principles and strategies that have been identified as critical to the success of green infrastructure initiatives. The principles provide a strategic approach and framework for conservation that can advance the sustainable use of land while benefiting people, wildlife, and the economy. This approach includes design, planning, acquisition, and decision-making guidance for agencies and organizations. Planners, developers, landowners, state and local officials, and others can use these principles as benchmarks for incorporating a green infrastructure approach into land use and economic development plans, projects, and policies.

Principle 1: Green infrastructure should function as the framework for conservation and development.

Most of our nation's land conservation programs have focused on protecting individual parks, preserves, or other isolated areas with important natural or cultural resources. Yet conservation biologists have found that, because wildlife populations cannot flourish and ecological processes cannot function if natural connections are severed, these islands are unlikely to meet their conservation objectives. By contrast, the nation's critically important roads and highways, which provide a framework for future growth and development, are planned, built, and maintained as a system of interconnected parts.

By making green infrastructure the framework for conservation, communities can plan for interconnected greenspace systems. Where isolated islands of nature exist, green infrastructure planning can help identify opportunities to restore the vital ecological connections that will maintain those protected areas. Green infrastructure planning also minimizes the adverse impacts of rapid growth on ecosystem functions and services, such as the disruption of wildlife migration corridors or the loss of riparian areas that absorb nutrients, recharge groundwater supplies, and reduce stormwater runoff.

Principle 2: Design and plan green infrastructure before development.

Restoring natural systems is far more expensive than protecting unde-veloped land, and engineered wetlands and other restoration projects often fail to function as well as their natural counterparts over the long term. Because green infrastructure provides communities with an eco-logical framework, it is essential to identify and protect critical ecolog-ical hubs and linkages in advance of development. Central Park in New York City could not be created today nor could the Forest Pre-serve System in Cook County, Illinois, or many other of the nation's best parks and preserves. Protecting green infrastructure up front ensures that existing open spaces and working lands are seen as essen-tial community assets and not left vulnerable to development.

In situations where development has already occurred, it is still important to assess where restoring green infrastructure would benefit people and nature. Green infrastructure plans should set acquisition and restoration priorities and help communities identify opportunities to reconnect isolated habitat islands as redevelopment opportunities occur.

Principle 3: Linkage is key.

The desired outcome for all green infrastructure initiatives is a green-space network that functions as an ecological whole. A strategic con-nection of system components—parks, preserves, riparian areas, wet-lands, and other greenspaces—is critical to maintaining vital ecological processes and services (e.g., controlling stormwater runoff, cleaning fresh water, etc.) and to maintaining the health of wildlife populations. In addition, green infrastructure requires linkages between different agencies, nongovernmental organizations, and the private sector. The Ecological Network Project of Florida's Statewide Greenways System and the state of Maryland's Green Infrastructure Assessment are examples of green infrastructure network design that is based on this principle.[2]

The nation's federal, state, and local highway networks holistically create a functional transportation system funded and supported by different levels of government. Green infrastructure should be designed in the same way, taking advantage of natural stream networks and terrain features to create physically connected greenspace systems that protect and restore vital ecological functions and linkages.

Strategy: Make connections between green infrastructure initiatives and other activities within and beyond the community.

Linking green infrastructure efforts to statewide, regional, and local smart growth programs provides a useful and satisfying framework for development. Integrating green infrastructure with programs that focus on growth and development will aid state and community efforts in the protection of vital agricultural and other working lands. Partnerships should also be forged among foundations, regional councils, government agencies, universities, nonprofits, and other organizations that are already funding projects and initiatives with similar goals to protect, restore, connect, or improve management of natural areas, parks, and greenways.

Principle 4: Green infrastructure functions across multiple jurisdictions and at different scales.

Green infrastructure systems need to be designed to connect across urban, suburban, rural, and wilderness landscapes and to incorporate greenspace elements at the state, regional, community, and parcel scales. Green infrastructure strategies can be used for initiatives of any size or scale, including:

- The project scale, involving individual parcels and within single real estate developments—e.g., the Fields of St. Croix in St. Elmo, Minnesota; or Prairie Crossing in Grays Lake, Illinois
- The community scale and regional scale, including park, recreation, and other open space projects—e.g., the Northern Illinois Regional Greenway Plan, which involves six counties in and around the Chicago metropolitan region

- The landscape scale, encompassing statewide and national conservation and open space resources—e.g., the Florida Statewide Greenway System for wildlife habitat, water quality, and recreation

Green infrastructure may be most successful when it functions at multiple scales in concert. For example, Toronto's "Greening the Portlands" project in Ontario, Canada, focuses on regional parks, neighborhood parks, wide habitat corridors, narrow trail corridors, and greenspace within developments.

Strategy: Work with all levels of government and private landowners at various scales to plan and implement green infrastructure.
State and local governments would never fund and construct highway systems without a multiyear transportation plan and an associated public communication plan that lays out all the implementation steps in a logical and orderly fashion. State and local transportation agencies even provide for volunteers to "adopt" highways. The funding, protection, and management of our green infrastructure systems deserve the same level of foresight and commitment on behalf of the community. It is important to note that green infrastructure systems do not require or even imply public ownership of all the land in the system. Clearly, privately owned land, particularly working farms and forests, can play an important role in any greenspace system.

Principle 5: Green infrastructure is grounded in sound science and land use planning theories and practices.
Conservation biology, landscape ecology, urban and regional planning, landscape architecture, geography, environmental engineering, and other related professional disciplines contribute to the successful design and planning of green infrastructure systems. Initiatives should, therefore, engage and incorporate the expertise of professionals from all relevant disciplines and should be based on sound science and up-to-date information.

Principle 6: Green infrastructure is a critical public investment.
The functions, values, and benefits of green infrastructure are available for everyone. Creating interconnected greenspace systems benefits

communities by providing land for resource protection and restoration, recreation, and other public values. More important, strategic placement of green infrastructure reduces the need for some gray infrastructure, freeing up public funds for other community needs. For example, in the 1990s New York City avoided the need to spend between $6 billion and $8 billion on new water filtration and treatment plants by instead purchasing and protecting watershed land in the Catskill Mountains for about $1.5 billion.

Green infrastructure also reduces a community's susceptibility to the risk of floods, fires, and other natural disasters. For example, Arnold, Missouri, has dramatically reduced the cost to taxpayers of disaster relief and flood damage repair by purchasing threatened properties and creating a greenway in the floodplain. Recognizing the public benefits of green infrastructure is an important first step in providing adequate funding. For all of these reasons, green infrastructure is an appropriate and necessary use of public funds.

Strategy: Make green infrastructure a primary budgetary item.
Our nation's gray infrastructure—transportation, water, electric, telecommunication, and other essential community support systems—is publicly financed as a primary budgetary item, in part to spread the costs of development and maintenance across a large pool of users and to ensure that all parts connect to one another to achieve the design function. State and local governments use dedicated taxes and other public funding mechanisms to pay for the planning, acquisition, construction, maintenance, and improvement of our highway systems. Green infrastructure should be included in the annual budget, as are roads, sewers, and other public works. While not yet on the same funding level as public works, states and communities have begun using conventional mechanisms to finance green infrastructure projects—including bond referenda, real estate transfer taxes, dedicated development fees, and direct budgetary line items.

In 1999, the Government Accounting Standards Board (GASB) issued comprehensive changes in state and local government financial reporting. The standards, known as "GASB-34," require governments to develop, maintain, and present capital accounts in their balance sheets. Two nonprofit organizations, the Center for Neighborhood

Technology and Urban Logic, are working with economists, account-ants, bond financiers, and others to explore using GASB-34 to help capture our natural environment's inherent capital. The new account-ing standard may be one method to incorporate green infrastructure into a city or state's budget by highlighting the economic trade-offs between built and natural infrastructure. It is also important to tap resources in state and federal agencies for planning and management activities, including protected public lands that can serve as building blocks for a viable green infrastructure.

Strategy: Document and promote the benefits of green infrastructure.
Green infrastructure provides a diversity of public and private func-tions and values that address both natural and human needs and ben-efit the environment and communities. These benefits need to be doc-umented, both in terms of their ecological values for people and the environment and their economic values to society. Just as all forms of built infrastructure are promoted for the wide range of public and pri-vate benefits they provide, green infrastructure systems need to be pro-moted actively for the wide range of essential ecological, economic, and social functions, values, and benefits that accrue to people and nature. Green infrastructure initiatives describe and define the values and functions of interconnected networks of open space in a context that enables citizens to understand the ecological, human, and eco-nomic benefits.

Principle 7: Green infrastructure involves diverse stakeholders.
The stakeholders of green infrastructure initiatives have diverse back-grounds and needs. Successful green infrastructure efforts forge alliances and interrelationships among various organizations—both public and private. The following are few examples of how diverse organizations have been brought together for a single purpose:

- The Chicago Wilderness is a grassroots collaboration of over 160 organ-izations representing all sectors with an interest in the region.
- Keep America Growing is designed to create partnerships to balance the demands for growth and development with the protection of vital work-ing lands.

- The Cooper River Wildlife Corridor Initiative in South Carolina uses an agreement for common land management practices with DuPont, Amoco, Medway Plantations, Cypress Gardens, and the Francis Marion National Forest.

Such voluntary community support is better than mandates or regulations, because the collaboration is lasting and sensitive to the economic value of the land, private property rights and responsibilities, and local home rule.

Strategy: Engage key partners and the general public.
By necessity, green infrastructure projects incorporate the experiences and programs of diverse public, private, and nonprofit partners. For this reason, it is critical to provide open forums that bring together key individuals, organizations, and agencies to coordinate and help guide the activities that will make green infrastructure a reality. To be successful, green infrastructure initiatives must excite people, engage them at the start, and keep them involved.

It is important to involve participants in the creation of a shared vision that can help drive the process and forge consensus. The community should be engaged in seeking ways to build on its history and existing assets and to extend the benefits into underserved and growing areas.

Successful citizen involvement programs go beyond traditional methods of engaging citizens to find informal and creative ways to get their attention. Among the strategies that might be effective are placing greenspace maps in post offices, libraries, schools, and city halls to invite input, and working with the media to get out the message, as was done in Anne Arundel County, Maryland. In creating its wetlands plan, the city of West Eugene, Oregon, used a variety of techniques to involve citizens, including direct mailings to landowners, marketing posters, news releases and newspaper stories, public surveys, and public hearings.

Examples of Green Infrastructure
Numerous conservation initiatives are occurring across the United States that embody green infrastructure concepts and approaches.

These projects encompass a diversity of scales and landscape types. The following are a few examples:

FLORIDA GREENWAYS COMMISSION: A NEW VISION OF THE FUTURE

The forty-member, governor-appointed Florida Greenways Commission engaged representatives of public agencies, conservation nonprofits, and the private sector in planning an interconnected statewide system of greenways and greenspaces to benefit Florida's people and wildlife. The following statements portray the commission's concept of the state's green infrastructure.

> The Commission's vision for Florida represents a new way of looking at conservation, an approach that emphasizes the interconnectedness of both our natural systems and our common goals and recognizes that the state's green infrastructure is just as important to conserve and manage as our built infrastructure. . . . We believe the recommendations in our report offer Florida an incredible opportunity to create a statewide greenways system that connects fragmented or isolated elements of the state's green infrastructure, and that connects people with their natural, historic and cultural heritage. . . . A healthy and diverse green infrastructure is the underlying basis of our state's sustainable future.[3]

The commission's vision statement helped guide the subsequent design of the statewide system and the development of its plan for implementation.

STATE OF MARYLAND: SMART GROWTH AND SMART CONSERVATION

In 1997, Maryland launched its Smart Growth and Neighborhood Conservation Initiative, which is designed to rejuvenate existing communities while preserving farms, forests, and other open spaces. Central to the success of this initiative are two related ideas. First, the state would no longer provide financial support for haphazard development but would instead redirect all of its financial resources to existing communities and areas approved for growth. Second, Maryland would take a much more aggressive and strategic approach to preserving open space.

The new strategic approach to land conservation manifested itself in two separate programs. Maryland's Rural Legacy Program seeks to protect large, contiguous blocks of farmland and other rural open spaces by working with local governments and nonprofit organizations to define preservation boundaries and then concentrating funding and preservation efforts in these areas.[4] Legislators appropriate bond funds each year to pay for the bulk of the program. A smaller percentage is drawn from Program Open Space money that is derived from the state's real estate transfer tax, in combination with general obligation bonds from the state's capital budget.

The state's new GreenPrint Program aims to identify and protect the state's most ecologically sensitive lands. Although Maryland has worked diligently to conserve its finest natural areas for decades, until the creation of GreenPrint, the efforts were not part of an overall long-term strategy. GreenPrint identifies the state's green infrastructure—a statewide network of large, ecologically significant hubs bound together by greenway corridors or links (see Map 6.1). Legislators provided $51 million over the first two years of the program (fiscal years 2002 and 2003), derived from general obligation bonds, to fund the program.[5]

CHESAPEAKE BAY WATERSHED: PROTECTING THE WORLD'S LARGEST ESTUARY

The Chesapeake Bay Program has undertaken one of the largest green infrastructure assessments in the nation's history—the 64,000-square-mile watershed that encompasses parts of five states and the District of Columbia. The Bay Program is a twenty-year-old regional partnership comprising the states of Maryland, Pennsylvania, and Virginia, along with Washington, D.C., the Chesapeake Bay Commission, the U.S. Environmental Protection Agency (EPA), and participating advisory groups.

A key driver behind the assessment, expected to be completed by 2004, is the goals of Chesapeake 2000, a watershed agreement signed by the partners that aims to improve water quality and protect living resources through voluntary measures that would preclude the imposition of federal regulations in 2011. The EPA has placed the bay and its tidal waters on the impaired waters list because of an overload of nitrogen and phosphorus nutrients. Two of many goals in the agreement are to permanently preserve from development 20 percent of the

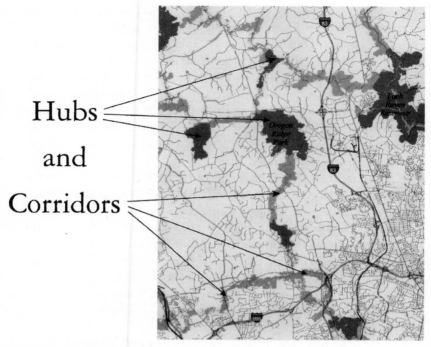

MAP 6.1. Maryland's hub and corridor system. *Map courtesy of Maryland Department of Natural Resources.*

lands in the watershed by 2010 and to reduce the loss rate of farm and forest land to sprawl development 30 percent by 2012.

The green infrastructure assessment builds on similar work that the state of Maryland completed to provide an ecologically based land protection strategy for its suite of land conservation programs. The assessment aims to identify the most valuable forests, wetlands, and farmland in the three-state study area. Once completed, the data and mapping will provide states, municipalities, land trusts, and watershed groups with information they need to be more strategic in the land protection activities and more efficient and effective in their funding of land conservation, said William Jenkins, who chairs a technical working group that is conducting the study. The Bay Program partners, which allocated $60,000 for data formatting and report writing while donating staff time for the overall project, would like to see their green infrastructure effort in the Chesapeake Bay watershed, which covers most of the mid-Atlantic Region 3 of the Environmental Protection Agency, linked to already completed EPA green infrastructure work encompassing all of Region 4 in the Southeast (see the following section).[6]

EPA's SOUTHEASTERN ECOLOGICAL FRAMEWORK: USING CONSERVATION GIS TO IDENTIFY GREEN INFRASTRUCTURE IN A MULTISTATE REGION

The Southeastern Ecological Framework Project is a geographic information systems (GIS) analysis used to identify ecological significant areas and connectivity in the southeast region of the United States. The states included in the project are Alabama, Florida, Georgia, Kentucky, Mississippi, North Carolina, South Carolina, and Tennessee. The project was conducted from 1999 to 2000 by the University of Florida Geo-Plan Center and sponsored by Region 4 of the U.S. Environmental Protection Agency.

Project goals and objectives include:

- Identifying primary ecological areas that are protected by some type of conservation or ecosystem management program
- Identifying a green infrastructure network that connects these primary ecological areas
- Identifying the important ecological characteristics of the ecological areas and connecting green infrastructure
- Developing an understanding of the spatial scale issues involved in analyzing the ecological connectivity at local, state, and regional scales, and developing a protocol for dissemination of the information.

This analysis was conducted with the use of landscape ecology principles and GIS tools. The product of the study can be used by local, state, and federal agencies to develop a regional atlas of environmental issues and threats to the natural ecosystems caused by human environmental impacts. State, local, and private entities can use the information to address various environmental resource allocation areas.[7]

Twin Cities Region, Minnesota: Metro Greenways Program Linking Partners and Programs for Resource Conservation and Restoration

In the past 150 years, urban development in the Twin Cities region has consumed nearly 96 percent of the presettlement habitat. Emphasizing the important role of natural resources, the Minnesota Legislature in 1998 established the Metro Greenways Program and provided $4.3 million in capital improvement bonds and funding from the state's Environment and Natural Resources Trust Fund to plan, protect, and improve significant natural areas in the seven-county metropolitan region. Administered and coordinated by the Minnesota Department of Natural Resources, Metro Greenways relies on partnerships with a wide range of nonprofit conservation organizations, government agencies, institutions, private businesses, and landowners. By assisting local government with planning grants and project funding, the program helps communities to protect and improve the natural resources that are important to them in a way that earns local support. At the same time, the seven-county scope assures that the individual projects contribute to the existing local and regional park systems as elements of a regional network of greenspaces and naturally functioning ecosystems.[8]

Saginaw Bay: Creating a Framework for a Twenty-Two-County Green Infrastructure Plan

Facilitated through a partnership of the Saginaw County Metropolitan Planning Commission and the East Central Michigan Planning and Development Region, the Saginaw Bay Greenways Collaborative is nearing completion of a green infrastructure plan for Bay, Midland, and Saginaw Counties in Michigan. The Saginaw Bay Watershed Initiative Network awarded a $130,000 grant to create the plan, the work of more than a dozen collaborative members representing nonprofit groups, local foundations, state and local governments, and the Rivers and Trails Program of the National Park Service. The collaborative has spent two years investigating the three-county area and completing a resource inventory. Computer modeling has identified and prioritized significant areas in the region for conservation and recreation based on principles of landscape ecology and conservation biology. The effort aims to establish the framework by which a twenty-two-county green-way vision can be formulated and implemented in the Saginaw Bay Watershed.[9]

PRAIRIE CROSSING, GRAYSLAKE, ILLINOIS: A CONSERVATION DEVELOPMENT INCORPORATING GREEN INFRASTRUCTURE CONCEPTS AND VALUES

Located 40 miles northwest of Chicago in Grayslake, Illinois, Prairie Crossing is a unique conservation development that shows how green infrastructure can add value to residential development. Prairie Crossing's 362 homes are located on a small portion of the site's 667 acres. The majority of the land is left in open space to protect environmental resources and the site's rural character. The 350 acres of open space include 160 acres of restored prairie, 158 acres of active farmland, 13 acres of wetlands, a 22-acre lake, three ponds, a village green, and recreational parks. Prairie Crossing's open space network is the western anchor of a 2,500-acre preserved area—the Liberty Prairie Reserve—making it part of a larger protected and functioning ecosystem. The project's design features have generated an estimated 15 percent premium over the local market and competition.[10]

TOPEKA, KANSAS: USING GREEN INFRASTRUCTURE TO REDUCE STORMWATER MANAGEMENT COSTS

In November 2000, Topeka, Kansas, initiated Green Topeka to holistically address stormwater quality and flood control issues. The partnership, which includes state agencies, Kansas State University, local government, nonprofit organizations, private stakeholders, and the U.S.D.A. National Agroforestry Center, is developing a set of best management practices to address stormwater concerns and increase green infrastructure throughout the community.

A 1-inch rainstorm over Topeka (pop. 124,000) yields 940 million gallons of water. The city is improving the quality of its runoff by filtering stormwater through natural vegetated systems, such as riparian forest buffers, bioswales, and reconstructed wetlands. This approach helps the city meet stormwater quality requirements under the Clean Water Act while expanding its green infrastructure as these natural systems are incorporated into street and parking lot designs, parks, and open spaces that serve surrounding neighborhoods.

Much of the funding for the "green" solutions to flood control and stormwater quality comes from existing stormwater management monies, in addition to a stormwater utility fee within water bills that is based on the amount of impervious surface on a property. The fee generates $3 million a year. Through the Green Topeka initiative, the city has found that a green solution rather than a hard engineering approach to remedy flooding is often less costly and can be funded with the money already set aside for stormwater management.[11]

MILWAUKEE, WISCONSIN: USING GREEN INFRASTRUCTURE TO REDUCE THE COSTS OF STORMWATER MANAGEMENT

Watercourse studies for three metropolitan Milwaukee rivers indicate that projected demographic trends will intensify existing flood problems. The Milwaukee Metropolitan Sewerage District (MMSD) is implementing an innovative program called the Conservation Plan to reduce future flooding through targeted land conservation. In 2001 MMSD allotted $15 million over nine years to acquire properties or purchase easements on at least 6,000 acres to protect against future flooding in the Menomonee River, Oak Creek, and Root River watersheds. As of March 2003, MMSD had completed seven acquisitions totaling 222 acres. More than forty sites have been identified by The Conservation Fund that could provide 4.7 billion gallons of floodwater storage for the Milwaukee area that complement the structural investments by MMSD. National studies have estimated that such green infrastructure investments can provide substantial savings compared with engineered, structural solutions to flooding. The land acquisition program, which could draw matching grants of $15 million, is part of a $300 million investment in flood management in response to devastating floods in the Milwaukee area in the 1990s.[12]

KINSTON/LENOIR COUNTY, NORTH CAROLINA: LINKING HAZARD MITIGATION TO CONSERVATION AND DEVELOPMENT

Two hurricanes that hit the Kinston/Lenoir County area in eastern North Carolina in the 1990s inflicted significant damage when the Neuse River overflowed its banks. Afterward, the local governments used Federal Emergency Management Agency disaster relief funds to purchase damaged properties lying in the floodplain.

As part of the flood recovery effort, a partnership of state, local, and nonprofit agencies and organizations developed two green infrastructure plans that outlined land conservation, recreation, and economic opportunities for the county and Kinston, the county seat. The "Kinston/Lenoir County Green Infrastructure Plan for the Neuse River Floodplain" identified opportunities to provide new green infrastructure along the Neuse River floodplain and adjacent areas in the county. A follow-up study, "Linking Natural and Historic Assets: Green Infrastructure as Economic Development in Lenoir County, North Carolina," provided guidelines for improving the quality of life in the county by connecting river-based recreation with heritage tourism opportunities, economic development, natural resource protection, and environmental health. Graduate students at the University of North Carolina's Department of City and Regional Planning researched and wrote the reports.

The first plan used green infrastructure planning principles and complemented existing community projects and goals such as the Kinston/Lenoir County Parks and Recreation Master Plan and the Greater Kinston Urban Area Growth Plan. The Green Infrastructure Plan presented ideas for how the Neuse River and its floodplain could provide Lenoir County and Kinston with additional recreational and environmental amenities. The report suggested ways to turn vacant buyout areas into a network of parks, trails, and habitats along the Neuse River and its tributaries that would connect downtown Kinston with other areas in the community.

The second plan had three focus areas: heritage tourism, passive recreation, and active recreation. It identified more than a dozen greenways and canoe launches that could be developed to connect Lenoir County's historic sites. With access to a linked greenway system, residents and visitors could travel throughout the county by foot, bicycle, canoe, or by car to visit a reclaimed battle site of Kinston along with existing historic districts and scenic millponds. Increased awareness of and access to heritage tourism sites could greatly increase revenues while creating positive economic impacts for the community, the study found.

Besides the "free" help from the UNC graduate students, and staff time from Kinston and Lenoir County, four foundations and the state of North Carolina funded the project.[13]

MONTGOMERY COUNTY, MARYLAND: PROTECTING GREEN INFRASTRUCTURE BEFORE AND AFTER DEVELOPMENT

Montgomery County (population 892,000) initiated green infrastructure planning for its stream valley park system in advance of the county's rapid growth. The county began buying land along all of its major stream corridors in the 1940s and 1950s—well before land development and population growth had made it impossible to preserve these ecologically important areas. As of 2003 the county had a system of stream valley parks encompassing over 32,000 acres. The county has begun making significant additions to this system with an innovative ten-year, $100 million initiative called Legacy Open Space.

The goal of Legacy Open Space is to complete a county-wide network of open space comprising of protected farmland, important ecological reserves, trail corridors, greenspace surrounding drinking water supplies, and urban and historic greenspace preserves, using a variety of land protection tools. As of 2003, the Legacy program had preserved over 2,400 acres of open space in the county through a combination of fee-simple acquisition and easements, with the majority of protection so far through outright acquisition. The Legacy Open Space program was established through the adoption of a Functional Master Plan after significant research, many levels of public input, and the review and approval of the Montgomery County Planning Board and the Montgomery County Council. Extensive research went into the design of the program, utilizing state-of-the-art GIS analysis and making use of the Green Infrastructure developed for the entire state by the Maryland Department of Natural Resources.

Legacy Open Space also uses an innovative funding approach. It is initially funded through the county's Capital Improvement Program (CIP) with a combination of funds from park and county bonds and current receipts. This county funding is intended to leverage additional funds from the private and public sector, including municipal, state, and federal funds as well as private donations and public/private partnerships. The county council set a target that $19 million of the entire $100 million program come from noncounty funding sources. In the first two years of the program (2001–2002), $31 million was committed for eleven acquisitions. Of that sum, $19 million in county funds as committed while partner contributions totaled over $12.5 million. The partner contributions break down into $7.2 million in state of Maryland GreenPrint funds (a program designed to protect the green infrastructure statewide); $3.5 million in state of Maryland Rural Legacy funds (a program that protects rural landscapes); municipal contributions totaling $1.36 million; and donation of a 106-acre parcel valued at $400,000.[14]

PITTSFORD, NEW YORK: A GREENPRINT THAT MAKES FISCAL SENSE

In 1993, the town of Pittsford, New York, commissioned a fiscal analysis of the revenues and expenses associated with existing and potential land uses. The analysis showed that it would be less expensive to implement a new land use plan rather than continue the current zoning policy. The proposed plan targeted 2,000 acres of land for permanent protection while also creating several enhanced economic development sites for commercial and light industrial expansion.

To implement the plan, the town issued $7.5 million in general obligations bonds and received about $2.5 million in open space and farmland protection grants from county, state, and federal sources. The town then purchased development rights on 1,200 acres of farmland and established zoning that requires 50 percent of the land in developments over 10 acres to be set aside as open space. Property taxes were raised 9 percent to pay off the bonds.

The community supported the plan, recognizing that protection of open space, including purchase of development rights, would cost taxpayers less per year than full build-out of the town. The town's fiscal impact analysis found that the bonds would cost homeowners $67 a year for twenty years while letting the land be developed would have cost $250 a year forever. Landowners supported the plan because they were compensated for the loss of their development rights. Today, Pittsford has a network of preserved open space that is a regional model.[15]

CHICAGO WILDERNESS: MOBILIZING HUMAN DIVERSITY ON BEHALF OF BIOLOGICAL DIVERSITY

In 1996, a coalition of organizations launched Chicago Wilderness. Their vision: a thriving mosaic of natural areas—200,000 acres of private, local, state, and federal protected lands connected by greenways and wildlife corridors—embedded within the nation's third largest metropolitan area, stretching from southeastern Wisconsin, through northeastern Illinois, and into northwestern Indiana.

On its seventh anniversary, Chicago Wilderness—once seen as a contradiction in terms—is becoming a reality, mobilizing human diversity on behalf of biological diversity. As of 2003 the partnership included over 160 agencies at all levels of government, centers of research and education, community groups, landowners, and conservation organizations that have joined forces and pooled resources to protect, restore, and manage Chicago wilderness. Financial support for Chicago Wilderness is provided by the member organizations, as well as through local, state and federal grants. Current funders include the U.S. Fish and Wildlife Service, the U.S.D.A. Forest Service, the Illinois Department of Natural Resources C2000 program, the U.S. Environmental Protection Agency, and the Grand Victoria Foundation.[16]

Conclusion

State and local governments have spent a lot of money on tools and techniques to conserve land across the United States. However well intentioned these programs are, many of them are limited in their ability to address overall quality of life and growth management issues because they are reactive in nature, haphazard, single-shot, or too small-scale. Increasingly, state and local officials, land use planners, and conservationists are looking toward developing a smarter, more cost-effective way to conserve land.

One approach to smart conservation is green infrastructure, a strategy that focuses limited resources on the best conservation. Green infrastructure is the ecological framework needed for environmental, social, and economic sustainability. It is our nation's natural life support system. Green infrastructure is an interconnected network of greenspace that conserves natural ecosystem values and functions and provides a wide array of benefits to people, wildlife, and communities. Green infrastructure can reduce a community's susceptibility to floods, fires, and other natural disasters. Documenting these public benefits is a key step toward securing adequate funding for this smarter, more comprehensive and ecologically sound approach to conserving land in America.

CHAPTER SEVEN

PROTECTING LAND CONSERVATION FUNDING IN TOUGH ECONOMIC TIMES

In the nine months it has taken to write this book, the economic picture for state budgets has darkened considerably. The National Conference of State Legislatures reported in February 2003 that states are facing at least a $68.5 billion budget gap for fiscal year 2004, this after addressing a $75 billion shortfall in FY 2003.[1]

Tough economic times make land conservation programs a tempting target for politicians looking to take an ax to state spending. For example, New York governor George Pataki asked legislators in 2003 to divert more than $53.4 million from legally dedicated money in the state's Environmental Protection Fund to help address the state's budget shortfall, after a $256 million diversion in 2002 following the terrorist attacks of 2001. In Florida, state legislators in 2001 appropriated $75 million of Preservation 2000 money to the Save Our Everglades Trust Fund. The next year, Governor Jeb Bush vetoed a second attempt to divert $100 million to pay for other state programs. And in Illinois, state legislators trimmed the state's budget in part by cutting $15 million from two programs: the Natural Areas Acquisition Fund and the Open Space Lands Acquisition and Development Program. But Governor George Ryan signed legislation in January 2003 that

BOX 7.1.

How to protect land conservation programs in your state budget

Given the serious budget shortfalls in most states, many land conservation programs are in jeopardy. The most critical element in saving these programs is communication. State departments of natural resources, statewide nonprofit organizations, and local land trusts must all work together to protect state funding for land conservation. Following are ten tips for protecting the programs in your state.

1. *Communicate.* Establish a regularly scheduled call or meeting with representatives from the state department of natural resources, national conservation organizations, statewide nonprofit groups, and local land trusts to discuss budget issues and the potential impact on land conservation.

2. *Anticipate the problem.* Make the case for land conservation now—before a crisis occurs. Demonstrate the benefits of land protection with hard numbers and facts. Commission studies on the economic benefits of land conservation efforts in your state. Compile statistics on land developed and land conserved, etc. Outline the specific benefits of programs administered by your state.

3. *Monitor the state budget.* Identify an individual familiar with the legislature, such as a state official assigned to monitor legislation on a regular basis, a lobbyist, or a representative of a statewide nonprofit group as the budget point person. Establish a regularly scheduled meeting with this individual. Understand all of the state-funded conservation programs within your state, including the funding source, funding level, and the specific beneficiaries of the program.

4. *Form alliances.* Look beyond natural allies for organizations with related policy goals. Attend the meetings of these organizations to see how your issues might overlap.

5. *Gather grassroots support.* Organize a statewide network of grassroots conservationists who can mobilize on short notice. Collect e-mail addresses for all activists so that communication can be quick and inexpensive. Work with local conservation and environmental organizations to share lists and e-mail addresses. Educate activists on your state's structure of government, including the legislative process

and governor's authority, and rules for lobbying by professionals, volunteers, or state officials.

6. *Develop relationships with state legislators.* Reach out to both Republicans and Democrats. Identify sympathetic legislators who can be recruited or are known to have an interest in preservation. Establish a program of year-round contact with elected officials through special events such as a legislators' breakfast or environmental rally or by inviting them to local meetings, conferences, and special events. Thank the legislators and supporters who have been friends of conservation in the past.

7. *Develop an effective message.* Develop a clear, succinct message. Gather real success stories from real people. Generate letters to the editor promoting land protection programs within your state. Collect visual images of important sites, representative of the state's heritage, and show how conservation programs played a role in their protection or revitalization. Host field trips to these places.

8. *Create an on-line advocacy network.* An efficient way to promote an issue is through electronic advocacy. The Land Trust Alliance and many statewide organizations have developed or are currently developing these systems. Advocacy web sites allow organizations to develop a broader base of activists and give activists direct contact to state legislators via e-mail. A web site allows for quick dissemination of information in the form of advocacy alerts and can easily be updated to reflect late-breaking developments.

9. *Develop good relationships with the media and use them.* Designate effective spokespersons to speak with reports and editors. Make sure those so designated have all the facts and feel comfortable in dealing with the press. Get your views in print early enough to influence debates—before key decisions are locked in. Develop compelling and concise fact sheets and brief position papers outlining your point of view. These can be given to reporters (and legislators) following meetings with them.

10. *Compromise.* Know what your priorities are and be willing to compromise.

Source: Adapted from National Trust for Historic Preservation.

restored the funding for both programs for the fiscal year that began on July 1, 2003. Even on the federal level, Congress has diverted more than $1 billion in spending from the Land and Water Conservation Fund between FY 1998 and FY 2003 for projects other than federal land acquisition and state grants for acquisition and development of parks.

With the economy lagging and budgets tight, open space funding is on the chopping block. This is because the public and local officials think open space is a luxury they can no longer afford. They think of it as an amenity, something that is nice to have. However, the same people understand that infrastructure is a necessity, not an amenity— something that communities *must* have, not just something that is nice to have. We view infrastructure as a primary public investment, not something we pay for with leftover money. Likewise, public officials understand that infrastructure must be constantly upgraded and maintained. It is not something we just buy and forget. People understand the need to invest in infrastructure—even in an era of deficits. Next to national defense, funding for roads, bridges, sewers, airports, and other forms of capital infrastructure is always at the top of the list. However, just as we must carefully plan for and invest in our capital infrastructure, so too must we invest in our environmental or green infrastructure.

These investments pay off. Many of the leading state land conservation programs have been demonstrably successful in leveraging additional funding for land protection.

- Between 1993 and mid-2001, the Florida Communities Trust state grant program partnered with local communities to acquire and preserve more than 40,000 acres using $242 million in state grants that leveraged $175 million in local funding (see Map 7.1).
- In New Jersey, residents of 20 of the state's 21 counties and 187 of its 566 municipalities will collect more than $158 million in 2003 to fund local open space and recreation plans and help attract $48 million in state grants made available each year for land conservation.
- Since Colorado's Great Outdoors Colorado (GOCO) program was created, 24 communities have approved open space tax or bond measures to protect open space. GOCO has awarded almost $295 million in grants, which have been matched on a three-to-one basis, to preserve 361,145

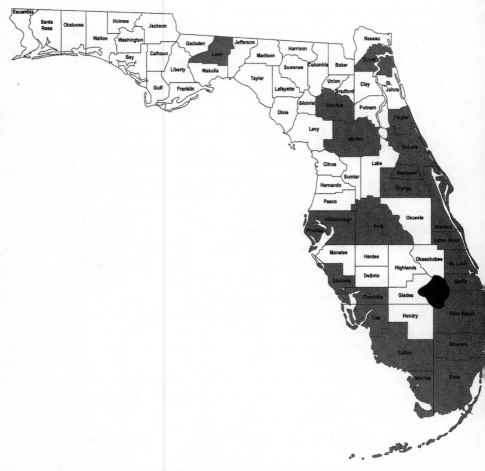

MAP 7.1. Since the state of Florida created the Florida Communities Trust program in 1989, it has awarded more than $240 million to local governments and nonprofit organizations to preserve parks and open space. Between 1990 and 2003, Boca Raton and twenty-three counties (shown here) have approved bond referendums or identified dedicated funding sources to help provide a 25 percent match for the state grant funding. *Map courtesy of Florida Communities Trust.*

acres of open space, acquire 47,041 acres for parks and wildlife areas, and build or restore 569 miles of trails.

- In Massachusetts, $26 million in annual matching grants from the state has spurred 58 of the state's 351 towns and cities to approve small property tax increases to raise $26 million each year for three purposes: acquiring open space, providing affordable housing, and preserving historic sites and buildings.

The success of these programs shouldn't go unnoticed. State and local governments and their citizens must come to understand that greenspace is a basic necessity. A popular bumper stickers says: "If you think education is expensive, try ignorance." Well, if you think greenspace is expensive, just imagine the future costs for clean air, clean water, and healthy natural systems if we don't invest in green infrastructure today.

NOTES

Chapter 1

1. The Conservation Fund, *Land and Water Conservation Fund: An Assessment of Its Past, Present and Future* (Arlington, Va.: The Conservation Fund, 2000): 2. www.conservationfund.org/?article=2012&back=true.

2. U.S. Government Printing Office, Senate Reports Vol. 1–4, Miscellaneous Reports on Public Bills, IV, 88th Congress, 2nd session, Jan. 7–Oct. 3, 1964, Senate Report 1364, Land and Water Conservation Fund Act, Committee on Interior and Insular Affairs, Aug. 10, 1964: 19.

3. The Appalachian Mountain Club has developed an excellent database listing all the projects funded through the Land and Water Conservation Fund, broken down by state, county, congressional district, project type, and federal land unit; see http://w3.netcapitol.com/outdoors/lwcf.cfm.

4. Jeffrey Zinn, *Land and Water Conservation Fund: Current Status and Issues* (Washington, D.C.: Congressional Research Service, Library of Congress, January 28, 2002): 2.

5. Mike McQueen, "The Land and Water Conservation Fund: Where Does Reform Effort Go from Here?" *Land Letter* 10, no. 25 (September 20, 1991) (Arlington, Va.: The Conservation Fund): 2.

6. Ibid., 2.

7. Natural Resources Conservation Service, *1997 National Resources Inventory* (revised December 2000); see www.nrcs.usda.gov/technical/NRI.

8. Land Trust Alliance, *Voters Invest in Parks and Open Space: 1998 Referenda Results, 3–6,* (Washington, D.C.: Land Trust Alliance, 1999). See www.lta.org/publicpolicy/refresults.pdf.

9. See www.state.nj/us/dep/greenacres/taxsummary.htm for a list of counties and municipalities in New Jersey with open space funding programs.

10. *Voters Invest in Parks and Open Space: 1998 Referenda Results,* (Washington, D.C.: Land Trust Alliance, 1999), 7–9.

11. Land Trust Alliance, *Voters Invest in Open Space: 1999 Referenda Results* (Washington, D.C.: Land Trust Alliance, 2000); see www.lta.org/publicpolicy/1999voters_inv.pdf.

12. Land Trust Alliance, *Voters Invest in Open Space: 2000 Referenda Results* (Washington, D.C.: Land Trust Alliance, 2001).

13. Trust for Public Land and Land Trust Alliance, *LandVote 2001: Americans Invest in Parks and Open Space* (Washington, D.C.: Trust for Public Land and Land Trust Alliance, 2002); see www.lta.org/publicpolicy/landvote2001.htm.

14. "How Propositions 40 and 45 Fared among Voters," *Los Angeles Times,* March 7, 2002; see http://a1022.g.akamai.net/f/1022/6000/10m/www.latimes.com/media/acrobat/2002-03/2235583.pdf.

15. The Conservation Fund, "The Environment, Community and Democracy: The Proposition 40 Victory," *Common Ground* 13, no. 2 (April–June 2002): 8.

16. Land Trust Alliance, *National Land Trust Census* (Washington, D.C.: Land Trust Alliance, 2001); see www.lta.org/newsroom/pr_091201.htm.

17. Mark Benedict and Edward McMahon, *Green Infrastructure: Smart Conservation for the 21st Century* (Arlington, Va.: The Conservation Fund Center for Conservation and Development, 2002). For more information on green infrastructure, see www.greeninfrastructure.net. A copy of the report may be downloaded from www.greeninfrastructure.net/pdf/sprawlwatch_gi.pdf.

18. Mark Benedict, "Green Infrastructure: A Strategic Approach to Land Conservation," American Planning Association PAS Memo, October 2000.

19. Edward McMahon, "Green Infrastructure," *Planning Commissioners Journal,* no. 37 (Winter 2000).

20. Mark Benedict and Edward McMahon, "Green Infrastructure: Smart Conservation for the 21st Century," *Renewable Resources Journal* 20, no. 3 (Autumn 2002): 12–17.

Chapter 2

1. See http://commpres.env.state.ma.us/content/cpa.asp for more details about Massachusetts's community planning efforts, including its Fiscal Impact Tool, Community Preservation Act toolkit, and publications such as "Building Vibrant Communities and the Buildout." Also, go to www.communitypreservation.org, a web site of the Community Preservation Coalition, consisting of sixty groups that back the state's effort.

2. For more details on New Jersey's Garden State Preservation Trust, see www.state.nj.us/gspt.

3. See www.state.nj.us/dep/greenacres for more information on New Jersey's Green Acres Program.

4. For more information on New Jersey's farmland preservation programs, visit www.state.nj.us/agriculture/sadc/overview.htm.

5. See www.njeit.org for more information about the New Jersey Environmental Infrastructure Trust.

6. For more information on Maryland's Program Open Space, visit www.dnr.state.md.us/pos.html.

7. See www.dnr.state.md.us/rurallegacy for more details about Maryland's Rural Legacy Program.

8. For more information on Maryland's GreenPrint Program, visit www.dnr.state.md.us/greenways/greenprint.

9. See www.mda.state.md.us/geninfo/genera3.htm for more information on Maryland's Agricultural Land Preservation Foundation.

10. For more details on the Maryland Environmental Trust, see www.dnr.state.md.us/met.

11. See www.dep.state.fl.us/parks/planning/FPS%202000-2001%20Economic%20Impact%20Assessment.pdf for the Florida State Park System Economic Impact Assessment for FY 2001/2002.

12. See http://p2000.dep.state.fl.us/about.htm for more information on Preservation 2000.

13. For more information about the Conservation and Recreation Lands and Florida Forever programs, see www.dep.state.fl.us/lands/carl_ff.

14. Go to www.dca.state.fl.us/ffct for more details on the Florida Communities Trust.

15. Florida Statutes, Title XI, Chap. 163, Sect. 3177. See www.leg.state.fl.us/statutes/index.cfm?App_mode=Display_Statute&Search_String=&URL=Ch0163/Sec3177.HTM.

16. For links to Florida's five water management districts—the Northwest Florida WMD, South Florida WMD, Southwest Florida WMD, St. Johns River WMD, and Suwannee River WMD—go to www.dca.state.fl.us/fdcp/DCP/Partners/wmds.htm.

17. See www.dep.state.fl.us/parks/bdrs/frdap.htm for more information on the Florida Recreation Development Assistance Program.

18. See www.floridadep.org/gwt for more information on the Florida Office of Greenways and Trails.

19. For more information on Minnesota's Environment and Natural Resources Trust Fund, see www.commissions.leg.state.mn.us/lcmr/trustfund/tfquestion.htm.

20. Go to www.commissions.leg.state.mn.us/lcmr for more information about Minnesota's Legislative Commission on Minnesota Resources.

21. For more information on land conservation programs in Minnesota's Department of Natural Resources, see www.dnr.state.mn.us.

22. See www.bwsr.state.mn.us for more information on the Minnesota Board of Water and Soil Resources.

23. For more information about Minnesota's agricultural land preservation programs, see www.mda.state.mn.us.

24. See http://dnr.state.il.us/ocd/newoslad1.htm for more information on Illinois's Open Space Lands Acquisition and Development Program.

25. Go to www.ilparks.org to visit the web site of the Illinois Association of Park Districts.

26. See www.openlands.org to download a copy of "Under Pressure: Land Consumption in the Chicago Region."

27. For more information on Illinois's Open Land Trust grant program, see http://dnr.state.il.us/ocd/newolt2.htm.

28. See www.goco.org for more information about grant making and other activities of the Great Outdoors Colorado program.

29. See www.dola.state.co.us/LGS/FA/ctf.htm for grant applications.

30. Go to www.parks.state.co.us rails for details on the trail program, grant information, and applications.

31. See the web site of the Colorado Department of Revenue's Taxpayer Service Division for more detail on the tax credit at www.revenue.state.co.us/fyi/html/income39.html.

32. See www.cedlink.org.

33. California Government Code, Section 65030. See http://ceres.ca.gov/planning/pzd/1997/plan_2.html.

34. Most of the historical information contained in this section on California ballot propositions comes from two Internet sources: lalaw.lib.ca.us/ballot.html and holmes.uchastings.edu/cgi-bin/starfinder/0?path=calprop.txt&id=webber&pass=webber&OK=OK.

35. See www.pcl.org for extensive information, links, and publications regarding many of California's key park and water bonds over the past two decades.

36. The California Legislative Analyst's Office provided much of the background information regarding the state's most recent park and water bond propositions. See www.lao.ca.gov for more. Of particular help was "California's Land Conservation Efforts: The Role of State Conservancies." See www.lao.ca.gov/2001/conservancies/010501_conservancies.html.

37. For more on trends in natural resource spending in California, see "California's Natural Resource Programs: Where Does the Money Come From and Where Does It Go?" by J. Fred Silva of the Public Policy Institute of California; www.ppic.org/content/pubs/R_702FSR.pdf.

38. Statistics on California's agricultural output are available at the California Department of Food and Agriculture. See www.cdfa.ca.gov/docs/CAStats01.pdf for a summary.

39. For more on the history of the Williamson Act, consult A. Sokolow, *The Williamson Act: 25 Years of Land Conservation* (University of California at Davis, Agricultural Issues Center, December 1990).

40. See www.consrv.ca.gov/DLRP/cfcp for more information on the California Farmland Conservancy Program.

41. For more information on California's Environmental Enhancement and Mitigation Program, see www.resources.ca.gov/eem.

42. See http://resources.ca.gov/conservancies.html and www.lao.ca.gov/2001/conservancies/010501_conservancies.html for more background on California's eight conservancies—Baldwin Hills Conservancy, California Tahoe Conservancy, Coachella Valley Mountains Conservancy, San Diego River Conservancy, San Gabriel and Lower Los Angeles Rivers and Mountains Conservancy, San Joaquin

River Conservancy, Santa Monica Mountains Conservancy, and the State Coastal Conservancy.

43. For more information on California's Natural Heritage Preservation Tax Credit Program, see www.dfg.ca.gov/wcb/tax_credit_program.htm.

Chapter 3

1. For more information on the Cape Cod Land Bank, see www.capecodcommission. org/landbank.

2. For more detail on the work of Lancaster County's Agricultural Preserve Board, see www.co.lancaster.pa.us.

3. For more information on the Lancaster Farmland Trust, see www.savelancasterfarms. org.

4. For more information on DeKalb County's Parks and Greenspace Program, see www.co.dekalb.ga.us/greenspace/index.htm.

5. For the 1998 Sierra Club report, "Sprawl: The Dark Side of an American Dream," see www.sierraclub.org/sprawl/report98.

6. For selected data on acres of open space per 1,000 residents, park and open space as a percentage of city area, and park-related expenditure per resident (excerpted from Peter Harnik's book *Inside City Parks*), see www.tpl.org/tier3_cd.cfm?content_item_id=5960&folder_id=985.

7. For more information on Preservation Project Jacksonville, see http://apps1.coj.net/preserve/default.htm.

8. For more information on Lake County's Forest Preserve District, see www.LCFPD.org.

9. For more information on the Metropolitan Park and Recreation District and the Metro East Park and Recreation District, see www.mprd.org and www.stlouis2004.org.

10. For detail on Douglas County's open space program, see www.douglas.co.us.

11. For more information on the Marin County Open Space District, go to www.marinopenspace.org.

12. For more background on the Marin Agricultural Land Trust, see www.malt.org.

13. For more information on the Marin Community Foundation, See www.marincf.org.

Chapter 4

1. Much of the material in this chapter was originally presented at "Creating and Expanding Public Funding Sources for Parks and Open Space," a seminar conducted by the Trust for Public Land at the Land Trust Alliance Rally held October 27, 2002, in Austin, Texas, and "Winning Ballot Initiatives for Conservation Funding," a workshop conducted October 29 by The Nature Conservancy at the rally. The Trust for Public Land provides assistance to communities to win voter approval of ballot measures for parks and land conservation. For more information on the Conservation Finance Program of the Trust for Public Land, see www.tpl.org/tier2_rp2.cfm?folder_id=708; telephone 617-367-6200. For information on The Nature Conservancy, visit www.nature.org. To find out more about the Conservancy's work

on ballot measures, please contact the Government Relations Department; telephone 703-841-8755.

2. "How Propositions 40 and 45 Fared Among Voters," *Los Angeles Times,* March 7, 2002. See http://a1022.g.akamai.net/f/1022/6000/1om/www.latimes.com/media/ acrobat/2002-03/2235583.pdf.

Chapter 5

1. To access more than 1,700 statistical tables on foundations and their giving, visit the Foundation Center's web site at www.foundationcenter.org/media/stats.html.

2. For more information on the Richard King Mellon Foundation, see http://fdncenter.org/grantmaker/rkmellon/index.html.

3. For more information on the David and Lucile Packard Foundation, visit www.packard.org.

4. For more information on the Resources Legacy Fund Foundation, see www.resourceslegacyfund.org.

5. For more information on the Gordon and Betty Moore Foundation, go to www.moore.org.

6. The 500-acre-per-week statistic comes from the 1998 Sierra Club report "Sprawl: The Dark Side of an American Dream," available at www.sierraclub.org/sprawl/report98.

7. For selected data on acres of open space per 1,000 residents, park and open space as a percentage of city area, and park-related expenditure per resident (excerpted from Peter Harnik's book *Inside City Parks*), see www.tpl.org/tier3_cd.cfm?content_item_id=5960&folder_id=985.

8. For more information about the Arthur M. Blank Family Foundation, see www.blankfoundation.org.

9. Mayor Franklin's Parks and Green Spaces Task Force Report is available at www.parkpride.org.

10. For more information on the land conservation programs of the Doris Duke Charitable Foundation, see www.ddcf.org.

11. For more information on the Turner Foundation, see www.turnerfoundation.org.

12. See John J. Havens and Paul G. Schervishi, "Millionaires and the Millennium: New Estimates of the Forthcoming Wealth Transfer and the Prospects for a Golden Age of Philanthropy," at www.bc.edu/research/swri.

Chapter 6

1. Much of the material in this chapter is excerpted from two publications: "Green Infrastructure: Smart Conservation for the 21st Century," a thirty-six-page Sprawl Watch Clearinghouse monograph written by Mark Benedict and Ed McMahon of The Conservation Fund (May 2002); and a seven-page article of the same title published by *Renewable Resources Journal* (Autumn 2002).

2. For more information on the Florida Ecological Network Project, see T. S. Hoctor, M. H. Carr, and P. D. Zwick, "Identifying a Linked Reserve System Using a Regional Landscape Approach: The Florida Ecological Network," *Conservation Biology* 14, no. 4 (2000): 984–1000; and www.biodiversitypartners.org/FL/FLENP.html.

For more on Maryland's Green Infrastructure Assessment, see T. Weber and J. Wolf, "Maryland's Green Infrastructure: Using Landscape Assessment Tools to Identify a Regional Conservation Strategy," *Environmental Monitoring and Assessment* 63 (2000): 265–277; and www.dnr.state.md.us/greenways/gia.

3. Florida Greenways Commission, *Creating a Statewide Greenways System: For People . . . for Wildlife . . . for Florida,* Report to the Governor, January 1995; www.1000friendsofflorida.org/PUBS/Greenways/contents.asp.

4. For more detail about Maryland's Rural Legacy Program, see www.dnr.state.md.us/rurallegacy.

5. For more information on Maryland's GreenPrint Program, visit www.dnr.state.md.us/greenways/greenprint.

6. For more detail on the restoration efforts in the Chesapeake Bay watershed, see www.chesapeakebay.net.

7. For more detail on the Southeastern Ecological Framework Project, go to www. geoplan.ufl.edu/epa/index.html.

8. For more information on the Twin Cities Metro Greenways Program, visit www.dnr.state.mn.us/greenways/index.html.

9. For more information on the Saginaw Bay Watershed Initiative Network, visit www.saginawbaywin.org. For more information on the Saginaw Bay Greenways Collaborative, go to www.saginawbaygreenways.org.

10. For more information on the Prairie Crossing conservation development, see www.prairiecrossing.com.

11. Mark Greene, "Topeka, Kansas: Getting Greener Gets the Job Done," *Inside Agroforestry, the USDA National Agroforestry Center Newsletter* (Summer 2001). For more information on Green Topeka, see www.topeka.org/greentopeka/greentopeka.htm.

12. For more information on the Conservation Plan of the Milwaukee Metropolitan Sewerage District, see www.mmsd.com and www.greeninfrastructure.net.

13. For the two green infrastructure reports on Kinston and Lenoir County, North Carolina, go to www.greeninfrastructure.net.

14. For more detail on the Legacy Open Space plan in Montgomery County, Maryland, go to www.mc-mncppc.org/legacy_open_space/index.shtm.

15. John L. Behan, "Planning and Financing Open Space Resource Protection: Pittsford's Greenprint Initiative," American Institute of Certified Planners, *Planners' Casebook* (Spring/Summer 1999).

16. For more detail on Chicago Wilderness, visit www.chicagowilderness.org.

Chapter 7

1. For more information on the National Conference of State Legislatures, see www.ncsl.org.

STATE CONSERVATION FUNDING MECHANISMS

Alabama

Tax Check-Off

The primary source of funding for Alabama's nongame program, the Tax Check-off, was established in 1982 by constitutional amendment. Funds generated by this mechanism are used primarily for nongame wildlife research and habitat protection. Revenues have declined significantly because of competition from other check-offs on the state income tax return. When the nongame program was the sole option for donations, $67,000 was generated; but with ten other check-off boxes on the form, revenues have declined.

Trust Fund: Oil and Gas Severance Tax

The Alabama Forever Wild Land Trust was established in November 1992 by a constitutional amendment approved by voters. It provides resources for the acquisition of land for wildlife habitat and natural diversity. The trust creates a permanent funding source for the Forever Wild Land Program (FWP), which coordinates land acquisition and stewardship of the state's unique natural resources through the appointed Forever Wild Board. The board has acquired more than 85,000 acres under the program.

Funding for the FWP, which has averaged $8 million to $10 million a year, is derived from 10 percent of the interest income, with a cap of $15 million a year, earned from the Alabama Trust Fund (which itself is generated from the oil and gas royalties within state waters). The amendment has a sunset provision and is set to expire in 2013 if not reauthorized by legislative action. The program leverages $3 million to $4 million a year in federal funds.

Alaska

Duck Stamp Program
The Alaska Duck Stamp Program provides annual funding for wetland acquisition and enhancement projects through the sale of duck stamps and prints to the public. This program, established in state law (AS 16.05.130), directs that money accruing to the state from waterfowl conservation tag fees from hunters may not be diverted to a purpose other than (1) the conservation and enhancement of waterfowl; (2) the acquisition, by lease or otherwise of wetlands that are important for waterfowl and public use of waterfowl in the state; (3) waterfowl-related projects approved by the commissioner; (4) the administration of the waterfowl conservation program; and (5) emergencies in the state as determined by the governor.

King Salmon Stamp Program
The Alaska King Salmon Stamp Program, established in state law at 16.05.340, provides annual funding for management, research, and enhancement of King Salmon in Alaska, through the sale of King Salmon fishing stamps to the public. Salmon stamp funds are often used to match federal funds for fisheries and fish habitat restoration and enhancement.

Fish and Game Fund
Receipts from the sale of Alaska state hunting and fishing licenses are used to fund a variety of conservation projects and initiatives that benefit the sport fisherman or hunter. Authorization for use of these funds is provided at AS 16.05.130: "Money accruing to the state from sport fishing, hunting, and trapping licenses, tags, or permit fees may not be diverted to a purpose other than the protection, propagation, investigation, and restoration of sport fish and game resources and the expenses of administering the sport fish and game divisions of the department." Projects related to fish and fish habitat include purchase of riparian wetlands, evaluation and typing of stream bank habitat, defining in-stream flow requirements, making in-stream flow reservations, and to restore degraded habitat. Wildlife-related projects include controlled burns and physical rehabilitation to improve ungulate and upland game bird habitat. These funds are also usable for the state match of wildlife education–related federal "CARA" funds.

Arizona

Tax Check-Off
The check-off generates approximately $280,000 per year, which goes toward the Arizona Game and Fish Department for nongame program sup-

port. This fund has been declining in the last few years because of competition from other tax check-offs.

Duck Stamp

The Duck Stamp Program generates approximately $100,000–$200,000 per year for wetlands acquisition or enhancement.

Lottery

Arizona Heritage Fund, established in 1990 through voter initiative, initially provided $20 million per year to the Arizona Game and Fish Department and the Arizona State Parks Board from state lottery revenues. In 1996, $3.5 million of this fund was used for habitat acquisition and management. However, lottery revenues have been steadily declining over the last few years, resulting in fewer dollars to fund heritage programs. Anticipated revenues for land acquisition in 2003 are less than $2 million.

Arizona Wildlife Conservation Fund

Established under the Indian Gaming Preservation and Self-Reliance Act of 2002, the Arizona Wildlife Conservation Fund directs 8 percent of funds deposited into the Arizona Benefits Fund (Arizona Benefits Fund revenues are derived from a percentage of the net proceeds of Class III gaming revenues) to Arizona Game and Fish for the conservation, enhancement and restoration of Arizona's wildlife resources and habitats. Funds can be used for land acquisition, and grants may be made to nonprofit organizations as long as reasonable access to the property is provided. The fund is anticipated to generate about $5 million per year for the first several years of the program.

Growing Smarter Grant Program

As part of the Growing Smarter Act, $20 million in grants is available each year until 2011 to acquire or lease state trust lands for conservation, with $2 million reserved for stewardship on ranch and farm land. The Conservation Acquisition Board oversees the grants program and makes grant recommendations to the Arizona State Parks Board for approval. The grants provide 50 percent of the appraised value of the land and associated costs. More than $22 million in grants has been approved over the program's first three years to acquire 2,620 acres, with more than $35 million available.

Water Protection Fund

The Arizona Water Protection Fund was established by the state legislature in 1994 to provide grants to private, local, state, federal, and Indian agencies for the protection and restoration of rivers and streams. The fund is generated by mandated direct appropriations by the legislature of $5 million per year and varying surcharges on sales of Central Arizona Project water to out-of-state utilities. Grants, which have totaled $5.5 million in the past, were zeroed out in the fiscal year 2002 budget but recovered to $2.5 million in the FY 2003 budget.

Arkansas

Real Estate Transfer Tax

At $2.20 per household, the real estate transfer tax generates about $12 million annually for state natural resource agencies other than the Arkansas Game and Fish Commission. The tax also provides monies for funding cultural and historic heritage programs on state-owned lands. The fund is overseen by the Natural and Cultural Resources Council with responsibility for reviewing and approving competitive bids for use of the money.

Sales Tax

A one-eighth-cent sales tax, created by a constitutional amendment, passed twice by voter initiative—once in 1994, but not implemented because of technicalities, and again in November of 1996. The sales tax generates about $32 million in annual revenue that is shared by Arkansas's Game and Fish Commission and Parks and Tourism Commission and by the Department of Arkansas Heritage.

California

Tax Check-Off

The Endangered Species Tax Check-Off generates approximately $1 million annually for the protection of endangered species and their habitat.

Cigarette Tax

The state cigarette tax generates about $400 million per year, of which 5 percent ($20 million) goes to the Public Resources Account for use by the departments of Fish and Game and Parks and Recreation. An additional $10 million per year goes to the Habitat Conservation Fund.

Bond Funds

California voters have approved two park and two water bonds between 2000 and 2002, totaling more than $10 billion.

Proposition 12. Voters approved the $2.1 billion Safe Neighborhood Parks, Clean Water, and Coastal Protection Bond Act of 2000 in March 2000. The money was split between funding for the state ($1.16 billion) to acquire and develop recreational facilities, natural areas, and fish and wildlife habitat; and local governments and nonprofit organizations grants ($940 million), which were geared toward recreation projects, particularly in cities.

Proposition 13. Voters approved the $1.97 billion Safe Drinking Water, Clean Water, Watershed Protection and Flood Protection Act in March 2000. The bond measure supports safe drinking water, flood control, Bay-Delta restoration, watershed protection, and water quality and supply projects.

Proposition 40. Voters approved the California Clean Water, Clean Air, Safe Neighborhood Parks, and Coastal Protection Act of 2002 in March 2002. The measure created $2.6 billion in new state funds for land and water protection.

Proposition 50. Voters approved the bond initiative Water Quality, Supply and Safe Drinking Water Projects. Coastal Wetlands Purchase and Protection in November 2002. It created $3.44 billion in new state funds for water quality, coastal protection, and water management.

Duck Stamp
The Duck Stamp Program has generated nearly $4 million for wetlands restoration.

General Fund, Tax Revenues
1. In 2000, California enacted the Natural Heritage Preservation Tax Credit Act, which allows private landowners to donate land or water rights to state or local agencies or nonprofit organizations for land conservation purposes and receive a tax credit for 55 percent of the value of the donation. The Wildlife Conservation Board awarded more than $40 million in credits in the first few years of the program, which was suspended for the budget year ending June 30, 2003, as part of the state's efforts to tackle its budget shortfall.

2. The California Wildlife Protection Act of 1990 dedicates a portion of tobacco tax monies to several state agencies for programs that protect wetlands, riparian and aquatic habitat, and mountain lion and deer habitat. Funding amount varies each year.

3. The California Farmland Conservancy Program provides grants to local governments, nonprofit groups, and resource conservation districts to conserve farmland through the voluntary acquisition of conservation easements. Propositions 12 and 40 made a total of $100 million available for the program, subject to legislative approval.

4. Through the Coastal Resources Grants program, funding is provided to local cities or counties for planning, mitigation, monitoring, and other activities related to offshore oil development, or to improve management of coastal resources.

Mitigation Monies
The Environmental Enhancement and Mitigation Program was established by the state legislature in 1989 with funding from state gas taxes. It offers $10 million each year in grants to local, state, and federal governmental agencies and to nonprofit organizations for projects to mitigate the environmental impacts caused by new or modified state transportation facilities.

Colorado

Tax Check-Off
The check-off is managed through the Division of Wildlife for nongame management activities.

Lottery Grants—Great Outdoors Colorado
In November 1992, Colorado voters approved the Great Outdoors Colorado (GOCO) Amendment. Under this constitutional amendment, a portion of lottery revenue is earmarked to award grants for parks, wildlife, outdoor recreation, trails, and open space. GOCO's share of lottery proceeds is 50 percent up to $35 million annually adjusted for inflation ($46.5 million in FY 2001/2002). From FY 1994 through April 2003, GOCO has awarded $338 million in grants for more than 1,800 projects.

Native Species Conservation Trust Fund
The Native Species Conservation Trust Fund was established in 1998 with a legislative appropriation of $10 million. The fund awards around $3 million annually and without further appropriations will be spent down by 2005. Funding is distributed by the executive director of the Department of Natural Resources for threatened and endangered species programs.

Connecticut

State Bond Fund
From 1998 to 2003, the Recreation and National Heritage Trust Program has received a total of $105 million. This bond money is used by the state Department of Environmental Protection to purchase additions to state parks and forests.

Matching Grants Program
Established in 1998, this program has received $59 million over five years to provide between matching grants to land trusts, municipalities, and water companies for open space acquisition.

Tax Check-Off
The check-off generates an average of $75,000 annually for endangered species, nongame, and natural area preserve programs.

Delaware

Tax Check-Off
In FY 2002, the check-off generated $27,700 for nongame programs and research.

Bonds for Land Acquisition
A ten-year, $70 million bond to provide monies for land acquisition passed in June 1990. A companion land protection act identifies priority areas for

protection. Debt service on bonds will be provided by any increase in baseline revenues from the Real Estate Transfer Tax. Six million dollars in existing bond spending was authorized for FY 1999 and FY 2000 for the state's Open Space Program.

Real Estate Transfer Tax

Delaware has a $10 million per year dedicated source of funding from its real estate transfer tax for open space, with $9 million for land acquisition and $1 million for land and resource management. Spending sunsets in 2020.

Direct Appropriation

The Open Space Program received direct general fund appropriations—$18 million in FY 1999 and $8 million in FY 2000. The state farmland preservation program received $5 million in FY 2001. The Natural Heritage Program receives $200,000 annually in general fund appropriations.

Florida

Bonds for Conservation and Recreation Land Acquisition, Documentary Stamp Tax

The Preservation 2000 (P2000) Program was created in 1990 and concluded its expenditures in 2001. It was succeeded by the Florida Forever program, and both are funded through the annual sale of bonds to raise $3 billion each over ten years. Florida Forever provides $300 million annually split between several state agencies for the acquisition of conservation and recreation lands, water resource protections, state forests, parks, greenways, trails, and local green space and parks. Funding authorization for P2000 and Florida Forever must go through the legislature every year. The annual bond is derived from revenues from the Documentary Stamp Tax, which is Florida's real estate transfer tax. The tax was increased three times in the 1990s to repay land acquisition bonds and other government services, including beach restoration and low-income housing.

A small amount of revenues derived from the Severance Tax on Phosphate is also contributed to the P2000 and Florida Forever Trust Funds. Of the $300 million in annual expenditures, $105 million of Florida Forever funds are earmarked strictly for the purchase of conservation and natural resource–based recreation lands, and another $105 million is earmarked for acquisition of land and capital projects for water resources.

Georgia

Tax Check-Off

The tax check-off was created in 1989 and yields about $250,000 each year. All revenue is earmarked for the Georgia Nongame Wildlife Conservation and Wildlife Habitat Acquisition Fund, but this income has declined in recent years, from a peak of nearly $500,000 in 1992. This decline can be attributed to competition from the State Human Resources Department's check-off, begun in 1993.

Hunting and Fishing Licenses

Surcharge on hunting and fishing licenses generates up to $400,000 per year and is the primary funding source for the Georgia Department of Natural Resources.

Bonds for Land Acquisition

From 1992 to 1999, Georgia had two land acquisitions programs—Preservation 2000 and River Care 2000—that were fueled by $115 million in bonds that are being paid for by the state's general fund.

Greenspace Program

The Georgia Greenspace Program, created through legislative action in 2000, establishes a framework within which developed and rapidly developing counties, and their municipalities, can preserve community greenspace. It promotes the adoption, by delineated counties and cities, of policies and rules that will enable them to preserve at least 20 percent of their undeveloped land areas and open greenspace, which can be used for informal recreation and natural resource protection. "Greenspace" means permanently protected land and water, including agricultural and forestry land, that is in its undeveloped, natural state or that has been developed only to the extent consistent with, or is restored to be consistent with, one or more listed goals for natural resource protection or informal recreation.

The statute creates a Georgia Greenspace Commission, which reviews and approves community greenspace programs submitted by eligible counties and municipalities. The law also created a Georgia Greenspace Trust Fund, which may include appropriated state funds, federal funds, donated funds, and any interest income. The Department of Natural Resources administers the fund. From FY 2001 through FY 2003, the state appropriated $30 million per year for the program, but the FY 2003 money was rescinded. Legislators cut funding to $10 million in FY 2004 because of budget problems.

Environmental License Plate Sales

Begun by administrative action in 1997, this voluntary license plate sales program generated $6.3 million dollars in its first year of operation. All revenue is earmarked for the Georgia Nongame Wildlife Conservation and Wildlife Habitat Acquisition Fund and is the primary funding source for the state Department of Natural Resources' Wildlife Resources Division.

Hawaii

Real Estate Transfer Tax

In 1993, the Hawaii State Legislature provided $1.2 million to the Natural Area Partnership Program and $500,000 to the Forest Stewardship Program through a 25 percent dedication of the real estate transfer tax. These programs provide matching management funds (2:1 and 1:1, respectively) to landowners who dedicate their important forestlands to conservation. This funding mechanism also provides about $400,000 yearly for landscape conservation management through watershed partnerships of multiple landowners.

Idaho

Hunting License

Revenues from the sale of hunting licenses contribute to the Idaho Fish and Game's Habitat Improvement Program and their habitat acquisition budget. The habitat program receives approximately $600,000 annually and provides technical and financial assistance for projects that improve upland bird and waterfowl habitat on public and private lands. The license revenue used for habitat acquisition is approximately $450,000 annually and goes toward easements and fee title acquisitions that benefit fish and wildlife.

Tax Check-Off

A check-off on state income tax generates between $40,000 and $50,000 for state nongame wildlife programs.

Wildlife License Plate Sales

For an add-on fee to vehicle registration, motorists can purchase a wildlife license plate that contributes to Idaho Department of Fish and Game's nongame wildlife program. The legislature voted to divert some of the revenue from these sales to fund wildlife disease programs and boating access in 2002.

Illinois

Tax Check-Off

Established in 1984, the tax check-off has raised nearly $3 million for the Illinois Natural Heritage Program. Fund revenues have decline in recent years from a yearly peak of $260,000 due to competition from other check-offs on the income tax return.

Real Estate Transfer Tax
This funding mechanism enacted by the legislature in 1989 places a tax of 50 cents per $500 of the property's assessed value. About $60 million is generated annually, with 35 percent ($21 million) earmarked for the Open Space Land Acquisition and Development (OASLAD) Fund to provide local matching grants for the acquisition, development, and rehabilitation of land for public outdoor recreation. Fifteen percent ($9 million) goes to the Natural Areas Acquisition and Management Fund for acquisition and stewardship of lands that are of statewide significance because of high-quality habitat or the presence of endangered or threatened species. In 2002, the Illinois General Assembly cut the formula for distributing the real estate transfer tax for both programs, resulting in a $15 million loss. The original formula was restored for FY 2004.

Bonds for Land Acquisition
In 1995, the Illinois General Assembly unanimously approved a six-year, $100 million program called the Conservation 2000 Initiative to take an ecosystem-level approach to tackle an array of local environmental problems. In August 1999, legislators extended the program until 2009, with $268 million in new funding authorized. The program is designed to take a broad-based, long-term ecosystem approach to conserving, restoring, and managing Illinois's natural lands, soils, and water resources while providing additional high-quality opportunities for outdoor recreation.

Of the first $100 million, 60 percent is allocated from the general fund and is generated by the state's income tax returns; 40 percent is provided by the state's capital budget and is generated through the sale of bonds.

In 1998, the state created the Open Lands Trust, the largest open space acquisition and development program in the state's history. The program authorized $160 million in state general obligation bonds over four years to step up land acquisition to protect more open space and wildlife habitat. It provides funding for state land acquisitions as well as loans and matching grants up to $2 million for local governments. Nonprofit land conservation groups are also eligible.

Indiana

Tax Check-Off
Begun by voter initiative in 1982, the check-off has averaged about $400,000 per year and $7.3 million in total and is the only source of funding for the state's nongame program. The revenues fund endangered species research and land protection.

General Appropriation

The Indiana General Assembly appropriated $17.5 million between 1995 and 2003 for the Indiana Heritage Trust Fund (IHT), the state's only dedicated land acquisition fund. Other funding has come from transfers of $3 million from a special environmental fund and $670,000 from dedicated wetland funds through the Indiana Department of Environmental Management, plus $1.7 million from interest and donations.

Through 2003, nearly 32,000 acres had been purchased through the IHT. Partner contributions of $25 million have been supplemented with $18 million in license plate revenues. The IHT has helped leverage funding from nonstate sources such as businesses, nonprofit organizations, individuals, and federal and local governments. Non-IHT funds have represented 48 percent of the total project costs. Beginning July 1, 1993, legislators cut off annual appropriations to the trust because of budget shortfalls, leaving environmental license plate sales as the sole state financial support for the program.

Environmental License Plate Sales

Proceeds from the sales of the environmental license plates go toward the Indiana Heritage Trust. The plates cost an additional $40, with $15 kept by the Bureau of Motor Vehicles (BMV) for administrative costs. Revenue from plate sales totaled $1.7 million in 2002. Between 1993 and 2002, 709,060 license plates were sold, generating nearly $18 million.

Iowa

Direct Appropriation, Lottery

Resource Enhancement and Protection (REAP) is funded from the state's Environment First Fund (Iowa gaming receipts) and from the sale of natural resource license plates. The program is authorized to receive $20 million per year until 2021, but it has only realized that level of funding in just one year (1991) since its inception in 1989. The state legislature usually appropriates $10 million each year for REAP. Interest from the REAP account and receipts from the sale of natural resource license plates add about $1.0 million to this appropriation for a total of $11 million per year. Legislators zeroed out funding in FY 2003, but restored it for FY 2004. This money goes toward open space, soil and water enhancement, county conservation, city parks, state land management, historical resources, and roadside vegetation.

Tax Check-Off

State residents donate about $135,000 per year to the Wildlife Diversity Program through income tax check-offs.

Wildlife and Duck Stamp Revenue
The Wildlife Habitat Stamp Program generates $600,000 per year and the state Duck Stamp Program generates $150,000 per year.

Kansas

Tax Check-Off
The Kansas "Chickadee Check-Off" generates $120,000 each year dedicated to various nongame wildlife programs administered by the Kansas Department of Wildlife and Parks.

Lifetime Hunting and Fishing Licenses
The Kansas Department of Wildlife and Parks' "Conservation Fund" is derived from the sale of lifetime licenses. Funds are dedicated to land acquisition. The FY 2003 budget for upland habitat acquisition is $500,000; that for wetlands habitat is $350,000.

State Waterfowl Stamp Revenue
Proceeds from the sale of the voluntary state waterfowl stamp are dedicated to wetlands development. The FY 2003 budget is $100,000.

Wildlife Fee Fund
Proceeds from the sale of hunting and fishing licenses fund various programs of the Kansas Department of Wildlife and Parks, some of which have private lands conservation components.

Kentucky

Tax Check-Off
Kentucky's tax check-off raises $70,000 each year for the Nature and Wildlife Fund, with proceeds split equally between the Kentucky Department of Fish and Wildlife Resources and the Kentucky State Nature Preserves Commission. The Nature and Wildlife Fund protects and manages state nature preserves and protects nongame wildlife. The two agencies cooperate on programs that protect rare plants and animals; acquire and protect forests, wetlands, and prairies; and manage wildlife.

Trust Fund: Mineral Tax, Penalties, Environmental License Plate Sales
In 1994, legislators passed enabling legislation for the Kentucky Heritage Land Conservation Fund, which provides a funding mechanism for the Kentucky Heritage Land Conservation Act (1990). Monies are derived from a portion of the unmined mineral tax, funds received from environmental penalties, and the sale of environmental licenses plates. This fund generated $4.1 million in FY 2002.

Louisiana

Tax Check-Off
A state income tax check-off generates $4,300 for the Wildlife Habitat and Natural Heritage Trust Fund, which was established in 1989.

Duck Stamp Fund
The Duck Stamp Fund provided $727,000 in FY 2002 that in part is used to acquire lands for migratory waterfowl habitat.

Trust Fund
Twenty-five percent of the state hunting license fees (about $1 million each year) goes into the Wildlife Habitat and Natural Heritage Trust Fund for land acquisition to preserve critical habitat for wildlife and unique natural areas.

The Wetland Conservation and Restoration Trust Fund, created by constitutional amendment in 1989, generates about $25 million each year in mineral revenues from oil and gas production on state lands to conserve and restore state coastal vegetated wetlands.

Maine

Environmental License Plate Sales
The Loon License Plate Program is a collaborative effort between the Maine Field Office and the Maine Department of Inland Fisheries and Wildlife. This program has generated more than $7 million from 1994 to 2003.

Bonds for Land Acquisition
The Land for Maine's Future Bond, a $35 million bond, was passed in 1987. This money was spent on open space, wildlife, parks, natural areas, endangered species habitat, and exemplary natural communities. In 1998 an additional appropriation of $3 million was made when the original bond was depleted. State voters approved a $50 million bond in 1999 to acquire land and conservation easements.

Lottery
Maine Outdoor Heritage Fund scratch-off ticket revenues are allocated to habitat conservation, land acquisition, and endangered species projects. The state awards about $1.5 million in grants each year. Between 1996 and 2002 more than $10 million in grant money was awarded for 365 projects. Slowing lottery sales in 2003 reduced grants by more than half for the year.

Affinity Card
An Affinity credit card was issued in 1996. By 2003 it had generated $336,000 for the Land for Maine's Future Program.

Endangered and Nongame Wildlife Fund

Maine taxpayers have the option of using what is called the Chickadee Check-Off to voluntarily contribute to the Nongame and Endangered Wildlife Fund when they fill out their annual tax form. From 1984 through 2001, taxpayers have contributed $1.5 million to the Nongame and Endangered Wildlife Fund.

Maryland

Environmental License Plate Sales

Maryland created a "Treasure the Chesapeake" license plate in 1990 that generated $567,828 in FY 2002. The money is distributed in grants by the Chesapeake Bay Trust.

Real Estate Transfer Tax

Program Open Space (POS) is the principal land acquisition and park development program for Maryland. Created in 1969, POS is funded by a 0.5 percent tax on real estate transfers, which generally brings in over $100 million a year. Administered by the Department of Natural Resources, POS funds are used for agricultural land preservation, protection of rare plant and animal habitat, local park acquisition, and other open space needs. Although POS is funded by a dedicated source, the distribution of the transfer tax revenue must go through the budget process each fiscal year. In FY 2003, half of the transfer tax revenue ($65 million) was diverted to the general fund to help balance the budget, and half of the FY 2004 revenue will be diverted as well.

General Obligation Bonds, Program Open Space Funds

The Rural Legacy Program was created in 1997 as part of then-governor Glendening's Smart Growth and Neighborhood Conservation Initiative. The program encourages local governments and private land trusts to identify Rural Legacy Areas (large intact landscapes of agricultural or forest land) in need of preservation and apply, through a competitive process, for funds to secure easements or fee-simple ownership of properties within these areas. Funding for Rural Legacy comes from Program Open Space (POS) funds and general obligation bonds. For FY 2003, the General Assembly authorized $15 million in general obligation bonds for Rural Legacy, in addition to $6.4 million from POS. During the period from FY 1998 to FY 2003, Rural Legacy received over $130 million in funding.

General Obligation Bonds, General Fund

Former Governor Glendening proposed in his FY 2002 budget a new program called GreenPrint to protect lands within the state's green infrastructure. The green infrastructure is a system of large intact natural areas and greenways, identified by the Maryland Department of Natural Resources, that will form the basis of much of the state's open space protection efforts for the foreseeable future. Glendening originally proposed spending $145 million over five years to support GreenPrint. The program received $51 million over its first two years, with $26 million in FY 2002 and $12 million in FY 2003 from general obligation bonds.

Agricultural Transfer Tax

Maryland charges a transfer tax on any agriculturally assessed land that is converted to another use, such as residential or commercial development. The transfer tax is assessed at settlement and can be as much as 5 percent of the purchase price, depending on the acreage. The agricultural transfer tax revenues go to the Maryland Agricultural Land Preservation Foundation (MALPF) for the purchase of agricultural easements. MALPF also gets funding from Program Open Space and the new GreenPrint Program. The amount of money generated by this transfer tax generally varies between $2 million to $3 million annually. For FY 2003, half of the agricultural transfer tax revenue was diverted to the general fund.

Tax Check-Off

Funding from the voluntary income tax check-off supports the Maryland Department of Natural Resources Wildlife and Heritage Program and the Chesapeake Bay Trust. In FY 2002, the check-off generated $1.1 million, which was split evenly between the two recipients. The funds going to Wildlife and Heritage are used for Natural Heritage Program operations. The Chesapeake Bay Trust uses their portion of the funding, combined with revenue from license tags, to provide grants to nonprofit organizations and government agencies in support of such activities as trail development, wildlife habitat enhancement, and Chesapeake Bay restoration. The trust disbursed $970,000 in grants over FY 2001.

Maryland Environmental Trust

The Maryland Environmental Trust (MET) is a state-sponsored land trust that holds conservation easements across the state to protect environmental values such as wildlife habitat and open space. MET has a revolving loan fund available for local land trusts for no-interest loans for fee-simple or easement purchases. In addition, MET provides a small grants program for local land trusts to provide funding for operating expenses and special projects.

Massachusetts

Wildlife Stamps, Hunting and Fishing Licenses

The Wildlands Acquisition Account is used to purchase land for wildlife habitat. Monies for this account come from the sale of wildlife stamps, hunting and fishing licenses, and other sources. This fund receives approximately $1.5 million annually.

State Operating Funds

The Massachusetts Legislature has appropriated operating funds for specific land acquisition projects at various times, depending on legislator/agency lobbying and availability or surplus tax revenue (lucrative in the late 1990s, and dropping quickly)

State Capital Funds

The Massachusetts Legislature has approved bond expenditures for environmental programs, including open space acquisition, in 1982, 1983, 1987, 1992, 1994, 1996, and 2000, and 2002. The Massachusetts Executive Office of Environmental Affairs (EOEA) had approximately $1 billion in authorized-but-unissued capital funding projects in 2003. EOEA's share of the state's overall bond spending cap has fluctuated from $65 million in FY 1993 (major state recession) to $132 million in FY 1996; generally, environmental programs account for approximately 10 percent of overall state capital spending. Between 1991 and 2003, state open space capital expenditures have been $30 million to $50 million annually.

Fish and Game Fund

The Massachusetts Inland Fish and Game Fund reinvests license fees for hunting, fishing, and trapping collected through the Wetlands Stamp Program (1990) for the Division of Fisheries and Wildlife's habitat acquisition.

Forest and Park Entrance Fees

The Department of Environmental Management's Second Century Fund (1996) collects forest and park entrance fees, camping fees, and special use charges, which are reinvested for improvements to state forest and parks system. The fees generate over $4 million annually, of which $2.3 million was authorized for spending in FY 2003 on the state forest and parks systems.

Land Acquisition Fund

The Department of Environmental Management's Land Acquisition Fund, established in 1994, collects 1 percent of the gross annual revenues from the Wachusett Mountain Ski Area, a private ski resort operating on state land, and reinvests receipts for land acquisition.

Real Estate Property Levy and Sales

The Commonwealth of Massachusetts has a proud and rich tradition of home-rule authority. In keeping with this heritage, the state has passed a number of home-rule bills to acquire open space.

The Community Preservation Act (2000) enables any municipality to impose a surcharge of up to 3 percent on local real property levies. In return, communities will receive state matching funds derived from a $20 surcharge on all recorded instruments at registries of deeds and land courts. The state revenue source raises $26 million annually. Funds are split between open space protection, affordable housing, and historic preservation.

The Cape Cod Land Bank (1998) enables the fifteen municipalities of Barnstable County (Cape Cod) to impose a surcharge of 3 percent on local real property levies. In return, communities received a total of $14.2 million in state matching funds during the first three years of the program, which were derived from state operating funds deposited in a trust in the state treasurer's office. Funds may be used for open space and aquifer protection.

The Nantucket Island Land Bank (1984) and Martha's Vineyard Island Land Bank (1986) enable Nantucket and Martha's Vineyard Islands to impose a transaction fee of up to 2 percent on real estate sales for open space acquisition.

Bonds for Land Acquisition

The Open Space Bond Bill, a program to protect and preserve Massachusetts's open space and critical water resources, authorized $399 million and was approved on in 1996. It included money for habitat restoration only on lands in which the state holds an interest, but where private groups can do the restoration work. The money is allocated in small amounts because of overall caps on capital spending and bonding.

Michigan

Tax Check-Off, Environmental License Plate Sales

The income tax check-off was established in 1983 and has generated more than $10 million ($600,000 annually) for the Nongame Wildlife Fund before it was ended in 2000. The fund supports projects that help endangered, threatened, and nongame animals, plants, and their habitats. In 2001, the state established an environmental license plate program, which raised $223,000 the first year for the fund.

Trust Fund: State Oil and Gas Revenues

Since 1976, the Michigan Natural Resources Trust Fund has provided financial assistance to local governments and the state Department of Natural Resources to purchase lands for outdoor recreation and/or the protection of natural resources and open space. It also assists in the appropriate development of land for public outdoor recreation. Money for the act is generated by the collection of oil and gas lease revenues, which produced $33.4 million in FY 2002. The fund has a $500 million cap, but has only reached $194 million as of September 30, 2002. Interest earnings from the fund, which totaled $14.5 million in FY 2002, plus one-third of the mineral revenues, which came to $11.1 million in FY 2002, is available for acquisition and development projects and program administration. The state legislature provides appropriations for projects each year that are recommended by a trust fund board. Nearly $600 million in appropriations from the fund have been made for more than 1,200 projects.

Property Tax Incentives, Penalty Fees
A state property tax incentive program—P.A. 116, the Farmland and Open Space Preservation Act—gives tax breaks to landowners who enroll their farmland in the program. When a party leaves the program or withdraws prior to expiration, repayment of tax credits received during the last seven years under the agreement is required. The program takes in $2 million a year for conservation purposes, including purchase of development rights on farmland. In 2000, state legislators overhauled the program to become a state grant program to localities that can use the money for purchase of development rights.

Bonds
In 1998, state voters approved a bond measure that included $50 million for parks and recreation.

Minnesota

Tax Check-Off
This check-off raises about $1.1 million annually for the Minnesota Department of Natural Resources Nongame Wildlife Program.

Hunting and Fishing Licenses
Revenue from hunting and fishing licenses, which totals about $120 million per biennium, goes into the Game and Fish Fund. The monies fund mostly game programs, but some of it goes to habitat stewardship, environmental review, enforcement, and trails.

Conservation License Plate Sales
Legislation establishing the conservation license plate program passed in the 1995 session, and the license plates were first sold in 1996. Proceeds amount to nearly $2 million annually and are directed as a public match to private donations of land and cash to the outdoor recreation system. Proceeds are used to acquire critical habitat.

Lottery
In 1988, voters approved two constitutional amendments that created the Environmental and Natural Resources Trust Fund and established the Minnesota Lottery. Forty percent of net state lottery proceeds are deposited to the trust fund (approximately $25 million annually). As of 2002 the fund totaled nearly $300 million. It is hoped the fund will reach $1 billion by

2025. Trust fund appropriations are intended for projects with long-term benefits—i.e., land acquisitions, biodiversity surveys, and innovative community-based conservation projects.

Bonds for Land Acquisition
The legislature approves capital budget projects, including selling bonds for land acquisition. Nearly $1 billion was appropriated for land acquisition and restoration between FY 1971 and FY 2001.

Sales Tax
In 2000, conservation advocates were successful in redirecting a sales tax on lottery tickets ("lottery-in-lieu") toward wildlife, state/metro parks, and zoo projects, for a total of $44 million per biennium. The sales tax on lottery tickets was enacted in the early 1990s to compensate for state budget shortfalls and had the effect of reducing deposits to the Environment and Natural Resources Trust Fund. The new "Heritage Fund" is appropriated annually, usually to one-time projects, by the legislature based on recommendations from the Department of Natural Resources.

Cigarette Taxes
A 2-cents-per-pack cigarette tax goes toward the Minnesota Future Resources Fund. The tax yields $7 million annually and is appropriated at the same time as Environment and Natural Resources Trust Fund earnings. Monies are used only to "accelerate" outdoor recreation programs, including land acquisition, but primarily parks and trails development. To address a budget shortfall, lawmakers diverted the cigarette tax to the general fund for the FY 2003–2005 biennium.

Mississippi

Tradelands/Tideland Leases, the Coastal Preserve Program
The Coastal Preserve Program is a partnership between The Nature Conservancy, the Office of the Secretary of State, and the Mississippi Department of Marine Resources focusing on coastal marsh and buffer land acquisition. Funds are generated from tradelands and tideland leases that casinos have provided on the coast, as well as state Department of Environmental Quality and U.S. Environmental Protection Agency grants and other grant funds obtained by the Coastal Preserve Program of the Mississippi Department of Marine Resources.

Environmental License Plate Sales
In FY 2001–2002, the state environmental license plates generated $832,380 for the Wildlife Heritage Fund.

Tax Check-Off
The state income tax check-off, created in 1985, generates $30,000 annually for the Wildlife Heritage Fund.

Missouri

Sales Tax
The State Parks/Clean Water Initiative, first approved in 1984 by voter initiative, provides $54 million through a one-half percent sales tax evenly split between State Parks and Soil Conservation Districts. In 1976, Missouri voters approved a statewide referendum called Design for Conservation. It included a permanent provision providing a one-eighth percent sales tax for the Missouri Department of Conservation (MDC) for conservation activities. Since then, MDC officials have spent more than $2 billion acquiring 774,000 acres, as well as starting programs and building infrastructure, giving Missouri the nation's third largest conservation budget per capita.

Montana

Hunting and Fishing Licenses and Fees
The Habitat Montana Program consists of five programs (including the mitigation program mentioned immediately following) that together generate more than $4 million each year to preserve land and water habitat. Funding comes from hunting licenses, duck stamp sales, and auctions of hunting permits for moose and bighorn sheep. The revenue can be used for outright purchase of land, but the state has primarily used the money to purchase conservation easements.

Mitigation
A $13 million mitigation fund established by the Bonneville Power Administration (BPA) in 1987, after BPA built dams in the Kootenay and Flathead Rivers for drainage, generates from $500,000 to $800,000 per year for the protection of wetlands and habitat for certain species.

Nebraska

Tax Check-off
About $50,000 from the state income tax check-off goes toward the Nongame and Endangered Species Conservation Act. This act authorizes habitat acquisition for species conservation.

Lottery
State legislators created the Nebraska Environmental Trust in 1992, which is funded by 49.5 percent of state lottery profits. The program generates

roughly $8.5 million in grant money each year for habitat, surface and ground water quality, waste reduction, and carbon management.

Nevada

Bonds for Land Acquisition, Capital Improvement, Planning, and Wildlife Protection

In 1990, Nevada voters approved the Nevada Parks and Wildlife Bond Act, which provided $47.2 million for the state divisions of wildlife and state parks for land and water right acquisitions and capital improvements at existing state facilities. Funds were also allocated to Clark County ($13 million) and Washoe County ($6 million) to assist those local communities in their open space planning and land acquisition needs.

In November 2002, state voters approved a $200 million bond measure to preserve water quality and protect wildlife habitat, open space, and historic and cultural resources. Included is $54.5 million for land acquisition and development at state parks and wildlife areas and $65.5 million in grants for state agencies, local governments, or qualifying private nonprofit organizations for various programs, including recreational trails, urban parks, habitat conservation, open spaces, and general natural resource protection projects.

Mitigation

Mitigation fees are collected by the California and Nevada Tahoe Regional Planning Agency to purchase conservation easements through the Tahoe Mitigation Program.

New Hampshire

Environmental License Plate Sales

Since 2000, the state's moose plate has raised $1.1 million for a variety of programs, including the Land and Community Heritage Investment Program, which offers communities grants for local conservation projects.

Migratory Waterfowl Stamp

The state Migratory Waterfowl Stamp Program generates monies for the acquisition of migratory waterfowl habitat.

Drinking Water Supply Land Grant Program

The state Department of Environmental Services provides up to 25 percent of the cost to acquire lands or protective easements for lands around public sources of drinking water to ensure the long-term protection of water quality. Current funding level is $1.5 million per year.

Land and Community Heritage Investment Program (LCHIP)
The LCHIP program, created in 2000, had by February 2003 invested $15 million to protect 28,102 acres and preserve and restore eighty-three historic structures. The program needs additional appropriations to continue its grant program.

New Jersey

Bonds for Land Acquisition
New Jersey voters approved nine Green Acres Bond Acts between 1961 and 1999, which provided a total of $1.4 billion dollars for open space and farmland preservation. In addition, in November 1998, New Jersey voters approved Public Question #1, which created a long-term stable source of future Green Acres funding by amending the state constitution to dedicate $98 million from existing sales tax revenues each year for the next thirty years, for a total of almost $3 billion in dedicated funds. This revenue stream will be used to support the issuance of revenue bonds and provide some "pay as you go" cash to continue the Green Acres and Farmland Preservation land acquisition programs. This measure is expected to provide more than $1.85 billion in bond revenues and cash payments for land acquisition over the next thirty years, with the balance of the dedicated revenues used to pay the debt service on the bonds.

State Income Tax Deduction
New Jersey allows an income tax deduction for donations or bargain sales of land for conservation purposes.

County and Local Dedicated Taxes
Twenty of New Jersey's twenty-one counties and 187 of its 566 municipalities have local dedicated taxes for open space purposes.

New Mexico

Tax Check-Off
The check-off generates over $30,000 a year, with the monies used for nongame wildlife programs.

Hunting Licenses
The Document Stamp Program, including hunting licenses, generates over $12 million annually. A portion of this money is dedicated to land acquisition.

New York

General Fund Appropriations
For FY 2002–2003, New York budgeted $1.4 billion on the environment. This includes the just over $125 million in non-general-fund appropriations below, and other non-general-fund programs.

Tax Check-Off
This check-off generates $1 million annually. One-fourth is allocated to the New York Natural Heritage Program.

Environmental License Plate Sales
Begun in January of 1996, all proceeds are dedicated to the state's Environmental Protection Fund (see immediately following) for projects that include open space protection. The license plate program generates about $100,000 annually.

Real Estate Tax
New York law dedicates $125 million annually from real estate transfer taxes to the Environmental Protection Fund, a dedicated fund established in 1993. The fund is used to support open space, parks, and solid waste management programs. Approximately $50 million is available for the fund annually for open space and farmland protection, and another $30 million for related programs. In FY 2002–2003 the state removed $235 million from this fund to provide emergency budget relief to the general fund.

State Bonds for Land Acquisition
In 1996, voters approved the $1.75 billion Clean Water, Clean Air Bond Act, which included approximately $150 million for land acquisition. Funds from these and previous bond acts had been spent or committed by 2002.

Local and County Bonds for Land Acquisition
In November 2002, ten communities approved municipal open space and community preservation funding mechanisms worth about $346.5 million. For 2002, twelve of thirteen local initiatives were approved providing about $364.5 million.

North Carolina

General Fund Appropriations
The North Carolina General Assembly appropriated $66.5 million to the Clean Water Management Trust Fund in FY 2002–2003. State legislators created the trust fund in 1996 to give grants to local governments, conservation nonprofit groups, and state agencies to finance projects to protect or restore water quality in the state's seventeen river systems. At the end of each fiscal year, 6.5 percent of the unreserved credit balance in the state's general fund (or a minimum of $30 million) goes into the trust fund. Between 1996 and 2003, the fund awarded 407 grants totaling $320 million, leveraging $533 million from other sources. The trust has helped protect 207,779 acres and 2,457 miles of buffers.

Legislators have appropriated $2.64 million for the state's Farmland Preservation Trust Fund between 1998 and 2003, leveraging more than $25 million in federal and other sources. Funding dropped to $200,000 annually in FY 2001–2002 and FY 2002–2003 because of budget shortfalls.

Tax Check-Off
Revenues go to the NC Wildlife Resources commission for nongame programs.

Personalized License Plate Sales
The sale of these license plates generates approximately $1.7 million annually for the Natural Heritage Trust Fund, which state legislators created in 1987 to provide grants to state agencies for land acquisition for parks, preserves, wildlife conservation areas, historic site properties, and other areas.

Conservation Tax Credit
A credit is allowed against individual or corporate income taxes when real property is donated for conservation purposes. Tax credit allowed equals 25 percent of the fair market value of the donated property interest, up to a maximum of $250,000 for individuals and $500,000 for corporations. Unused credit can be carried forward for five succeeding years.

Real Estate Transfer Tax
Of every $2.00 generated from the real estate transfer tax, $1.00 goes to conservation, the other to local governments. Of the "conservation dollar," 75 cents goes to the Parks and Recreation Trust Fund, which legislators created in 1993, to fund land acquisition, capital improvements, local park projects, and public beach access. The remaining 25 cents goes to the Natural Heritage Trust Fund, used primarily for land acquisition. Most of the Natural Heritage Trust Fund supports protection of natural areas; a small portion is used for cultural preservation. License plate sales and real estate transfer taxes generate $12 million each year that is available for funding.

North Dakota

Direct Appropriation
The state legislature appropriated $8 million to the Private Lands Initiative Program for the FY 2003–2005 biennium. The program has three goals: (1) conservation for habitats for fish and wildlife populations, (2) cost-share assistance to landowners interested in wildlife conservation for developing and protecting wildlife habitats, and (3) access to private land for hunting.

Ohio

Tax Check-Off
The Natural Areas/Scenic Rivers Check-off was established in 1984 to provide funds for the Division of Natural Areas and Preserves, which is housed

in the Ohio Department of Natural Resources (ODNR). In 2002, 114,400 Ohioans contributed a total of $821,226 to these funds: $442,936 for natural areas and preserves and $378,290 for wildlife habitat and endangered species protection. The ODNR Division of Natural Areas and Preserves uses tax check-off funds solely for land acquisition, new facility development, and special projects at Ohio's state nature preserves and state scenic river segments.

Wildlife Habitat Stamps, Hunting and Fishing Licenses
In 2000, the Division of Wildlife received $28.5 million from the sale of hunting and fishing licenses and game permits, most of which was used for operations. The sale of Wetland Habitat Stamps generated $385,121 in 2000 for the Division of Wildlife.

Environmental License Plate Sales
Ohio has four license plate programs that generate resources for natural resource protection. The Lake Erie License Plate Program, the oldest of the four, provides monies toward the Lake Erie Protection Fund for water quality monitoring and shore protection. The program is run by the Lake Erie Commission and from 1993 to 2003 generated $8.2 million in grant money. The Scenic Rivers License Plate Program and the Wildlife License Plate Program are part of the Diversity and Endangered Species Fund run by the Division of Wildlife, which includes income tax and plate sale profits. Sales of 58,053 Wildlife License Plates in 2002 generated $870,795 for the fund. Between 1995 and 2002 sales of 77,000 Scenic Rivers License Plates garnered $1.2 million for the ODNR's Scenic Rivers Protection Fund. The newest license plate option is the Bald Eagle plate, created in 1999 to benefit the ODNR's management program for the endangered bird. From 1999 to 2002, sales of 41,000 plates generated more than $600,000.

Bonds for Land Acquisition
The $200 million NatureWorks bond issue, passed by voters in November 1993, funds annual grants for major renovations and improvements for Ohio's state and local parks, state forests, nature preserves, wildlife areas, and other natural resources facilities. From 1995 through 2003, the program awarded more than $55 million in grants, which require a 25 percent match with local funds. In 2003, the program awarded 104 grants totaling $3.43 million.

Clean Ohio Fund
Voters approved a $400 million, four-year statewide bond measure passed in November of 2000 for various environmental purposes: $200 million for brownfield revitalization, $150 million for greenspace and stream preservation, $25 million for farmland preservation, and $25 million for multiuse

trail creation. Applicants for the bond funds may be local government or nonprofit entities whose mission coincides with the application request. Applicants must provide a 25 percent local funding match, which can be in-kind services.

Oklahoma

Tax Check-Off
Money from the check-off goes to the Wildlife Diversity Program. FY 2002 sales were $164,425.

Hunting and Fishing Licenses
The state received more than $10.9 million in FY 2002 in hunting and fishing license revenue, which is used for wildlife conservation programs.

Wildlife Conservation License Plate Sales
In FY 2002, $143,000 was raised through license plate sales, which went to the Wildlife Diversity Program.

Oregon

Tax Check-Off
Established by voter initiative in 1979, the tax check-off was one of the first in the nation. Money goes to the Wildlife Diversity Program in the Habitat Conservation Division of the Oregon Department of Fish and Wildlife. Check-off revenues have declined from $350,000 at their inception because of increased competition from other check-offs to $135,000 from 2000–2002.

Interest Income
A unique source of funding for the Wildlife Diversity Program, implemented by legislative action in 1989, is a provision that provides the program with 50 percent of the interest from the department's checking account. The revenue from this mechanism has fluctuated greatly, with an average yield of $125,000.

License Surcharges
A $2 surcharge on hunting licenses, authorized by the state legislature in 1993, generates $550,000 a year for the Access and Habitat Program. This program, administered by a seven-member governing board, funds habitat restoration projects through grants. Varying surcharges on sport fishing licenses, commercial fishery permits, and commercial salmon poundage fees, authorized by the legislature in 1989, generate $1.7 million yearly for the Fisheries Restoration and Enhancement Fund. This fund, administered by an appointed board, funds projects to restore fisheries and their habitat through grants.

Lottery
Fifteen percent of Oregon's lottery profits are split evenly each year ($50 million each) between Oregon Parks and Recreation, which buys, maintains, and restores parks at the state and local level, and the state Watershed Enhancement Board, which devotes 65 percent of its share to capital projects that restore salmon habitat.

Migratory Waterfowl, Upland Bird, and Nonresident Game Bird Stamps
The Migratory Waterfowl (begun in 1983), the Upland Bird (begun in 1990), and the Nonresident Game Bird Stamps are $5 document stamps purchased in conjunction with sport licenses. Collectively and including the sale of associated artwork, they generated $651,168 in 2002. Monies from the stamps are distributed by the Oregon Wetlands Joint Venture, a coalition of conservation groups.

Pennsylvania

Tax Check-Off
The Wild Resource Conservation Fund tax check-off has generated $6.2 million over twenty years, but annual revenue has declined from a high of more than $600,000 annually to $140,000 in 2002 because of increased competition from other check-offs.

Direct Appropriation
In 1999, legislators approved a $645 million "Growing Greener" program, a proposed five-year environmental plan. Legislators intended to fund the program at about $130 million each year, with funding coming from the General Fund, Recycling and Hazardous Sites Cleanup fund, and landfill closure accounts. In 2002, the legislature extended the program for ten years, with funding coming mostly from a $4.25 per ton tipping fee on solid waste disposed in municipal waste landfills. The new funding is expected to be $100 million a year for parks, open space and watershed protection, acid mine drainage cleanup, and water and sewer infrastructure.

Hunting and Fishing Licenses
The money generated through fishing and hunting fees is allocated to their respective commissions for the management of game species. A small portion goes toward the nongame program.

Environmental License Plate Sales
In 1995, $3 million was generated from the sale of license plates for the Wildlife Resources Conservation Fund. In 2002, plate sales had declined to $40,000.

Real Estate Transfer Tax
Of the state share of the real estate transfer tax revenues, 15 percent is designated for the Keystone Recreation Park and Conservation Fund. Of that amount, approximately $38 million is allocated to the Department of Conservation and Natural Resources for projects on state park and forest land, grants to local governments for recreation development and acquisition projects, as well as grants to land trusts and conservancies.

Bonds for Land Acquisition
The Key 93 initiative provided a total of $50 million in bonds over three years for land acquisition, improvement and rehabilitation of parks, recreation facilities, educational facilities, historic sites, zoos, and public libraries.

Cigarette Taxes
Each year, about 6.5 percent of state cigarette tax goes into the Farmland Purchase of Development Rights Program. The program raises about $20 million yearly.

Rhode Island

Bond for Open Space
A 2000 bond initiative provides $34 million over five years for open space and recreational development. Of the $34 million, $23.5 million is allocated for state and local open space preservation, including preservation of habitat, farmland, forest, greenways and protection of public drinking water supplies; $10.5 million is allocated for development of recreational facilities and parks. A 1998 bond initiative provided $15 million for acquisition of open space, protection of greenways and development of bike paths.

South Carolina

Tax Check-Off
Monies from this check-off go to the Nongame Wildlife and Natural Areas Fund. The check-off generates about $80,000 annually for the fund.

State Appropriations
The Heritage Trust Program had been receiving a state appropriation of $500,000 annually, but budget cuts dropped funding to $300,000 in FY 2002–2003. Legislators also appropriate money for special acquisitions occasionally.

Real Estate Transfer Tax
The state Heritage Land Trust Fund receives $3.2 million annually from a portion of the state's real estate transfer tax: 20 cents per $1,000. The fund

has protected 60,000 acres of endangered species habitat through acquisition of land and conservation easements.

Environmental License Plate Sales
The sale of these endangered species license plates generates about $50,000 annually for wildlife management and conservation.

Conservation Incentives Act
This law provides a state income tax credit for voluntary donations of land for conservation easements.

Conservation Bank Act
Beginning in July of 2004, a portion of the real estate transfer fee ($9 million per year after phase-in) will fund grants and loans to acquire parks, endangered species habitat, farmland, open space, and other lands through the purchase of land and conservation easements.

South Dakota

Hunting and Fishing Licenses
In FY 2002, hunting and fishing license revenues totaled $21.6 million, some of which goes toward habitat conservation.

Tennessee

Hunting and Fishing Licenses
The sale of fishing and hunting licenses generates about $8 million annually. All of these monies are used for conservation.

Real Estate Transfer Tax
The state of Tennessee uses 17.6 percent of its real estate transfer tax of 37 cents per $100 to fund three land protection programs. Of the 37 cents, 3.25 cents (about $7 million annually) goes to the Tennessee Wildlife Resources Agency's Wetland Acquisition Fund for acquisition and maintenance of wetlands and easements, 1.75 cents (about $3.5 million annually) goes to the Local Parks Land Acquisition Fund for matching grants to cities and counties to buy and develop parks, trails, natural areas, and greenways. An additional 1.5 cents (about $3 million annually) goes to the State Lands Acquisition Fund, which funds the acquisition of land and easements for state parks, state forests, state natural areas, boundary areas along state scenic rivers, and the state's trail system.

Natural Resources Trust Fund
Interest from the revenue acquired from the sale of state lands, which is deposited in the Natural Resources Trust Fund, is spent on state and local

recreation grants. In 2003, about $1 million in the fund was earmarked for use on the Cumberland Trail.

License Plate Program

Tennessee has four specialty license plates that generate money for conservation. The Watchable Wildlife plate raises $410,000 each year for the Watchable Wildlife Endowment Fund that preserves nongame and endangered wildlife species. The Sportsman plate produces $165,000 yearly for the Sportsmen's Wildlife Foundation to protect, propagate, and conserve game species. The Fish and Wildlife Series plates produce $160,000 a year for the wildlife resources fund to protect fish and wildlife species and their habitat. The Radnor Lake plate generates $70,000 annually for the state lands acquisition fund.

Texas

Document Stamp

Document stamp revenues from the sale of hunting and fishing licenses generated about $48 million in 1995.

Sporting Goods Tax

The sporting goods tax is a major source of funding for conservation measures in the state. The tax generates more than $90 million each year, of which a maximum of $32 million can be appropriated by state legislators for state and local parks. Traditionally, $15.5 million goes to the State Parks Fund and $15.5 million to local government entities for matching grants for local parks. The remaining $1 million goes to the parks capital account. For FY 2004 and FY 2005, lawmakers cut the local park appropriation to $8 million each year. From FY 2001 through FY 2005, legislators agreed to boost local park grants by $4 million to $5 million.

License Plate Program

The state offers five license plates that have raised more than $1 million for fish and wildlife conservation and state parks between 1999 and 2003, including the horned lizard and bluebonnet plates that depict the state reptile and state flower, respectively.

Utah

Tax Check-Off

The check-off generates over $48,000 per year for the Utah Division of Wildlife Resources to support nongame programs.

Environmental License Plate Sales

The sale of environmental license plates generated over $140,000 in FY 2002 for programs of the Division of Wildlife.

Hunting and Fishing Licenses
These licenses raise over $2 million each year for the Habitat Council's work with easements and habitat restoration,

Conservation Grants
The LeRay McAllister Critical Land Conservation Fund, created in 1999 by the Quality Growth Act, provides matching grants and loans to local governments, private individuals, and nonprofit organizations to preserve or restore critical open or agricultural land in Utah. Legislators approved $2.75 million in funding annually for the first three years of the program, but budget constraints reduced appropriations to $486,200 for FY 2003 and FY 2004. From 1999 through 2002, $8.8 million in state grants have leveraged $43.4 million to preserve 33,553 acres.

State Appropriations
State legislators also appropriated $250,000 from FY 1999 to FY 2003 that the state Department of Agriculture used to purchase easements on farmland. The funding was cut off after FY 2003 because of budget problems.

The state direct appropriation is a general fund appropriation of $80,000 a year that goes toward the Utah Division of Wildlife Resources for Heritage Program.

Vermont

Tax Check-Off
This check-off generated about $141,390 in 2002. The money goes toward the Nongame and Natural Heritage Program.

Conservation License Plate Sales
Conservation license plates generated $180,290, split evenly between the watershed program and the Nongame and Natural Heritage Program in 2002.

Real Estate Transfer Tax
Since 1988, roughly half of the state property transfer tax collected each year ($11 million) has funded the Vermont Housing and Conservation Board (VHCB), which makes grants to support conservation and affordable housing. About 43 percent of the VHCB money since 1998 has been awarded in grants to state and local governments and nonprofit groups for purchase of natural areas and easements on farmland.

Direct Appropriation
In some years, the legislature makes direct appropriations in support of VHCB land conservation programs, including $4.5 million in 1999 for a special appropriation.

Virginia

Tax Check-Off
For FY 2002, the income tax check-off for the Virginia Nongame Wildlife Program raised $188,000; the Virginia Open Space, Recreation and Conservation Fund raised $69,000; and the Chesapeake Bay Restoration raised $382,000.

Virginia Land Conservation Foundation
The Virginia Land Conservation Foundation (VLCF), established in 1999, received appropriations of $1.75 million in FY 1999 and $6.2 million in FY 2000, before legislators zeroed out funding beginning in FY 2001 because of budget problems. Under a statutory formula, any money received by the foundation is divided as follows: 25 percent to the Virginia Outdoors Foundation (which protects mostly farmland) and 75 percent divided equally between natural area protection, open space and parks, farmland and forest production, and historic area preservation.

Motor Vehicle Registration Fee
In 2002, legislators approved a bill that allows the Department of Motor Vehicles to impose a $2 "opt-out" fee to generate $5 million for the 2007 anniversary of the Jamestown settlement. If everyone pays the fee, it will generate $15 million per year. All of the money generated above $5 million will go to the VLCF.

Bonds for Land Acquisition
In November 2002, voters approved general obligation bonds for parks and natural areas that included $13.2 million for natural area land acquisition and $22.5 million for state parkland acquisition. Also in 2002, the General Assembly directed the Virginia Public Building Authority to issue $20 million in bonds for Department of Conservation and Recreation land acquisition. About one-third of this amount is slated to be spent on natural area acquisition. The rest will be used to purchase land for state parks.

Washington

Real Estate Transfer Tax
A two-year transfer tax was enacted in 1987. This tax generated $18 million in the two years it was in existence and was used to acquire land for natural area preserves, natural area preserves, natural resources conservation areas, and other conservation programs. In 1990 county governments were authorized, with the approval of the majority of voters in the county, to impose a 1 percent tax on the sale price of real property. The proceeds of the tax are to be used for acquisition and maintenance of conservation areas. One of the thirty-nine counties (San Juan) has imposed this tax.

Direct Appropriation

The legislature established the Trust Land Transfer Program in 1989 to address the management of state school trust lands by the Department of Natural Resources (DNR). For the FY 2001–2003 biennium, DNR received a capital budget appropriation of $50 million for the program. From 1989 to 2003, the legislature has appropriated more than $420 million under this program, which has allowed the legislature to transfer over 70,000 acres of ecologically valuable land out of the timber harvest revenue producing school trust and into protected status.

In 1990, the legislature established the Washington Wildlife and Recreation Program to fund the acquisition of lands for wildlife conservation and outdoor recreation and to provide recreation facilities. From 1990 to 2003, the legislature has appropriated more than $360 million, funding over 600 projects ranging from critical habitat, natural areas, and urban wildlife habitat, to local parks, state parks, trails, and water access sites.

In 1999, the legislature created the Washington Salmon Recovery Funding Board to guide spending of state and federal appropriated funds for state and local salmon habitat protection and restoration projects. Since its inception, the board has distributed $45 million to a total of 231 projects. In 2001, another $56 million was appropriated for grants in the FY 2001–2003 biennium.

The Washington Natural Heritage Program is part of the Washington Department of Natural Resources. The program depends on an appropriation of approximately $1 million per biennium to support its operating budget.

West Virginia

Environmental License Plate Sales

A conservation license plate for Nongame Wildlife and Natural Heritage programs yielded about $125,000 when it was first issued in 1998, but competition is increasing from other special interest plates. The money from this source is essentially earmarked for the Nongame/Natural Heritage program but basically substitutes for dollars previously allocated as a line item in the state budget.

Wisconsin

Tax Check-Off

In 2002, this check-off on the personal income tax form generated $631,000 for endangered resources fund. In 2000, the check-off was also added to corporate tax returns. The state has been matching the contributions with a cap of $462,000.

Wisconsin Stewardship Program

Originally passed in 1989, this program allocates $60 million per year for state and local matching grants for land protection and capital improvements on conservation lands. Of the $60 million, up to $53 million is for state and local matching grants for land acquisition. Over its life, the program has protected 225,000 acres. The program is supported by twenty-year general obligation bonds.

Wisconsin Outdoor Wildlife Trust Fund

In 2002, legislators created the Wisconsin Outdoor Wildlife Trust Fund to provide the Department of Natural Resources with another potential source of funding for land conservation. No appropriations have been made as of 2003.

Environmental License Plate Sales

The Endangered Resources Timber Wolf license plate, established in 1995, raised $625,000 in 2002 for the Bureau of Endangered Resources.

Wyoming

Wildlife Conservation Stamp

The state Wildlife Trust Fund receives money from wildlife conservation stamp licenses to improve wildlife habitat nongame wildlife. About $800,000 to $1 million is available each year, derived from interest on the $15 million fund.

Source: Adapted from The Nature Conservancy.

USEFUL WEB SITES

American Farmland Trust — www.farmland.org

Appalachian Mountain Club — www.outdoors.org

Arthur M. Blank Family Foundation — www.blankfoundation.org

California ballot history — lalaw.lib.ca.us/ballot.html
holmes.uchastings.edu/
cgi-bin/starfinder/o?path=
calprop.txt&id=webber&pass=
webber&OK=OK

California Conservancies — resources.ca.gov/conservancies.
html

California Department of Food and Agriculture — www.cdfa.ca.gov

California Environmental Dialogue — www.cedlink.org

California Environmental Enhancement and Mitigation Program — www.resources.ca.gov/eem

California Farmland Conservancy Program — www.consrv.ca.gov/DLRP/cfcp

California Legislative Analyst's Office	www.lao.ca.gov
California Natural Heritage Preservation Tax Credit Program	www.dfg.ca.gov/wcbax_credit_program.htm
Cape Cod Land Bank	www.capecodcommission.org/landbank
Chesapeake Bay Program	www.chesapeakebay.net
Chicago Wilderness	www.chicagowilderness.org
Colorado Department of Revenue (state tax credit)	www.revenue.state.co.us/fyi/html/income39.html
Colorado State Parks	www.parks.state.co.us
Community Preservation Coalition	www.communitypreservation.org
Congressional Research Service (reports)	www.ncseonline.org/NLE/CRS
The Conservation Fund	www.conservationfund.org
David and Lucile Packard Foundation	www.packard.org
DeKalb County Parks and Greenspace Program	www.co.dekalb.ga.us/greenspace/index.htm
Doris Duke Charitable Foundation	www.ddcf.org
Douglas County, Colorado	www.douglas.co.us
Florida Communities Trust	www.dca.state.fl.us/ffct
Florida Forever Program	www.dep.state.fl.us/lands/carl_ff
Florida Office of Greenways and Trails	www.floridadep.org/gwt
Florida Recreation Development Assistance Program	www.dep.state.fl.us/parks/bdrs/frdap.htm
Florida Preservation 2000 Program	p2000.dep.state.fl.us/about.htm
Florida State Parks	www.dep.state.fl.us/parks
Florida Water Management Districts	www.dca.state.fl.us/fdcp/DCP/Partners/wmds.htm

Foundation Center	www.foundationcenter.org
Gordon and Betty Moore Foundation	www.moore.org
Great Outdoors Colorado	www.goco.org
Green Infrastructure	www.greeninfrastructure.net
Illinois Association of Park Districts	www.ilparks.org
Illinois Open Land Trust	dnr.state.il.us/ocd/newolt2.htm
Illinois Open Space Land Acquisition and Development Program	dnr.state.il.us/ocd/newosladı.htm
Jacksonville Preservation Project	appsı.coj.net/preserve/default.htm
Lake County Forest Preserve District	www.LCFPD.org
Lancaster County Agricultural Preserve Board	www.co.lancaster.pa.us
Lancaster Farmland Trust	www.savelancasterfarms.org
Land Trust Alliance	www.lta.org
Marin Agricultural Land Trust	www.malt.org
Marin Community Foundation	www.marincf.org
Marin County Open Space District	www.marinopenspace.org
Maryland Agricultural Land Preservation Foundation	www.mda.state.md.us/geninfo/genera3.htm
Maryland Environmental Trust	www.dnr.state.md.us/met
Maryland GreenPrint Program	www.dnr.state.md.us/greenways/greenprint
Maryland Program Open Space	www.dnr.state.md.us/pos.html
Maryland Rural Legacy Program	www.dnr.state.md.us/rurallegacy
Massachusetts Community Preservation Act	commpres.env.state.ma.us/content/cpa.asp
Milwaukee Metropolitan Sewerage District	www.mmsd.com

Minnesota Board of Water and Soil Resources	www.bwsr.state.mn.us
Minnesota Environment and Natural Resources Trust Fund	www.commissions.leg.state. mn.us/lcmr/trustfund/ tfquestion.htm
Minnesota Department of Agriculture	www.mda.state.mn.us
Minnesota Department of Natural Resources	www.dnr.state.mn.us
Minnesota Legislative Commission on Minnesota Resources	www.commissions.leg.state. mn.us/lcmr
Montgomery County, Maryland Legacy Open Space	www.mcmncppc.org/legacy_ open_space/index.shtm
National Conference of State Legislatures	www.ncsl.org
Natural Resources Conservation Service	www.nhq.nrcs.usda.gov
The Nature Conservancy	www.nature.org
New Jersey Environmental Infrastructure Trust	www.njeit.org
New Jersey Garden State Preservation Trust	www.state.nj.us/gspt
New Jersey Green Acres Program	www.state.nj.us/dep/greenacres
New Jersey Farmland Preservation Program	www.state.nj.us/agriculture/ sadc/overview.htm
Openlands Project	www.openlands.org
Prairie Crossing	www.prairiecrossing.com
Resources Legacy Fund	www.resourceslegacyfund.org
Richard King Mellon Foundation	fdncenter.org/grantmaker/ rkmellon/index.html
Saginaw Bay Greenways Collaborative	www.saginawbaygreenways.org
Saginaw Bay Watershed Initiative Network	www.saginawbaywin.org
Southeastern Ecological Framework Project	www.geoplan.ufl.edu/epa/ index.html

St. Louis 2004   www.stlouis2004.org

Trust for Public Land   www.tpl.org

Turner Foundation   www.turnerfoundation.org

Twin Cities Metro Greenways Program   www.dnr.state.mn.us/
                                             greenprint/metrogreen.html

SELECTED BIBLIOGRAPHY

Behan, John L. "Planning and Financing Open Space Resource Protection: Pittsford's Greenprint Initiative." *American Institute of Certified Planners, Planners' Casebook.* Spring/Summer 1999.

Benedict, Mark, and Ed McMahon. "Green Infrastructure: Smart Conservation for the 21st Century." The Conservation Fund. May 2002. www.greeninfrastructure.net/ ?article=2047&back=true.

_____. "Green Infrastructure: Smart Conservation for the 21st Century." *Renewable Resources Journal.* Autumn 2002. www.rnrf.org

Brookings Institution Center on Urban and Metropolitan Policy. "Growth at the Ballot Box: Electing the Shape of Communities in November 2000." 2001.

The Conservation Fund. "Land and Water Conservation Fund: An Assessment of Its Past, Present and Future." 2000. www.conservationfund.org/?article=2011.

Environmental Law Institute. "Smart Links: Turning Conservation Dollars into Smart Growth Opportunities." 2002. www.eli.org.

Florida Greenways Commission. "Creating a Statewide Greenways System: for People . . . for Wildlife . . . for Florida" Report to the Governor. January 1995. www. 1000friendsofflorida.org/PUBS/Greenways/contents.asp.

Greene, Mark. "Topeka, Kansas: Getting Greener Gets the Job Done," *Inside Agroforestry, the USDA National Agroforestry Center Newsletter* (Summer 2001).

Harnik, Peter "Inside City Parks." Urban Land Institute and Trust for Public Land. 2000. www.tpl.org/tier3_cd.cfm?content_item_id=5960&folder_id=985.

Havens, John J., and Paul G. Schervishi. "Millionaires and the Millennium: New Estimates of the Forthcoming Wealth Transfer and the Prospects for a Golden Age of Philanthropy." www.bc.edu/bc_org/avp/gsas/swri/documents/m&m.pdf.

Hoctor, T. S., M. H. Carr, and P. D. Zwick. "Identifying a Linked Reserve System Using a Regional Landscape Approach: The Florida Ecological Network." *Conservation Biology* 14, no. 4 (2000):984–1000.

Land Trust Alliance. "Voters Invest in Parks and Open Space: 1998 Referenda Results." 1998. www.lta.org/publicpolicy/refresults.pdf.

———. "Voters Invest in Open Space: 1999 Referenda Results." 2000. www.lta.org/publicpolicy/1999voters_inv.pdf.

———. "Voters Invest in Open Space: 2000 Referenda Results." 2001.

Lerner, Steve, and William Poole. "The Economic Benefits of Parks and Open Space: How Land Conservation Helps Communities Grow Smart and Protect the Bottom Line." Trust for Public Land. 1999.

Lyndon Baines Johnson School of Public Affairs, the University of Texas at Austin. "State Growth Management and Open Space Preservation Policies." Policy Research Project Report No. 143. 2002.

"Mayor Franklin's Parks and Green Spaces Task Force Report." 2002. www.parkpride.org.

Sierra Club. "Sprawl: The Dark Side of an American Dream." 1998. www.sierraclub.org/sprawl/report98.

Silva, J. Fred. "California's Natural Resource Programs: Where Does the Money Come From and Where Does It Go?" Public Policy Institute of California. August 2002. www.ppic.org/publications/reports.html#calnaturalres.

Sokolow, Al. "The Williamson Act: 25 Years of Land Conservation." Agricultural Issues Center, University of California at Davis. 1990.

Trust for Public Land and Land Trust Alliance. "LandVote 2001: Americans Invest in Parks and Open Space." 2002. www.lta.org/publicpolicy/landvote2001.htm.

———. "LandVote 2002: Americans Invest in Parks and Open Space." 2003. www.tpl.org/download_landvote_02.cfm.

Trust for Public Land and the National Association of Counties. "Local Greenprinting for Growth." 2002. www.tpl.org.

Weber, T., and J. Wolf. "Maryland's Green Infrastructure: Using Landscape Assessment Tools to Identify a Regional Conservation Strategy." *Environmental Monitoring and Assessment* 63 (2000): 265–277.

INDEX